GRANNY'S PLACE

Arvis Marie Taitt

Granny's Place by Arvis Marie Taitt

ISBN 978-1-970072-92-1 (Paperback)
ISBN 978-1-970072-93-8 (Hardback)

This book is written to provide information and motivation to readers. Its purpose is not to render any type of psychological, legal, or professional advice of any kind. The content is the sole opinion and expression of the author, and not necessarily that of the publisher.

Copyright © 2019 by Arvis Marie Taitt

All rights reserved. No part of this book may be reproduced, transmitted, or distributed in any form by any means, including, but not limited to, recording, photocopying, or taking screenshots of parts of the book, without prior written permission from the author or the publisher. Brief quotations for noncommercial purposes, such as book reviews, permitted by Fair Use of the U.S. Copyright Law, are allowed without written permissions, as long as such quotations do not cause damage to the book's commercial value. For permissions, write to the publisher, whose address is stated below.

Printed in the United States of America.

New Leaf Media, LLC
175 S. 3rd Street, Suite 200
Columbus, OH 43215
www.thenewleafmedia.com

"Full of adventure and places to go
when I wanted peace of mind.
I felt more at home there than anywhere else!
It had the smell of welcome,
The aroma of comfo
And…
You always had an open invitation to stay.
That's how I remember…
South Fourth Street!"

The author:
Arvis Marie Taitt now…
And then!

My daughter, Kassandara L. Johnson, read the makings of this book and then wrote the above poem for me. I took her to Suffolk to view the remnants of part of my past. I will cherish the words she has written to capture the essence of where I spent my summers.

CONTENTS

Chapter 1:   April Fool's Day 1
Chapter 2:   Preparations 6
Chapter 3:   The Train Ride Home 8
Chapter 4:   The Cab Driver 11
Chapter 5:   Arvis Marie 15
Chapter 6:   A Team 25
Chapter 7:   I'll Miss You 30
Chapter 8:   The Faithful Crew 31
Chapter 9:   The Final Farewell 34
Chapter 10: The Untimely Guest 42
Chapter 11: Petula Clark 47
Chapter 12: One Morning 51
Chapter 13: The Dream 56
Chapter 14: Good Old Suffolk 61
Chapter 15: Once Again 64
Chapter 16: 139 South Fourth Street 68
Chapter 17: The Front Porch 74
Chapter 18: Best Friends 79
Chapter 19: The Biscuits 81
Chapter 20: T.J. Jones 95
Chapter 21: Braids and Beads 109
Chapter 22: The Last Piece of Chicken 118
Chapter 23: Glenda Marie Johnson 126

Chapter 24:	And Now There Were Three	135
Chapter 25:	The House	145
Chapter 26:	The Hikers	152
Chapter 27:	The Shopping Spree	153
Chapter 28:	The Saga Continues	162
Chapter 29:	The First Adventure	170
Chapter 30:	Searching	182
Chapter 31:	Rescued	183
Chapter 32:	Good News	186
Chapter 33:	Still In The Cave	187
Chapter 34:	It's Not Your Fault	195
Chapter 35:	The Johnsons	199
Chapter 36:	Finally Revealed	201
Chapter 37:	Jasper's Final Conflict	202
Chapter 38:	Mr. Percy's Place	207
Chapter 39:	The Plan Unfolds	209
Chapter 40:	Uptown	211
Chapter 41:	The Letter	217
Chapter 42:	The Fishing Trip	221
Chapter 43:	Jericho Cemetery	226
Chapter 44:	The Enigma	235
Chapter 45:	Joy's Third Dream	240
Chapter 46:	The Last Preparations Begin	242
Chapter 47:	The Warning	248
Chapter 48:	The Final Adventure	250

APRIL FOOL'S DAY

It was 1958 and old folks still seemed to have a saying for everything… especially in Suffolk, Virginia. One such saying was, if a baby took eleven months to arrive on this side of the hereafter, that same baby would meet its guardian angel, but there is more to say about such a mystic birth. If the baby was born with a thin membrane of skin covering its face, the baby would also have the gift of predicting the future. If the child experienced the death of a parent as well as numerous harsh circumstances, the child would have dreams of the exact situations before they happened. Most significantly, every obstacle in the child's path would be victorious. Disguised as an earthly human being, the assigned angel would intervene for the child when all circumstances seemed hopeless only if the child was pure of heart.

Such was the case of thirteen-year-old Joyce Ann Bailey. Her home was in Eatontown, New Jersey. Her mother, Arvis Marie, gave birth to her in Suffolk, Virginia at the home of her parents, Eva and Pervis Tazell.

She was nicknamed "Joy" by her Mom. She'd inherited an artistic gift of drawing and was an honour student too. From an early part of her life, problems began. While other female students in her homeroom at Eatontown Elementary School bragged about the daily writings in their diaries, Joy drew her thoughts for that day and attached together each drawing to the day, until a scroll formed.

Every evening after supper, she'd race upstairs to the privacy of her bedroom, stretch out on her bed, and sketch an event that had grabbed her attention that day. She smiled as she scrolled through her past drawings. One drawing was labelled "October 31, 1948". The day was Halloween and the day belonged to her because it was her birthday.

In one birthday drawing, she'd drawn a picture of herself dressed in a colorful clown costume her Mom creatively sewed out of bright sheets of crepe paper. She imagined her homeroom Halloween school party was in celebration just for her. Each night, she'd pretend the ring at the door was a signal of trick-or-treaters getting a handful of birthday candy, but... something was about to change...something was in the air. Joy continued to draw but failed to notice that shades of blue, red, and green began to be replaced by brown, tan and black. Then... on April 1st...it began.

The sun shone bright that day. Joy rushed out of the massive glass front doors with the rest of the junior high students of Eatontown Elementary School. The two-day Easter vacation coupled with the weekend had begun. Joy ran home at top speed. The hem of her powder blue dress and white cotton petticoat bounced against her knees as she raced through familiar shortcuts and down sidewalks with galloping strides. Joy's heart thumped hard with the anticipation of trying out her new April Fool's joke on her Mom. As she got closer to home, she repeated the joke she had memorized in her head to make certain to get every word right.

"568...570...572 Pinebrook Road and I'm home at last!" Joy's breathless running approach slowed down to halted steps. She caught sight of many people getting out cars parked by the curb in front of her apartment door. She recognized the faces of out-of-state relatives who only showed up for weddings and...funerals.

Joy started panting heavily again. As she stepped into the living room, she sensed a lingering atmosphere of sadness. People were seated and standing in any available space whispering and mumbling in low tones. Mrs. McDonald, the AVON lady who visited once a month, was

GRANNY'S PLACE

in the living room too. Apologetic and tearful faces made Joy uneasy. After excusing herself numerous times to get to the small dining room and combination kitchen, Joy saw them seated at the table…Eva and Pervis Tazell…her Mom's parents.

"Hello, Sweetmeat," Pervis said, choking back tears. Eva grabbed her grandchild and smothered her with hugs and kisses.

"Granny, why are you crying? Why are all these people here? Granddaddy, what's going on? Where's Mom?" In her gut, Joy was afraid to hear the answers to her questions.

Like swallowing a bitter pill, Eva said, "Baby, your Mamma passed away early this afternoon,"

Joy broke free of her grandmother's embrace, blindly pushed through the living room guests and bolted upstairs to her bedroom. She sat on the edge of her bed. She felt hollow inside. Her mother, her best friend, was gone. She thought of her April Fool's joke. Hurts suddenly turned to disappointments, disappointments to frustration, frustration turned to vehemence, and vehemence turned into a vow.

"The only other people in this whole sticking world I'll ever care about and love are sitting downstairs at the dining room table," Joy hissed.

She heard someone tipping softly upstairs on the wooden steps her Mom had polished only a week ago. It was Lois Eddleston, her grandfather's niece. Lois stared at Joy's bowed head and assumed she was saying a little prayer. Joy raised her head slowly but the expression on her face was not one of grief.

"How would you like to live in Suffolk with your grandparents for a while, Joy?" Lois asked.

With a blank angry look on her face, Joy stared at Lois. She studied the small framed, dark-skinned, elderly woman dressed in an out of fashion, cream color silk blouse and black cotton tweed straight skirt.

"What planet did this boob fall off?" Joy said herself.

"You want me to help you pack up a few things, Joy?"

"I'm not a baby. I can do that myself. Leave me alone please."

"I understand, honey. I'll go back downstairs and let Eva and Pervis know you'll be getting ready to go back with them."

"Fine, you do that."

GRANNY'S PLACE

Joy listened as Lois' footsteps descended the stairs. She went over and over the conversation they'd just had in her head. She didn't mean to be rude to Lois, but her Mom had just died and that's all she wanted to think about now.

Joy's father, Jasper Bailey arrived home from that last hospital visit. Without the courtesy of greeting anyone present, he let the back-screen door slam close to announce his entry. He walked straight to the refrigerator, opened the freezer, took out a handful of ice, reached on top of the refrigerator, retrieved a half empty quart bottle of Tanqueray gin and fixed a drink. He swished the ice cubes around with his finger and closed the freezer with his elbow. He dragged a dining room table chair across the linoleum floor and sat down next to Pervis and Eva. The black rubber cover protectors on the end of the chair legs left a trail on the newly waxed kitchen floor Arvis had recently waxed. He plopped his shiny black combat boots up on the table and seemed more annoyed than grieved. He didn't care about the intense stares of Eva and Pervis. He never liked them anyway.

"Country bumpkins," he sneered to himself. He gloated over the fact that he'd mentally punched Eva and Pervis in the face by marrying their daughter. A warped grin spread across his lips and gloated over the fact that this would be the last time they saw their precious daughter. In the meantime, Joy came back downstairs and made her way back to the warm arms of her grandmother.

"It'll sure be nice to know Joy will be staying in Suffolk with her grandparents," Lois said, sheepishly.

"Who says she going to Suffolk? Joy will do just fine right where she is," Jasper slurred drunkenly. "Come over here, girl and give your old man a squeeze." Hesitantly, Joy left the protective arms of her grandmother. Her stomach churned and she felt like throwing-up. Jasper snatched her towards him roughly. Joy tried her best to squirm free of his vice grip on her arm.

"It's going to be just you and me, kiddo," Jasper hissed, while breathing his gin soured breath in her face. Pulling free, Joy ran back into the arms of Eva. Pervis saw it all.

"She's going to stay with us," Eva said. "Arvis, Pervis and me already discussed the matter."

"Arvis didn't tell me about it," Jasper said angrily. "Oh, I know! This is some sort of trick!" Because of his loud, drunken behaviour, all heads had turned towards dining room.

"I don't care what Arvis said or didn't say. Joy stays with me and that's it."

"I wonder what your commanding office would say about you having a dependent without having a wife," Pervis said.

"I don't care what the commander has to say. This is family business."

Jasper concluded the standoff with the Tazells with a look that could have taken the rust off an old battery. He concluded his conversation with Eva and Pervis by rudely storming through the living room, pushing through the guests, stomping upstairs, and slamming his bedroom door. Eventually, everyone said 'good-night' and filed out the door. Eva immediately began collecting coffee cups and glasses left around the living room and dining room.

"Rest yourself, Eva."

With tears in her eyes she said, "My child was always neat and clean and that's that!"

PREPARATIONS

Pervis got what little sleep he could on the thin, pull-out-couch bed. It was four in the morning and the train bound for Suffolk was to depart at 4:45 am. All during the night, Eva's soft weeping awakened him periodically. Words could not express how much Eva missed her baby daughter, Arvis. He thought about Arvis but also thought about their other daughter Barbara too and about the incident that happened to them both, including Henry Morgan, who was now Barbara's husband. His thoughts drifted back to the past when Arvis' health began to go downhill with each and every episode of Jasper's mean antics.

Barbara and Arvis had always been close and shared numerous sisterly secrets. Whenever Arvis had to go the hospital and a telephone call came, he and Eva would cringe. Barbara's questions to him ran through his mind and the words rang out like loud clanging bells.

"Why didn't Jasper call sooner and let us know that Arvis had been taken to the hospital, Daddy? Why did he wait for two weeks before telling us of her dire health situation?"

Pervis had no answers to give Barbara and knowing the kind of man Jasper was didn't leave much for the imagination either.

Henry was a contract attorney and Barbara's speciality was teaching advanced English classes at Oneonta University. Now living in Oneonta, New York, Barbara received the call about her sister. Glenda, their twelve-year-old adopted daughter who was sick with the flue. She and Henry left her to the discretion of a twenty-four-hour home care registered nurse.

The drive to Suffolk in their black BMW was comfortable but quiet. Six long hours of early morning driving passed. They finally reached the sleepy town of Suffolk. When Big Mama, the next-door neighbor, spotted the New York tags on the car, she spit out her mouthful of snuff, gave her condolences to Barbara and Henry, and hurried home to call Eva and Pervis about the visitors coming to their house. She had promised to keep an eye out…among other things.

Wasting no time, Barbara began making the necessary phone calls in preparation for her sister's funeral. Mr. Hewlett, the editor of the Suffolk News Harold was the first call she made. Mr. Hewlett set type and prepared the announcement for the evening edition. The news of the loss of Arvis spread fast. Mr. Leon Jenkins, President of the only bank in town and Mr. Johannes, the owner of the only Black owned supermarket, read the morning edition of the Suffolk Harold the next day and were shocked and saddened. The news about Arvis spread quickly around town. A once healthy, good-natured, soft-spoken compassionate woman left Suffolk's boundaries never to return to spread her contagious smile all over town. However, everybody knew whom she married. Suffolk was a community of strong traditions and a belief in old-time superstitions and the premature death of this precious being caused folks to frown and raise an eyebrow.

THE TRAIN RIDE HOME

Jasper's snoring was the only sound heard in the small apartment. He was still dressed in his military uniform with his untied army boots hanging off the edge of the bed. He was a drunken mess but despite his drinking, he managed to keep an exemplary record with the military. A dark-green Lincoln Mercury was the family car and Jasper kept it shinned like new. Joy hated the car. Its massive chrome bumpers resembled alligator's teeth about to devour some unsuspecting prey. The car's wide white-walled tires reminded her of the blank, wide eyes of a hoot owl. Every Saturday morning, Jasper spent hours washing, waxing, and shining the dark green monstrosity.

It was early morning and orange sunrays blanketed the Eatontown apartment complex. Eva was moving about in the kitchenette. The smell of hot coffee filled every room of the apartment. Pervis stretched himself, yawned and scratched his ribs. He smiled when his eye caught sight of the Cinderella alarm clock on the coffee table. It was a present sent to Joy by he and Eva five Christmases ago. He smiled tenderly. He and Eva always used a biological alarm clock for years, but he let the Cinderella clock tick away to enjoy the attention given by his granddaughter.

"Good morning, Pervis. Here's a steaming hot cup of strong coffee fixed just as like you like it," Eva said, sitting down next to her husband.

The aged but wise couple sipped from their cups and nibbled on pieces of buttered toast and strips of bacon. They sipped in silence as each embraced their thoughts about the events upon them and of course...Joy.

"Pervis, you clear off the table and wash up these few dishes while I go upstairs and wake Joy up."

"No problem, honey. I want to get back to the friendly territory of Suffolk as soon as possible."

"Lord, I know what you mean, Pervis."

Eva's knees ached as she climbed the stairs. "Goodness gracious, this arthritis of mine is really acting up today."

Tipping into her room, Eva stood over Joy's bed looking at the strong resemblance of her and Arvis. Tears ran down her pump brown cheeks, but she wiped them away with the back of her hand.

"Wake up, sleepyhead," Eva whispered. "It's time to get up and get ready for our train ride so get dressed and come downstairs for some breakfast. Your plate is saved and waiting in the oven for you."

"Gee, Granny. I don't feel like eating anything this morning. In fact, I don't feel like eating anything for the next hundred years."

"All right Joy, but a hundred years is an awful long time," Eva said to lighten the moment.

The taxi arrived right in time to get the two generations to the train station. The train engine hissed and chug-a-lugged out of Eatontown, New Jersey bound for Suffolk, Virginia where Eva and Pervis had been residing for over twenty-five years. Joy snuggled down on the seat between her grandparents feeling safe and protected. Soothed by the click clacking of the train wheels speeding over the iron tracks, Joy feel asleep.

This was not the first time she'd ridden the train to her grandparents' home. Ever since she was six years old, Arvis had packed her off to Suffolk to enjoy her three-month summer vacation.

"Fresh air and plenty of sunshine is the best medicine for you Joy," Arvis would always say but, Joy knew her visits were mainly because of Jasper. It was during those visits Joy longed to confide in her grandparents. She wanted so desperately to tell them of the goings on in Eatontown. She wanted to tell them of Jasper's appallingly vicious immorality. She wanted them to know what he'd said and did but, she was obedient to her mother's request for silence.

Jasper warned Joy. *"What happens in this home better stay in this home and you better not breathe one word of our family business to 'Pegged-legged Pete' and 'Battle Axe Annie'. If you do, I'll blister your hide so bad you won't be able to sit down for a year. Remember to be on your P's and Q's!"*

His threats also included shipping Joy off to a reformatory charged with bad behaviour and sexual misconduct and would never to see her Mom again. Joy was willing to do anything her Dad dictated because she didn't want any kind of separation from her Mom. What Eva and Pervis didn't know was Joy got the same warning threat last night.

"Wake up, honey child," Eva said, gently shaking her granddaughter. "We're home! We're back in Suffolk!"

THE CAB DRIVER

Harvey Ellis was the owner of the only Black taxi service in Suffolk. His competition was two other cab companies that serviced the white areas of town, but his current activity was a strong contrast of his past.

He had nothing else to do but read the morning edition of the Suffolk News Harold, but his thoughts would drift and focus on the most turbulent time of all his thirty-four years of life. It seemed like ages ago when he started out as an obscure taxicab driver picking up Blacks here and there and occasionally making a long distance run to Norfolk. There were only three drivers servicing the Black residents of the city. Most of his workdays were ten hours of a six-day week.

Born in 1926 and married at twenty, Harvey and Janet now had a six-month-old son and he had nowhere job. He joined the army by the time his son celebrated his first birthday. Because of tough times, joining the army was the only way he could support his family and stop his wife's constant complaints of 'not enough money'. He got an honourable discharge upon his return from a fifteen-month stint of duty in 1948 but the horrors of war left him an emotional mess.

On his return to Suffolk, everything seemed mundane and meaningless. He spent most of his time in the seclusion of his darkened bedroom. A brief interaction with his son was the only time he seemed to relish life.

When he'd come home from his job, he'd greet Janet, go to his bedroom, sit in a corner chair…in the dark…while images of wartime tragedies repeated over and over in his mind like horrific commercials. He began to neglect Janet and son even more. The core of his activity was staring out the bedroom window as if he were waiting for someone to arrive or if he was waiting to say 'good-bye'…for good.

One incident harassed his mind above all his wartime memories. The Suffolk Warriors were Thomas Hargrove, Melvin Dixon, Lewis Jones, Calvin Holden and of course, Harvey. Dressed in their military best, the boys greeted Harvey at his home to say their farewells to

Harvey's parents. However, as a good-bye surprise, Harvey's parents secretly organized a going away party.

Everyone had a joyous time while laughing, joking, and posing for pictures, which included some old town folks the warriors didn't even know. It seemed as if the whole town was there to bid them a final farewell.

Thoughts of Melvin haunted him the most. He relived the vivid screams of the injured and dying men on the battlefield. In the confusion of attempting to explode grenades, bombs and the roar of machine guns firing at the enemy, Harvey got separated from the rest and was trapped in a foxhole. Thomas, Lewis, and Calvin fought valiantly but, where was Melvin? Where did Melvin go?

A grenade landed three feet away from Harvey, but it did not explode. To save his friends, Melvin suddenly appeared. He climbed out of a hidden manhole yowling like a mad animal and threw his body over the grenade. It exploded tearing his body to shreds. Harvey and the rest of the warriors stared in disbelief as pieces of their friend covered their faces and helmets. Melvin was no more. Somewhere in the confusion of battle, Thomas, Lewis and Calvin became no more too. Only Harvey remained somewhat sane.

With a limited budget as a working mother and a fulltime homemaker, Janet became perturbed with trying to manage the household by herself. Harvey's robotic actions and refusal to embrace life finally got to her. One night she decided she had enough, packed up herself and their five-year-old son, and left for parts unknown. After six months, Harvey learned of his wife's whereabouts by answering a knock at the front door. Serviced with divorce papers, he couldn't handle life's punches anymore and had decided to end it all by committing suicide. At that very moment, the phone rang. Harvey decided to answer one last time.

"Harvey, can you go to 139 South Fourth Street for a pick-up right away?" Lucille asked.

"10-4, Lucille," Harvey answered. Lucille Phillips was the middle-aged taxi radio dispatcher that tried to hide her real age with loads of make-up. Her favourite hobby was gossiping on the phone, but she was top-notch on her job.

GRANNY'S PLACE

When Harvey arrived at the Tazell address, all the lights in the house were off. Irritated, he blew the taxi horn and waited for some kind of response. Finally, Pervis stepped onto the front porch and held up his hand to shade his eyes from the taxi's headlights. He was still chewing a mouthful of a late night snack and was somewhat annoyed with the sudden interruption.

"What's up, son?" Pervis yelled when he recognized the taxi logo.

"I'm here because you called for a pick-up, didn't you?"

"No son, you must have gotten your addresses mixed up or something."

"Okay, I'm gone then," Harvey said, obviously annoyed.

"Wait, son. How about having a cup of coffee with Eva and me to answer for all this trouble? After all, you came all the way across town and at this hour," Pervis shouted from the porch. "Well…come on in. There's plenty of room for another plate on the kitchen table."

As the evening wore on, Eva offered more rich smelling coffee and a plate of apple dumplings. Through Pervis' sound advice and wisdom of his conversation, Harvey could feel an inner strength welding up inside and it electrified him with a new outlook on life. A mistaken call became his redeeming grace that developed into a long lasting relationship with the elderly couple.

As the night wore on, Harvey remembered one summer night especially. After finishing his taxi route, Pervis and Eva invited him to relax on the front porch and down some of Eva's excellent dessert after eating a hearty supper. The sound of soft playing harmonica music somewhere in the distance interrupted their conversation. The hypnotic melody floated over the trees as if carried by a gentle summer breeze but, Eva and Pervis didn't hear it. The melody seemed to linger over the top of the Tazell home. Harvey could feel a warmth flow from the top of his head down to the soles of his feet.

"Something is happening to me, Miss Eva!"

"Let it happen son, and don't fight it. Hold on to it!"

It what was a hypnotic moment. Harvey emancipated every negative thought while he continued listening to the harmonica tune. He could feel his mind emptying of every bad episode in his life as if the memories now became a fog receding to reveal a sunny shore. Harvey stood to his feet with hands held high thanked God for his deliverance.

Tears rolled down his face. He was free! Free from the memories of the ravages of war, his divorce and everything that tangled him emotionally and embodied his soul. Never again, did dreams of the death of his comrades beset his slumber. He had a new energetic zeal for life.

As he and the Tazells praised the Lord for his deliverance, the harmonica music faded into the night. For the first time in long agonizing months, Harvey sensed a quiet calmness inside of his being, and his mind was as clear as a bell. That next morning, he went to the bank and borrowed the money to start his own cab business. As a result, he became the first Black owned cab company in the city of Suffolk.

ARVIS MARIE

The train from Eatontown screeched to a stop and halted at the station door. Harvey was waiting. Pervis, Eva, and Joy were the first to step down with the assistance of a porter. Harvey greeted the Tazells and Joy with an enthusiastic hug and welcome.

"Glad your home but, I'm so very sorry to hear of your loss," Harvey said. He tenderly kissed Joy on the forehead. He had always secretly imagined how things would have been if he had been her father instead of Jasper.

After the luggage was secure in the taxi trunk and everyone was inside, Harvey began the five-mile drive to South Fourth Street. At first, no one uttered a single word but instead let the sultry breeze flow through the opened taxi windows to distract the already rising heat. Eva began to weep again. From the back seat, Pervis leaned forward and put his hand on his wife's shoulder to comfort her and then sat back to wipe away tears of his own. Joy stared out the opposite rear seat window. As she observed the city, she could see that nothing had changed but, all were thinking the same thing…somebody special would never see Suffolk again.

Pervis' memory drifted back to an incident that happened long before Arvis and Jasper were married. He remembered every detail as if it had happened only yesterday.

Arvis introduced Henry Johnson to her sister, Barbara. The girls were in Barbara's bedroom busily getting dressed for a college spring break dance. Barbara was a senior at Norfolk Division of Virginia State College majoring in English Education and Arvis was a junior at the same college majoring in Music. Henry, Barbara's perspective date, was a senior at Howard University's School of Law. He'd come home to visit his folks who also lived in Suffolk but secretly, he came home to see the one person that had stolen his heart the year before…Barbara.

Sheila Porter and Arvis were best friends and Sheila was Henry's cousin. Arvis and Sheila had known each other since their early high schools days and were excited to know they majored in the same curriculum at college. Sheila had introduced Arvis to Henry as a potential love interest, but Henry flipped head-over-heels for Barbara. During one of their girl-talks, Barbara told Arvis she was not interested in Henry, and didn't have time for flirtations of any kind and especially didn't have time to get involved with anybody. Even though Barbara insisted that she had her mind on being a professional, Arvis never took her seriously and just giggled.

"Marriage is not for this girl, I can tell you that," Barbara said to her teasing sister. "I'm going to join the ranks of all black female pioneers who have braved social obstacles and burned trails of success for all women who have the visualization…"

"Blah! Blah! Blah! Oh please, Barbara," Arvis mockingly groaned. "Give it a rest. You can impress somebody else with that speech, but you can't fool me. I saw that sparkle in your eye when you were first introduced to Henry Morgan."

As far as Arvis was concerned, she knew Barbara and Henry were a twosome. She didn't know all the whys but was determined to help things along anyway. Unfortunately, Arvis failed to listen to Sheila's advice about Jasper.

After graduation, Barbara and Henry were married and moved to Oneonta, New York. Jasper had staked his sinister claim on Arvis. Pervis and Eva objected venomously to the actions of the man but had to give up because they found out through the confession of Arvis that Joy was on the way and would arrive in seven months. Eva and Pervis were devastated but did not condemn Arvis but rather they condemned Jasper. Pervis mentally recorded it all.

Harvey made a right turn off Main Street and onto South Fourth Street. Neighbours waved at the Tazells to welcome them home despite the reason for their the reason they had to leave. Harvey parked in front of the house, got out and unlocked the trunk to get the luggage. Henry and Barbara gave their salutations and hugs on the front porch to the train travelers. The Tazells had always been fond of Henry and loved him as if he were their own son. Not only was he their son-in-law but, he was their family attorney too.

"Thanks for everything, my friend," Pervis said, reaching out a hand to pay the taxi fare.

"No charge, Mr. Tazell."

"Bless you, my boy."

"Don't hesitate to call me if you need a ride for anything, Mr. Tazell," Harvey said.

Pervis stood on the front porch until the taxi was out of sight. His attention turned back to the house when he heard Barbara's voice.

"I'm so glad you're here Mama," Barbara said. For the moment, she was able to hide the pain she felt for the loss of her sister.

Eva immediately went into her kitchen and began to rummage through her refrigerator until she found a snack to fix for everybody. Being in her own kitchen was relaxing to her.

"I don't want anything to eat, Mama," Barbara said.

"Me either, Mrs. Tazell," Henry said.

"That makes three," Pervis said.

"I couldn't eat a thing either." Joy said.

"Let's all get some rest then", Eva said.

"We have a lot to deal with and our bodies are tired. I agree with Miss Eva. Let's all get some rest." Henry said.

"Wonderful suggestion, Henry," Barbara said.

Everything he said was wonderful to her. Since there was so much to plan, everybody decided to take an afternoon nap was a good idea. They all wanted to be mentally fresh for the upcoming activities. Barbara had been up early for the long drive from New York. Her mind kept tossing and turning as thought after thought of her sister raced through her mind. Joy was lying next to Eva in Eva and Pervis' bedroom.

In Arvis' old bedroom, now shared with Henry, Barbara buried her head under her pillow trying not to think but sleep never came. She could hear snoring and envied the sleep that allowed her Mom to relax a bit and escape the hurt of the loss of a sibling. However, Barbara just couldn't stop thinking about Arvis and didn't want to awaken Henry with her tossing. A little smile crept across her face and tears filled her eyes as she remembered an incident that happened back in December of 1948.

It had been a harsh winter that year. Snow blizzards were a common weather report too. Arvis was chatting and giggling while both sisters dressed for a New Year's party held at Sheila's house.

"The word among friends is that Sheila has all the latest tunes at every party she hosts. That's why everybody has so much fun. She's the absolute best and…" Arvis rattled on excitedly.

"…and what?" Barbara asked.

"…and a certain guy named 'Henry' will be there too!"

"Okay, little sister of mine. Here we go again. Don't you ever give up? You tried this before at the college spring break dance. All I know is this party had better be all you say it's cracked up to be. I can't stand getting all dressed up for nothing especially on a miserably cold night like this one. The snow is coming down by the boatload. I've never seen snowflakes so big!"

"Oh, Barbara, don't be such a party pooper."

"I hope Harvey can get here on time. The snow on the streets is really starting to pile up. I wonder why the streets weren't salted. Say Arvis, speaking of Harvey, why haven't you two hooked up yet? Haven't you given him a little love encouragement?"

"Be serious, Barbara. Harvey Ellis?"

"Why not? He's a perfect gentleman and Mama and Daddy love Harvey to death and you already know he's had his eyes on you."

"I know, Barbara. I've had my eyes on him too but, what about Jasper?"

"That bum…that absolute street hood. I wouldn't waste my breath even speaking his name. Harvey is the one for you."

Arvis knew her sister was right but what Barbara didn't know was the strange hold Jasper had.

"Oh, I forgot to tell you something, Barbara."

"Forgot to tell me what, Arvis?"

"Harvey called Daddy and told him he was tied up with cab calls because of this snowy weather. He won't be able to pick us up but is sending Gus Jones instead."

"Gus Jones is a slick-haired, flirting demon," Barbara shouted while struggling to close the side zipper of her dress.

"Calm down, Barbara. Gus is the only driver available tonight. The others called in sick and left Harvey and Gus to do all the driving tonight."

"I hope Gus doesn't expect big a tip from us tonight just because we're having terrible weather." Arvis chuckled as she remembered the last time Gus tangled with Barbara and wound up with a black eye. He was in real trouble if he messed with Barbara on a night like this.

"Is that a new dance step you're practicing, Barbara?"

"You know darn well I'm trying to zip up this blasted dress. It's stuck!" Arvis laughed while watching her sister twist and wiggle while she struggled to zip up her sequined, form fitting, black velvet party dress.

"Oh-o-o-o-o, look at you!" I haven't seen you make such a fuss over primping and dressing up since you took your senior class picture. Henry's eyes are going to pop out of his head when he sees you in that outfit!"

"You can be a real pest sometime, Arvis," Barbara grinned sheepishly while kicking off her bedroom shoes to put on her black patent leather pumps. Gus blew his car horn!

"That's Gus," Arvis said.

"I'm ready," added Barbara.

Four inches of snow had already fallen. Roads were slippery and dangerous. Unfortunately, the only snowplough in town for Black folks belonged to Benjamin Boone's Repair Shop. Ben was a mechanic that could be trusted to fix any mechanical problem. Despite the junky appearance of engines and car parts in front of his business, he was a top-notch mechanic. His ability to fix anything mechanical was uncanny. He was so talented that all he had to do was listen to an engine and he could tell you the problem. However, tonight Ben was laid up at home with a sprained ankle. Suffolk's roads were on their own tonight. Black folks stayed off Suffolk's wintry covered icy roads since Ben was home bound except for Arvis and Barbara and all the brave young people who dared to venture out.

"You girls be careful. Why yawl want to go out on an awful night like this to jitterbug is beyond me!"

"Now Mama, Arvis and I will be just fine," Barbara said, as she and Arvis gave her a see-you-later kiss. Gus honked his horn again.

"Hold your horses, Gus Jones! The girls are coming out now!" Eva yelled through the porch screen. "That man can be so frustrating sometimes."

Eva watched her girls get into the taxi. The taillights of the car vanished behind a curtain of windblown fluffy snowflakes. She didn't

GRANNY'S PLACE

understand why but she felt a chill way down deep in her bones. She wrapped her thick shawl around her shoulders even tighter.

"Shucks! It's nothing but the cold weather that's got me shaking in my shoes. I know I've got nothing to worry about when it comes to my girls but…maybe…I should have put my foot down harder and said no party," Eva thought to herself. All she could do was pray to the One she bowed to every night and ask for the safety of her daughters. Had she remained on the porch a minute longer, she would have heard the sound of a harmonica playing louder than the noise of a distant train whistle.

"Would you please slow down at bit, Gus Jones? Slow down this minute!" Barbara shouted. "We want to get where we're going in one piece!"

"Don't fret so much, Miss Barbara. I've got everything under control," Gus answered, as he looked behind him through his rear-view mirror and grinned at Barbara with a stupid look on his face.

"Watch out! You're going to hit that deer," Arvis shouted.

Gus slammed on the brakes. The car spun around in circles on the icy road, tipped over, rolled on its side, and finally slid to a stop in a deep muddy ditch on the side of the narrow two-way road. A deer stared into the headlights, as if in a daze and calmly walked to the other side of the rode.

Disoriented, Arvis managed to crawl through the broken back window cutting her knee on the broken glass. Holding her hand over the bleeding gash she had on her forehead above her left eye, she struggled to stand to her feet. Blood ran through her fingers as she staggered down the middle of the icy road as two blinding car lights came closer and closer.

"Oh Lord have mercy," Harvey said. He gasped at the sight before him and quickly moved his cab closer to the wreckage by the side of the road.

"Help me somebody! Please help me," Arvis muttered before collapsing onto the snow-covered road.

"Arvis, can you hear me? Arvis, speak to me!" Harvey picked her up off the cold road and carried her to the back seat of his taxi.

"Barbara…Gus…taxi…" Arvis whispered, in Harvey's ear.

"Don't say anymore, Arvis. Save your strength," Harvey replied softly as he placed her on the back seat and covered her with a blanket. He left his car motor running to keep the car heated and called Lucille.

"Lucille, there's no time to give you the details but send an ambulance to Bryon Crossing. There's been a terrible accident."

Without hesitation, Lucille made the call. Not wanting to waste precious time, Harvey retrieved his flashlight from the glove compartment of the cab. Using the light shining from his flashlight, Harvey followed the skid marks made by Gus' cab on the dark snowy road. He followed the tire skid marks until he saw the mangled mess.

"Gus, are you there? Are you okay?" There was no response. "Is anybody in there?" This time, Harvey heard a low moan. Cautiously, he climbed up on the overturned taxi and aimed his flashlight through the back window.

"Barbara! Hold on, honey! Help is on the way."

"Harvey…" Barbara repeated softly.

"Yes, Barbara, I'm still here with you. I won't leave."

"Arvis…is…she…is she…" Her voice was getting weaker. "Arvis is okay, Barbara. She's lying on the backseat of my cab. Just be still."

Harvey tried to disguise the panic in his voice. At last, he heard screaming sirens and saw the flashing red and blue lights of three ambulances, two fire trucks and three county police cars.

"Good old Lucille," Harvey said to himself. "Thank you, Lord God for Your mercy, from the bottom of my heart."

With lightning speed and precise efficiency, the paramedics removed Arvis from the backseat of Harvey's taxi, laid her on a gurney and rolled her to an ambulance. Meantime, fire fighters were using the jaws-of-life to get Barbara and Gus out of the wreckage. Gus didn't make it. His neck was broken. Harvey called Lucille again to give her an update on what was happening.

"Oh no, Harvey, I'm sorry to hear that Gus is gone. I can hardly believe it. What a shame," Lucille lamented.

"It's a pretty ugly sight out here, Lucille but right now I need you to call Eva and Pervis to fill them in on all the details and tell them that I'm already on the way to get them to take them to the hospital."

"Already done, Harvey but you watch yourself on the roads too. The storm is getting worse by the hour."

"Okay, Lucille."

Harvey took advantage of speed of one of the ambulances and drove close behind. The route it was taking passed directly by South Fourth Street. He reached the anxious parents in eleven minutes flat. They waited on the front porch while Harvey turned the taxi around in the front yard. Emotionally, Eva was one-step away from hysteria.

"Come now, honey bunch. I know this is a tough one, but we've been through worse times than this," Pervis said. "Chin up now. We are almost to the hospital. I'm sure all is not as bad as you think."

"I know you're trying to lighten the load a bit for me, Pervis but those are my babies in there. That's all I can think about now."

Harvey pulled up to the hospital emergency doors at Louise Obici Memorial Hospital. Eva swung the taxi door open and stepped briskly through the wide, automatic glass doors without breaking her stride. Pervis was right behind her.

"I'll be in the lobby waiting for you and Miss Eva, Mr. Tazell."

"Okay, Harvey" Pervis yelled as he walked as rapidly as he could to keep up with his wife.

Out of breath, Pervis walked to the end of the hall and rested his elbow on the counter next to Eva. She was impatiently drumming her fingers on the counter and waiting for the nurse to hang up the phone from a humdrum conversation. Finally, the nurse finished her call and gave Eva the information she needed to find her girls. Even though Eva now knew the room number, she investigated every room as she hurriedly walked by the doors just in case the nurse at the desk got things a little mixed up. With Pervis close behind, she came to an abrupt stop. Pervis knew she had found the right room.

"My babies!" she screeched, clasping her mouth to muffle her loud cry.

Despite needles attached in her hand and arm, Arvis looked to be resting. A thick gauze bandage was over her eye and around her head. To Eva, it made the injury look worse than it was. Arvis was resting under the watchful eye of a nurse who remained in her hospital room and attentively checked the attached IV needle and recorded data.

Barbara was in the next room. The extent of her injuries was more serious. Hospital staff x-rayed her and gave her a head-to-toe MRI. They discovered internal bleeding. She was unconscious during the

GRANNY'S PLACE

whole procedure and in dire need of surgery. Eva and Pervis watched as the nurses rolled Barbara into an operation room. Eva and Pervis waited for news of Barbara's surgery results by the side of Arvis' bed. A head nurse in Barbara's room who was an administrator also, interrupted her thoughts and directed her attention towards Eva and Pervis.

"Mrs. Tazell? Mr. Tazell?"

"Yes," Pervis answered.

"I'm Miss Fidler, Dr. Jamieson's assistant. He will be with you shortly but he's attending to your daughter, let me see, Barbara right now. I know this must be upsetting to you both but the best way you can help your daughters is by being as calm as you can." Ser was very lackadaisical and emotionless.

"Let me tell you something, Miss Fidel, or whatever your name is. That's our daughter in that operating room," Pervis said, irritated to no end. "My wife has been crying since we got here and all you can do is show off your so-called professionalism. I'll tell you what, Miss 'whatever-your-name-is', leave my wife and me alone. If we need anything, we'll call you. Now, would you please vacate the premises?" Miss Fidler vanished saying nothing. Then, he guided his wife to the waiting room.

Weak from anxiety, Eva leaned on Pervis' shoulder. Pervis could feel her body relaxing against his. He spotted the waiting room coffee table and got up to fix a cup for his wife.

All that happened back then but this is now. What happened to his daughters in the hospital seemed like yesterday. Arvis recovered with a tiny scar on her forehead near her hairline. Barbara was less fortunate. Unforeseen complications from the accident left her unable to bare children.

Barbara knew that Eva secretly bla`med herself for letting her girls go out on such an angry, stormy night. Arvis blamed herself for failing to get Harvey as the taxi driver on that night instead Gus but, only Jasper is to blame now for what has happened to Arvis now.

"Jasper," Barbara hissed the name to herself. "He's a disease that needs to be stopped." Her eyelids began to weigh heavily with the blessed sleep she needed. Her mind finally found the solitude of an interlude of repose.

Henry and Pervis went to the kitchen for a tall glass of lemonade. Neither one could sleep. As soon as their wives fell asleep, Pervis and Henry quietly went downstairs. Henry had to wait for what seemed like an eternity for Barbara to fall asleep.

"Eva sure knows her way around the kitchen," Henry said, breaking the silence.

"Your wife knows a few tricks of the trade too," Pervis said, as he poured himself another glass of lemonade.

"Do you think we should check on the ladies, Pervis?"

"Nope, give them some space. Time for them and to be left alone with their memories and thoughts is the best medicine for them now."

"Oh well, I suppose your right Pervis," Henry replied, ending the conversation.

A TEAM

After a restful slumber, Eva was out of bed. It was early evening when she quietly tipped out of her bedroom not wanting to wake Joy.

"Poor baby," Eva whispered to herself as she walked down the hall to the kitchen.

"Hi Mama, did you get plenty of rest?"

"Yes, I was just lying there doing more thinking then sleeping."

"Thinking about what, Mama?"

"I was thinking about the next few days of planning for the service for Arvis. It's going to be a trying time for everyone."

"What do you mean, Mama?"

"Well here's a list I managed to jot down on the train. It's all that must be done and the order of each task to be completed."

"Wait, Mama. Here's a list I made too. Let's compare notes and see if we've cover everything that needs attention. Arvis deserves the best and that's what we're going to give her."

"You're certainly right, Barbara. Mr. Crocker of Crocker's Funeral Home assured me that he has taken all the necessary steps to have Arvis body brought from New Jersey by train on Friday evening. Reverend Leyton knows all the information and has a completed program for the services for Sunday at one o'clock. Pervis made those arrangements before we left New Jersey."

"This is Thursday. The timing is good, Mama. Oh, while you slept, the phone has been ringing off the hook. Calls have been coming in from so many of Arvis' friends who want details of the services so they can be at the service to pay their respects. For example, The Mayflower Carole Singers want to sing a song in Arvis' honour since she was a member too. They'll be coming all the way from Rhode Island."

"Isn't that nice of them, Barbara? So many loved my lamb but… actually I have two little lambs and it will always be two." For a moment they embraced each other and let tears flow.

After some time, Barbara said, "By the way Mom, the Suffolk News Harold will run the obituary tomorrow. Mr. Hewlett printed up a special memorial statement for the services and should be included in the paper too. He wanted to express his sentiment. Henry and Dad have gone to his office and make sure all the particulars are worded the right way and then they're going to go over to the church to be with Reverend Leyton today too to make sure he gets everything just right."

"God bless Mr. Hewlett," Eva said. "Let's sit on the front porch now and go over this plan of action for the folks from out of town and where they'll stay. The Express Hotel says they have our reservations for the rooms we need. How about we take a tall glass of ice tea with us?"

"Okay, Mama," Barbara said. Eva sat in her metal rocker and Barbara relaxed on the glider, which sat at the end of the porch by the living room windows.

"You know something, Mama?"

"What, Barbara?"

"Joy is still sleeping."

"I know, honey. That child hasn't budged either. In all my years, I've never known anybody to sleep as sound as that. Her breathing was very heavy at one time. It's like she's in some kind of stupor and…I've noticed something else."

"What, Mama?"

"Every time Joy vacations with me and Pervis, the first day she would always go into a deep sleep…just like now. Girl, one summer she slept for two whole days when she got here. Pervis told me that sleep like that isn't natural."

"Under the circumstances, I can see why. With a jackass for a Dad, it's a wonder she's not disturbed mentally."

"I think you've said it best, Barbara. The man is a 'jackass'. Lord, have mercy on my granddaughter."

"Don't worry yourself about Joy, Mama. She's here now and is getting a much-needed break from meanness. You and Dad are giving her that break."

"Now…let's get back to the schedule. I've contacted Mrs. Bremond, chairperson of the Women's' Building Fund Committee. She and ten members of the W.B.F.C. have volunteered their assistance with organizing all the cooking, supervision here after the funeral services and anything else that needs to be done."

"That's more than anybody could ask, Barbara. They're a faithful, hardworking bunch."

"What about Arvis' personal belongings, Mama?"

"Before Pervis and I left Eatontown, we convinced Jasper to have all her things shipped here for storage. Pervis' strong notion was all Jasper was going to do was hand her things out to those hussies that use to sneak calls to the house when Arvis wasn't around. I reminded Pervis and Henry to make sure everything arrives with her at the train station. The night before we caught the train to come home, Pervis told Jasper not one thing of her's had best be missing or…"

"The company commander!" the two said together.

Then, both sat quietly as if listening to a sound nobody else could hear. Eva gazed into nothingness and mechanically poured another glass of ice tea for herself and Barbara. Barbara was first to interrupt the momentary silence.

"Number nine on the list has been completed." Numbers ten, eleven, twelve, thirteen, and fourteen are completed too. I don't know about you, Barbara but I think that's enough for today."

"I agree, Mama," Barbara said. "The rest can wait."

Pervis and Henry pulled up in the front yard driveway and parked right in front of Pervis' workshop. The two men talked about this and that as a way of relieving themselves of the events to come. After piddling around in Pervis' workshop, they decided to join their wives on the front porch. Henry sat next to his wife on the glider and Pervis sat in the matching metal rocker opposite the house door.

All four sat quietly as sounds of nature enveloped them. A lazy afternoon had turned into an early evening. The sounds around them included a squawking bullfrog splashing into a muddy stream down the hill from the house. Pervis began to whistle softly as the fireflies danced around the white flowered snowball bushes that graced the front porch's white concrete steps. The smell of honeysuckles escaped into the evening air and perfumed the front porch. Pervis contemplated the business of the next few days but there was one thing that dominated his mind more than anything else. Since he was to deliver

Arvis' eulogy, he wondered deeply how he could say what would represent his daughter's life in only half of an hour.

"You know something, Henry," Pervis said, interrupting the silence.

"What's that, Pervis?"

"Well…I got this strange feeling in my gut and I can't toss it to one side."

"…a feeling?"

"It just can't end like this, Henry. It just can't."

Eva and Barbara were puzzled but knew not to step in front of their competent husbands. Besides that, they were anxious to hear what else they were going to say. Eva knew her husband was concentrating on something of extreme importance.

"Rest in peace, my little dove," Pervis said, tenderly. "Your Daddy will know what to do when the time comes."

Henry knew his father-in-law didn't have a revengeful bone in his body but believed that there were certain principles in this life that were not to be crossed. Jasper had crossed the line.

"Come along everybody and let's get an early rest. We have lots to do in the next few days and we'll need every bit of our strength," Eva announced.

"You're right, Eva," Pervis agreed. "What about Joy? She's still sleeping. If she gets up during the night and we're sleeping and she's hungry or something, what then?"

"She's a big girl Eva and knows where the kitchen is. She knows she can get whatever she wants to eat or drink. Does that suit you?"

"Everything's fine Eva," Pervis said, with a smile. It was always the custom in the Tazell home for Pervis to check the locks on the front and a back door to make certain the house was secure. He was about to step onto the landing to go upstairs when the phone rang.

"Hello? Oh! Sure, I remember you. Thank you. Same to you and your words are very comforting. Yes, she was a wonderful person. I'm sad you won't be able to come but, I thank you for calling. That was very thoughtful. Thanks again and goodnight to you too."

After hanging up the phone, Pervis continued upstairs once again and prepared for bed. Joy was still sleeping. Henry came in and gently picked up her limb body and carried her in his arms to her bedroom, which was next to the back porch that Pervis had constructed. Once placed on her bed and covered, all said their goodnights.

The only light that penetrated the darkness of the slumbering household was a small nightstand lamp next to Eva's side of the bed. She silently mouthed the words of her favourite Bible verse. It was Psalms 91. Reading the Bible before bedtime sleep was a nightly episode that she had faithfully practiced for many years. Tonight, verse five of Psalm 91 exploded with what she had faithfully done for so many years. *"Now you don't need to be afraid of the dark anymore, nor fear the dangers of the day; nor dread the plagues of darkness, nor disasters in the morning."*

"Goodnight, my baby girl." Eva turned off the small nightstand lamp and after a few sniffles, fell into a deep sleep.

I'LL MISS YOU

The next day, Harvey stopped for a hamburger and ice cream cup at Dairy Queen taking a much-needed break. His heart was heavy as images of the lovely woman soon to be eulogized, to scroll across his mind. He had tuned out the hustle and bustle of uptown shoppers going by and imagined what it would have been like to hold Arvis in his arms after a hard day at work and feel the warmth of her body against his. He started to tremble as he thought of stroking her long black tresses as he pressed his mouth against her full, moist lips whispering soft words of love in her ear as he spread…

Lucille's husky voice ripped into his thoughts. "Yeah, Lucille, go ahead."

"Mrs. Tucker and Barbara need a ride to Hoffheimer's Shoe Store. Her husband and Pervis had to make a run out of town today so there's no transportation at the house."

"10-4, Lucille, I'm on the way."

Harvey stuffed the last of his vanilla ice cream cone in his mouth and backed his taxi out of the Dairy Queen parking lot.

"I will always miss you desperately, my beloved Arvis. You'll always be my secret love," Harvey said to himself.

THE FAITHFUL CREW

It was early Saturday morning and the W.B.F.C. had already begun their tasks. They vacuumed every room up and downstairs, dusted, washed windows, ironed whatever needed ironing, shook out every throw rug in the house, and ran any last minute errands. Mrs. Bremond was the chairperson of the industrious bunch and assigned all chores. The women moved like an army of African ants. The most Barbara and Eva could do was answer the telephone and make certain not to get in the way of the W.B.F.C. clean-up crew. Not only was the group extremely detailed, the younger members had the energy to trim the hedges and cut the grass. The organized chaos whirled about the house until every assignment was finished with time to spare.

"Don't you worry one bit, Sister Tazell. We'll all be back one hour early tomorrow ready to begin our service to you and your family again."

"Thank you so much, Mrs. Bremond but won't you and the ladies have some refreshments before you go? It's awfully hot outside and you and the ladies have been working non-stop," Eva asked.

"Good gracious no Sister Tazell, you have enough to deal with already. We'll be on our way. You need this time to spend with your family."

"Thanks again!" Barbara waved to the women, as they crammed their brooms and mops in their two cars.

"Let's relax now, Mama."

"Lord yes," Eva said, flopping down in her metal rocker. "By the way, has Joy gotten up yet?"

"Yes, Mama. I heard her running water in the tub."

The telephone rang just as Eva passed to go to the kitchen.

"Hello Mr. Crocker," Eva said. "All the programs were expertly done and are on their way to the church? I'm so glad to hear that. Thanks for calling and letting us know. Bye now."

GRANNY'S PLACE

Joy wasn't sleeping as Eva thought but was lying across her bed peering out of her bedroom window. As she looked, she made sure that the hair curlers attached to her hair were in place. Even though they ached on her head a bit, she knew they were in place for a special reason. She could see the east side of the yard that included Granddaddy's workshop and the entire side yard where four peach trees and an ancient magnolia tree swayed in the breeze. She watched a hummingbird busily gather nectar from inside an enormous white magnolia blossom.

Spread out all over her bed was her picture diary, colour markers, and pencils. For some reason, many black charcoal pencils were now included among her drawing tools. In her picture diary, using her black charcoal pencils, Joy drew rolling hills silhouetted by dozens other trees. The sky, filled with various size clouds, overlapped each other while suspended in a coral blue sky. Far in the distance of the drawing, sitting on a hill was an insignificant looking plantation mansion fashioned like one of those down south mansions seen in one of those old southern movies. Tall columns supported an upstairs porch wrapping all around the mansion. She didn't know why, but she felt the mansion had a secret.

"Joy, honey," Eva shouted. "Come on downstairs and get something to eat!"

"Coming down right now, Granny," Joy shouted back while rolling up her picture diary and putting it back into the dresser drawer.

As always, Pervis sat at the head of the table. A tall glass of sweet ice tea completed his plate setting. Filled with the rest of the tea, Eva positioned a round pink pitcher next to his plate. No other drink ever filled the pitcher. Barbara and Henry sat opposite of Eva and Joy and Pervis sat at the end of the table. An oscillating fan set on the highest speed hummed as it automatically turned from side to side in an effort to relief the heat of the early morning.

Only a few months ago, Suffolk had been enjoying the cool pleasantness of spring weather. However, on this day, Mother Nature had decided that she would remind all within her domain that she was boss on today by releasing a sample of what the summer season would really be like. Hanging by the front porch door, a thermometer registered ninety-eight degrees and it was only ten o'clock in the morning.

"Let's bow our heads," Pervis said. "We thank you Lord for this food we are about to receive. May it nourish our feeble bodies in Jesus' Name…Amen." "Amen," all others chimed together.

After the grace, the hush at the breakfast table was deafening. Unknowingly and out of habit, Eva had put a plate setting across from Barbara for Arvis. All pretended not to notice.

All would end the day on the front porch.

THE FINAL FAREWELL

A thump on the front porch door signaled the beginning of events that would test the faith of the Tazell family. The Suffolk News Herald had arrived. With big pink curlers bobbing from her shoulder length hair, Barbara excused herself from the breakfast table to retrieve the paper off the front porch. A note from Mr. Hewlett attached read: *No fees for the next three month. Sincerely, Hank Hewlett.*

"How sweet of him," Barbara commented to herself. Walking back down the hall with paper in hand, she went back into the kitchen. Everyone was anxiously waiting to read the announcement written about Arvis. Barbara began to read aloud for everybody. They all held hands as she read:

SUNDAY RITES FOR ARVIS MARIE BAILEY

GRANNY'S PLACE

Funeral services for Mrs. Arvis Marie Bailey will be held Sunday at 1:00 pm at Tabernacle Christian Church. She left this life to join her Creator on Tuesday, April 1, 1958 in a New Jersey Hospital after a short illness. Mrs. Bailey is survived by her husband, Sgt. Jasper Bailey and one daughter, Joyce Ann Bailey; her parents, Mr. and Mrs. Pervis Wendell Tazell; one sister, Mrs. Barbara Gwendolyn Tazell-Johnson; a brother-in-law, Henry Johnson of Oneonta, New York; one aunt, Ms. Georgia Woods of Mt. Clair, New Jersey; four uncles: Stanley Tazell of Flint, Michigan; Rupert Tazell of Cape Charles; and Peter Tazell of Bridgetown, Barbados; and a host of other relatives and friends.

The family asks that all floral donations be forwarded to the Crocker Funeral Home. All financial donations will be forwarded to the W.B.F.C.

After the announcement was read, Eva couldn't contain her emotions any longer. Bowing her head, she wailed for Arvis. She wailed for her lost child as if a knife had pierced her heart. Barbara wrapped her arms around her mother's trembling shoulders…Joy wrapped her arms around Barbara…and Pervis and Henry embraced all of them. Finally, Eva raised her head, wiped her face with the corner of her apron, and sighed deeply. All was well with her soul now. She gently cupped Barbara's face and hugged Joy to assure them that all was fine. The men dried their eyes. As they did, everybody was startled as Eva slammed her fist down so hard on the corner of the table that the top of the sugar dish popped off, fell on the floor, and broke.

"Barbara, hand me that bowl! I'm going to make the best coconut cream cake that you've ever tasted. It was Arvis' favourite. She's safe and in a place where she'll always be happy and never suffer or hurt again. So, yawl get out of my way unless you want an apron tied around your waist too!"

Very befuddled, Henry and Pervis made a beeline to the front porch. As they did, Pervis smiled quietly because he knew the moods of his wife and knew that she had a good reason for her actions this morning.

"You know, Henry. Eva's actions are like the seasonings she cooks with."

"What do you mean, Pervis?"

"Well, everything about this family is held together by special ingredients all blended and cooked together. The result is something delicious. After a while…you'll know what I mean."

Joy went upstairs to her bedroom and got out her picture diary and crayons again. Barbara joined her husband on the front porch after she'd helped Eva clean and prepared the kitchen for the W.B.F.C. The scent of baking vanilla cake layers careened down the hall to the front porch. All except Eva sat and relaxed before the soon coming event. Pervis pulled out his notes he'd written for the eulogy from his pocket. He was to read about his daughter. Henry sat next to Barbara on the glider and comforted her while she laid her head on his shoulder.

"Well, we better start getting ready," Pervis said, rising from his rocker.

"Oh! Look what's coming down the street," Henry said.

"Eva! The W.B.F.C. is heading down this way," Pervis yelled to Eva."

"Let them in when they get here, Pervis."

"Okay, Eva." Pervis waited patiently for their approach. Finally, they were on the front porch steps.

"Come on in, ladies," Pervis said. "The house is yours." He and Henry scurried out to the workshop like two scared jackrabbits. Looking at them from her upstairs bedroom window, Joy laughed at her uncle and granddaddy.

"Whew! Those ladies have more get-up-and-go than some of the executives in my office building," Henry smiled.

"I don't know much about 'big wigs' and such but those gals look like they can change your socks without taking your shoes off," Pervis said, holding his sides and laughing hard. The men continued their workshop antics.

"Mrs. Tazell!" Mrs. Bremond yelled upstairs.

"Yes, Mrs. Bremond?" Eva answered.

"We're ready to get started and the announcement about the food donations was made at the prayer meeting Saturday night but Radonia Bemory donated a bowl of potato salad that night anyway."

"That's okay and thank you for telling me, Mrs. Bremond."

Mrs. Bremond took the bowl of potato salad and placed it in the already overcrowded refrigerator. After Eva was halfway dressed, she

GRANNY'S PLACE

went back down to the kitchen to put the final changes on her vanilla cake and then hurriedly back upstairs.

The W.B.F.C. made quick work of setting up serving tables in the dining room. All forks, spoons, knives, plates, napkins, cups and all other serving utensils were placed in the proper positions for serving.

"Pervis, Henry! Yawl come on in and get ready now. We women have finished with the bathroom", Eva yelled from the upstairs back porch.

"Okay, Eva. We're coming right now!" Pervis hollered back.

Barbara and Eva descended the stairs like coronate queens in their best stylish attire. Eva was dressed in a straight black skirt with a split on the side. A black silk collar accented her asymmetrical matching jacket. Two large bejewelled Victorian buttons on either side of the jacket opening finalized the style. A wide brim black hat, black silk gloves, and black patent leather shoes completed her outfit.

Barbara was richly dressed too. She wore a wide bottomed, black taffeta dress with a low-necked top accented by a wide black silk collar. The bottom of the outfit was styled with a narrow hem of black satin. A pillbox hat adorned her pageboy hairstyle. Black silk gloves, a small black purse and patent leather shoes were equally matched. It was obvious the she and her mother had shopped together at one of the most exclusive shops in town.

Driving the family limousine, Mr. Crocker had arrived. He soberly opened the rear door for Eva, Barbara, and Joy. Then Pervis and Henry sat on the facing seat inside of the majestic vehicle. The limousine started moving slowly up South Fourth Street. Neighbours stood on their porches and watched the sober sight pass. Men took off their hats and women dabbed their tear-filled eyes with their aprons. All loved Arvis. They knew how she died. In fact, all Suffolkonians knew.

Tabernacle Christian Church was comfortably air-conditioned due to the persistent fundraising efforts of the Women's Christian Building Fund. Deacon Dave Wilson directed all activities to assure everything ran smoothly. He and his wife Debra were long-time friends of Eva and Pervis. Like Pervis, Dave was a staunch believer in punctuality and saw to it that there wasn't the slightest deviation of the specified schedule of events. Reverend Leyton, Pastor of the church, sat reservedly in his chair on the podium. According to the program, he held written remarks given to him by Pervis because he had a habit of not sticking to the point. He had been the pastor of the church way beyond his years of retirement but refused to step down and let a younger voice take his position.

All female ushers dressed in all white and the male ushers dressed in black suits alternated in their standing positions at the end of each pew. The family walked quietly down the left church aisle and sat on the first pew. Jasper was already sitting at the opposite end of the pew. Nobody knew when he got in town because he stayed at his cousin's house. He was dressed in full military attire. Even today, of all days, he showed distain for the Tazells by refusing to acknowledge their arrival as they took their seats. Pervis was last to be seated. Next to him sat Eva then Joy, Barbara, Henry and then…Jasper. Eva placed her arm around Joy's shoulders as if to protect her from the deadly virus sitting on the end of the pew.

Seated in the second pew behind the Tazell family were: Mr. Jenkins, President of Main Street Bank; Mr. Hank Hewlett, Editor-in-chief of the Suffolk News Harold and his wife Freda Hewlett; Mr. and Mrs. Percy Barnes, owners of Percy's Ice Cream Place at which Arvis and Barbara had frequented many times. On the third pew sat: Lenny Jackson, Pervis' boss at the shipyard; Lucille Phillips, radio cab dispatcher and Harvey Ellis, owner of Suffolk's only Black cab service. The rest of the pews were filled to capacity with acquaintances whose lives Arvis had touched with her bright personality and contagious 'million dollar smile'. Joy leaned forward to peek at her father. He stared straight ahead never moving a single muscle.

Before he sat down beside his wife, Pervis reached into his suit jacket pocket and retrieved the eulogy he had written for Arvis. The nagging gut feeling of such a waste of life remained in the recesses of his mind. As he thumbed through his notes, his only thought was of honoring his daughter.

"Granny," Joy said, tugging at her grandmother's sleeve.

"Yes, darling," Eva whispered.

"Is Mom in heaven?"

"Yes, sweetie, heaven is her new home."

"Do you think she misses me like I miss her?"

"I have no doubt in my mind that she does."

"Will I ever see her again?"

"Yes, baby. We all will…one day."

The senior choir finished its rendition of *How Great Thou Art* and seated themselves in union with a gesture from the choir director. In their starched white uniforms, the Deaconesses sat in the four pews in the front left side of the church. The seats had long been designated as 'Pews For The Deaconesses.'

Reverend Leyton delivered a brief invocation and words of bereavement to the Tazell family. Dressed in his black robe that showed years of shine on the derrière, he returned to his seat. Kassandra Porter rose to read Psalms 91. The Mayflower Coral Singers sang: *Peace Be Still*. Feet patted in time to the music. A few 'Yes, Lord' could be heard throughout the church. Acknowledgements of condolences were read, and the Tabernacle Senior Choir sang a selection that rang with perfect harmony. Eva was grateful for that.

TA-FLAP! TA-FLAP! Fluttering cardboards fans with advertisements of the local funeral home on the backside and a picture of the Tabernacle Church on the other side swung back and forth. The air conditioner was going at full blast but the number of folks that packed the church building made the temperature humid and the air conditioners were not able to ward off all the heat of the day.

Joy leaned forward and looked at Jasper again. His head was bowed, and snot dribbled from his nose. He was crying crocodile tears like a kid caught doing something wrong. He'd done something wrong alright, and his error was lying in the coffin. Joy shifted her position back into her weeping grandmother's arm.

"…and now," Reverend Leyton said. "Mr. P.W. Powell will deliver the eulogy."

Once on the podium, Pervis eyes quickly observed a sea of tear streaked faces. Everyone gave their undivided attention to one of Suffolk's most beloved citizens.

"Dear Friends,

Last Tuesday, Almighty God looked down with tender compassion on a child of His in a hospital in Eatontown, New Jersey and whispered, 'My child, come home.' And so…the spirit of Arvis Marie Tazell Bailey took its flight up to the first heaven, up above the second heaven, up to the third heaven, and finally to the realm of peace and glory where changing scenes of earth are left and feared no more. She was born to Eva and Pervis Tazell in Riverhead, New York on July 6, 1929. She spent most of her life growing up in Suffolk where she received her high school education. She went on to attend the Norfolk Division of Virginia State College and finished her degree requirements in music and taught music for five years until her illness.

In 1948, she married Jasper Bailey. To that union, was born Joy, or formally named, Joyce Ann Bailey.

Arvis was a loving daughter, a faithful wife, a patient mother, a kind sister and always someone's sympathetic friend. This is why our loss we feel so deeply. Yes, we weep and sigh but not as those who have no assurance. Thanks we extend to our God who gave her courage to at last say... 'A better thing I do than I have ever done. A far better rest I shall know than I have ever known and a far better home up there with mansions bright and fair away from sickness, toil and pain in that land of no despair'.

And in that 'land up there', Arvis will continue to sing. Perhaps she may be singing as she did here with glad Hosannas to the Christ, Our Lord and King.

The life she lived and the service she gave merit her peaceful existence away from this land of sorrow where she'll weep no more. Yes...in that land up yonder, around the Great White Throne, we'll meet her when our own travelling days are done."

Greetings and sincere thanks to each of you for your presence here today and thank you for each thought and each word and deed of kindness extended to me and my family on this sad occasion."

Pervis stepped down from the podium and re-joined his family on the front pew. As the senior choir stood in unison to sing its last song, *Amazing Grace,* family was the first to be ushered down the aisle past the casket to bid Arvis farewell one last time.

While lying in repose as if in a quiet sleep, Arvis resembled a sleeping queen. She was attired in a sparkling long pink mesh lace dress edged with white satin. Tiny gems speckled the entire dress. A diamond necklace bejewelled her neck and the rounded bodice of the top of her dress was fashioned of silk. Her head lay on a white satin pillow. Her black shoulder length hair cascaded in soft waves and framed her face like a professionally done portrait. Her wedding rings sparkled as if to announce what marriage was really supposed to be like. All that was needed was a crown on her head and she even had that now in her new home.

Joy stood transfixed by her mother's casket. She let her eyes fill with the image before her. She stroked her Mom's hand gently for some time and smiled quietly as if to say, "I'll see you again". She burned the image of her mother into her mind for one last time. Feeling the gentle nudge of Eva's hand, Joy moved on. Pervis and Eva looked at the face of their daughter. Eva dabbed her cheeks with her handkerchief, leaned down, and gently kissed her daughter's cheek.

"My child, my little girl," Eva cried.

"Lord, forgive me but that man has to pay for this," Pervis said, silently.

When Henry and his wife passed by, the reality of not ever again having a midnight chat with Arvis reverberated every nerve in Barbara like a horrible explosion. She wept out loud while Henry held his arms around her waist. He supported her sagging body as she started to faint. Pervis helped Henry steady her on her feet.

Jasper had slipped past the Deacon's pews, past Mr. Crocker who was sitting there and hurried out of the side door of the church annex. Mr. Crocker eyed the man with a frown and with disdain. Pervis saw it all.

THE UNTIMELY GUEST

Mrs. Bremond and her W.B.F.C. members left the funeral services a half hour early and drove to the Tazell home to position themselves at their posts before to begin phase two of their strategies for the day. They wanted to make certain that the traditional aftermath remained decent and in order. The dining room table turned into a masterpiece decorated with flowers with perfect arrangements of the silver utensils, drinking glasses and bowls. The dullest mind could determine where the food line began and ended. Arranged chairs were set in a specific place on the front porch and along the driveway as cars would be instructed to park on the street when there was no more room in the Tazell yard. A single rose lay in wait in the chairs of Eva and Pervis. Three other roses lay on the glider. One was for Barbara, one was for Henry, and one was for Joy.

    The family limousine arrived first. Barbara, Henry, Eva, Pervis followed by Joy entered the house and went straight upstairs without exchanging a word with each other. They changed into less formal outfits and went back downstairs to prepare for the arriving guests. Dave and his wife arrived first. Then Harvey came. All sat reverently for a moment in the living room while more guests continued to arrive.

    Mrs. Bremond shrewdly positioned her three-hundred-fifty pound, five foot torso right in front of the kitchen door. It was her ways of letting folks know the area was strictly forbidden except to immediate family. She firmly requested inspection of all containers of fluid brought on the premises when it was doubtful as to the contents of each container. The only fluids offered in the house were already set up on a special table in the dining room. Any fluids stronger than fruit punch were poured straight down the kitchen drain. The other W.B.F.C. members placed themselves around the dining room and living room to keep order and remained standing like impassive statues.

    Dave Wilson volunteered to settle the parking chaos by directing each car to a parking area in the yard. He used the large side lawn as a

GRANNY'S PLACE

parking lot also making sure to stay clear of the magnolia tree and being careful not to ruin the thick grass on the huge lawn. The yard soon resembled a major sale at J.C.Penny's. The modest house was bursting at the seams with hungry relatives, friends, and unrecognizable faces.

Eva and Pervis took their perspective seats on the front porch. They resembled pillars of strength and loving forbearance as they listened to words of condolences repeated by each guest who greeted them. The flapping cardboard fans of the guests weren't a match for the sultry heat of the day. An unforeseen additional number of guests didn't help matters either. Mrs. Bremond instructed one of the committee members to place a small oscillating fan on the front porch to try to bring momentary relief as it created a cooling gust of air across the sweating brows of Eva and Pervis.

"Where's Joy?" Barbara asked, sitting next to Henry on the glider.

"She said she wasn't hungry and just wanted to take a nap. That sounds extremely relevant now," Henry replied, continuing to keep a close eye on his wife. The conversations held throughout the house consisted of childhood memories, places once visited, whose birthday was on what date, were second helping available.

Suddenly, all attention on the front porch was directed towards a car barreling down the street well above the accepted speed limit. Dust and pebbles filled the humid afternoon air as the green Mercury halted dangerously close to the freshly painted white porch steps. The car was turned around and parked as if preparing for a fast getaway. The driver of the car got out. It was Jasper. He mounted the porch steps and entered but was not offered a seat. Eva was glad Joy chose to remain upstairs. The silence was so thick that the only sound heard was the whirling of the porch fan and ta-flap.

"What's on your mind?" Pervis asked, rising from his rocker never taking his eyes off the unwelcome visitor.

"I'll be here to get Joy day after tomorrow," Jasper said, dispassionately.

"What!" Eva said, obviously frustrated with the insensitivity of the man and his abrupt visit. "Why not let the child stay here for the rest of the school year. Barbara can have Joy enrolled into Suffolk Middle School without any problem. Then she can go right into summer vacation as she usually does when school gets out."

"Besides that, who's going to look after the child now that her mother is gone?" Pervis asked.

"I've worked all that out," Jasper answered.

"Worked what out? What's your plan, Jasper?" Pervis asked.

Before he could answer, Barbara repeated her father's question. "Joy will need much attention after what she's gone through. You'll be doing whatever it is you do on the army base all day. What about Joy? Who is going to care for her?"

"If you give me a chance to answer, I'll tell you," Jasper said. "My family, namely my cousin, will take charge of things from now on and Joy will have all the attention she'll need. Besides, I was talking to Pervis…not you," Jasper sneered. Because of his remark, Henry was standing too and was about to answer the smart mouth soldier but Pervis answered first.

"You'd better watch how you address my family," Pervis said, with an intimidating tone like an agitated grizzly bear. Jasper got on Pervis' nerves and Pervis was in no mood for his foolishness. Jasper, realizing he was out-numbered and in the "enemy camp", decided to humble himself only as a survival tactic rather than go one-on-one with the head of the Tazell family.

"What do you mean by 'you've everything worked out'?" Pervis asked.

"Well…err…what I meant to say was Petula Clark, my sister, is coming down from New York. That way Joy can finish up her schooling in Eatontown, be supervised by an adult, and of course spend her last summer in Suffolk as she's always done since…since…"

"What are you trying to say, boy? Spit it out! Let's have it all," Pervis said gruffly.

"…err…since it may be a good while before she'll be able to visit Suffolk again since this will be her last summer here."

"What do you mean? Why will this be her last summer?" Eva asked, standing to next to her husband.

"I've got traveling plans for the future. My battalion is sending me to Europe. I have to travel as a family and Petula completes the picture," Jasper said, delighted that he'd found a new nerve to pinch.

Henry listened intensely to the warped soldier's explanation carefully and sensed something was desperately wrong. He knew Jasper was up to no good and Joy was in impending danger if her father carried out his so-called overseas travel plans. Henry continued to listen keenly to every word said. His legal mind made numerous mental notes. He had dealt with men of no integrity before but Jasper was on top of the list. He smelled the rotten undercurrent of a wicked mind. Barbara trembled with anger. She was thinking of Arvis while having to listen to the ramblings of the imitation of a man whose words of nonsense only made her even sicker. By this time, Eva and Pervis seethed with rage and were astonished at Jasper's insolence.

"Well, that's all I have to say. Guess I'll shove off now because I've got some business to take care of uptown." With that he rolled his shoulders back, swung open the porch door and got into his Mercury. Tires spun and pebbles flew. Looking through his rear-view mirror, Jasper giggled devilishly. He felt maliciously victorious one more time and was proud of the fact that he had left injuries in the enemy camp.

Most of the folks in the house knew what kind of man Jasper was and the path of cruelty that usually followed him. However, Jasper had forgotten the unspoken code. It was something known by the black townsfolk and was never violated...until now. It was a kind of "do unto others" code. If it were discovered that someone intentionally did an injustice to one of the townsfolk's own, unspeakable torments would be the unfortunate result. All sensed and knew that Jasper had spun a web from which there would be no escape. He had broken the Suffolkonian code.

The events of the day, the endless stream of guests, Jasper's surprise visit, and the sultry heat had finally taken its toll on the weary family members. Two by two and three by three, friends and relatives filed past Eva and Pervis as they bid them farewell. The W.B.F.C. members and Mrs. Bremond were the last to leave. It had taken the women only an hour to replace moved furniture, clean the kitchen and put leftovers in the refrigerator.

"Sister Tazell, we'll be leaving now. Remember, we are only a call away," Mrs. Bremond said.

"I'm at a loss for words for all that you have done, Mrs. Bremond," Barbara said.

"Miss Barbara, if you only knew of the debt of gratitude folks in this city owe to your Mama and Daddy, you'd understand that what we did today was an honour and a privilege."

Joy was sitting on the top step. She had heard everything and felt sick to her stomach. She heard what her Dad had said about going overseas, Petula, and the whole mess.

"Oh, Mom," she whispered to herself. "Why did you have to leave me all alone?" She cried…for the first time.

PETULA CLARK

Eatontown, New Jersey seemed desolate and barren without Arvis. Joy could hardly wait for the last three weeks of school to end when she could return to Suffolk and her grandparents.

Joy's teacher, Mrs. Cottcreeve was the kindest yet firmest teacher in the building. She painstakingly watched her list the lessons to be reviewed for the final exams of the year and remembered the lovely bouquet of silk flowers placed among the floral arrangements at her Mom's funeral were from Mrs. Cottcreeve.

On the other hand, there was Petula, a walking alcoholic nightmare. Obviously, she was one of Jasper's kinfolk because the physical resemblance was strong. Joy couldn't stand the sight of Petula and the thought of having to share her bedroom with a constantly inebriated, living cartoon was heartbreaking. She felt as though her room was being invaded by a monster from outer space.

During one of their shouting conversations constantly heard by next-door neighbors, Petula told Jasper under no circumstances would she be considered as a live-in babysitter and that her privacy and her other activities would totally be her own. Bitter experiences had transformed the academically aggressive young woman into a manipulative, loudmouth shrew. She had learned to use men to her advantage and because of her positive physical attributes, they were like putty in her hands. She knew Jasper inside and out and was well aware of his intimidating tactics and bulling and, they didn't work on her. That evening Jasper came home and immediately met Petula's raspy voice.

"Well…hello soldier boy," Petula mockingly greeted with the smell of gin on her breath.

"Don't start with me, Petula. I'm tired and don't feel like any foolishness."

"Listen, mister sergeant," Petula spewed. "We're two of a kind and I learned well because of your meddling in my life. So, don't think you can dish out to me what you dished out to your dead wife."

"Shut-up about her!"

"Oh, seems as though I stepped on a sore toe. Try anything funny with me and you'll be gasping for air, understand?" Mildred hissed.

"Take it easy, Petula. Everything is everything, know what I mean? Why are you coming on so strong?" Jasper asked.

"Like I said, I was dumb enough to listen to you years ago and your advice turned out to be rotten. Then you marry one of the nicest girls in town and that goes rotten too."

"Come on, Petula. Give me a break. What are you trying to say?"

"Just this, lover boy. I know you like the back of my hand so if you want me to do this favour for you and Uncle Sam just pay me like you promised and keep your brat out of my face. Now...where's the cash you promised for this deal?"

"I told you already, half of the cash now and half once I get things straight on the home front in Germany."

"Nothing doing, buster, you promised you'd give me everything upfront so give me all the cash you promised now or the deal is off!"

"Then the deal is off!"

"Fine with me, buster, step to one side because I've got some packing to do!"

"Now wait a minute, Petula. You drive a hard bargain but you win," Jasper said, rubbing his forehead as he rolled a tumbler of scotch between his hands. "Have it your way." He reached into his wallet and handed her the money. Petula snatched the hundred dollar bills, licked her forefinger and began to count.

"All one-thousand dollars is here and now we're back in business," Petula grinned. "Don't try anything else, okay? Remember...we're two of a kind."

Joy closed her bedroom door to shut out the pathetic bickering of her father and Petula. Taking out her picture diary from under her socks in her dresser drawer, she lay across her bed and began to draw. When she finished, she lovingly rolled up a drawing of her grandparent's home on South Fourth Street.

Petula's story was told through the Suffolk grapevine in several versions but one fact veined true through them all and that was Petula was an alcoholic monster because of a love affair gone sour. Even though she and Arvis had been in the same senior class in high school, they'd only one-met-on one or two occasions. When they finally met, it was at the East Suffolk High School graduation ceremony. Arvis had graduated as summa cum laude and Petula magna cum laude. Not only that, Arvis had received a full scholarship at the Norfolk Division of Norfolk State College in music and Petula was awarded a full scholarship at Fisk University in engineering.

Petula's future was bright and secure. She would have been the first woman to select engineering as a field of study. During her first year, Petula maintained a perfect four-point grade average. Then Jasper came on the scene.

Before her sophomore year at Fisk and during her first summer vacation, Jasper introduced Petula to one of his corner boys. He knew that his naïve cousin was no match for the smooth talking nincompoop he picked out. Some of Petula's closest friends saw Jasper's plan and tried to warn Petula but nothing would sink into her intellectualized mind. Petula seemed to be void of common sense where affairs of the heart were concerned and Jasper took advantage of that fact.

To this day, Petula's friends couldn't figure out her deep attraction to Thomas Lewis because he was uncouth, loudmouthed and jobless at twenty-three. He had been a tenth grade dropout that expressed his no-nothing opinion every time he opened his mouth. A first level reading book would have been mind boggling for him.

His appearance was always disheveled. Craters in between razor bumps disfigured his high-yellow complexioned face. His teeth would have been a medical challenge to any dentist. A lye-slicked, combed-back hairdo always needed a touch up around what little hairline the lye had graciously left. His hygiene was questionable until he exposed his armpits then another of his problems was evident. Despite the pleas from her friends and other family members, Petula fell head over heels in love with the man as if he were some kind of school experiment that could be salvaged. Maybe she saw something nobody else could see. Maybe she saw a diamond in the rough to which all others were blind. Maybe she had x-ray vision too. He was an eyeful indeed but he wasn't a diamond.

College bells rang for the sophomore school year but Petula wasn't able to answer the academic call. Thomas had whispered sweet nothings in her ear and Petula was going to have a baby. Of course, bumpy-faced Thomas denied having anything to do with the matter and skipped town with Jasper's help. Petula pleaded with Jason to tell of Thomas' whereabouts by Jasper pretended not to know anything. To this day, she'd not forgiven Jasper for that fact.

Early December, Petula gave birth to a seven pound, eight ounce handsome baby boy. There was no doubt that the father was Thomas Lewis. Having never quite recovered her wits after Thomas deserted her, Petula began to drink heavily. Any liquid that was a least one hundred twenty proof had pickled what mothering skills she'd had and the constant care of her son fell on her already overworked parents. At present, her ten-year-old son had gotten a visit from her only three times since his birth. He never knew who she really was. It was a sad scenario because Petula would have been the first in her family to earn a college degree.

ONE MORNING

Each night before going to bed, Joy made sure she'd set her alarm clock for six o'clock sharp. School didn't begin until nine o'clock but she needed the extra time to fix a good lunch, clean up the kitchen, and do other assignments Jasper gave her before going to school. While wrapping her sandwich, she remembered how her Mom use to fix two meaty sandwiches with cheese and tomatoes, wrap up two large homemade oatmeal cookies, pour a thermos of chocolate milk or Kool-Aid sweetened like she wanted, and a surprise dessert that was always delicious. That was then and this is now. A cheese-and-mayonnaise sandwich and a thermos of watered down Kool-Aid represented lunch. Besides that, Jasper refused to except any excuse for school tardiness. Joy knew the punishment would be a whipping with switches that stood as tall as the refrigerator in the corner of the kitchenette. However, this morning when she woke up, something was different. Joy had an awful stomachache.

"Maybe it was that weird concoction Petula cooked last night," Joy said, rubbing her stomach. Fear gripped her as she threw back her bed covers.

"Oh no, what do I do now?" Joy made a mad dash for the bathroom to try to wash out her pajama bottoms. The thought of being late for school drove her into near hysteria.

"Petula, wake up! Please, wake up!" Joy pleaded, while shaking the comatose woman.

"Huh? What's wrong with you, fool?" Petula snarled while squinting through eyelids swollen from late night rabble rousing. Without saying another word, Joy held up her pajama bottoms.

"You mean to tell me this is what this nonsense is all about?"

"But what do I do?"

"You mean to stand there and tell me that you've never heard of this happening? Of all the…"

GRANNY'S PLACE

Petula got out of bed and staggered towards the bathroom with Joy tipping behind her. She reached under the bathroom sink and retrieved a long white cotton object from a dark blue box.

"Here…take this. I'll show you how to put it on and what this strap is for."

Petula gruffly read the instructions to Joy and showed her how to use the apparatus.

"Yes…but…but…"

"Do as I say because you'll only have to deal with this once a month." With that, Petula stomped back into the bedroom and resumed her morning sleep. Joy tried to hold back her tears and keep her sanity but lost the fight.

"Quit your blubbering. Get out of here and get your tail ready for school. You know what your Dad will do if you're late. Don't just stand there slobbering! Get out of here and get going! I need my beauty sleep."

"…then you'll need to sleep for the next twenty years," Joy sniffed.

Joy looked at her alarm clock. It was getting dangerously late. She skipped her daily morning ritual of pouring herself a bowl of corn-flakes. She pulled her long black hair back into a mangled ponytail and dashed out the front door. As an additional precaution, she wore two pairs of shorts under her poodle skirt. She was unnerved by the new sensation of stomach cramps and felt strangely different and more grown up.

"I'll die if this is found out. I wish Mom were here to explain what's happening to me." Joy said, trying not to let tears come to her eyes.

The tardy bell rang just as Joy sat down at her desk. Out of breath, she took out her notebook and pencil and tried to fit in with the rest of the class. A sharp pain shot through her abdomen like a fiery arrow as she wiped beads of perspiration from her brow with the sleeve of her blouse. The announcements were read and it was time to stand and salute the flag. It was an effort to stand. Joy repeated the pledge along with everyone else. The class sat down in their desks again to listen to the school announcements.

"Our librarian, Mrs. Augustine is asking that all teachers remind their students to return all library books before the end of the day. Also, a cart will be send around to each classroom by the homeroom library assistants to collect library books," concluded the student announcer.

After the announcements were made, Mrs. Cottcreeve directed the class to open their history textbooks to page one hundred eight.

"Make sure you have your notebooks open too," Mrs. Cottcreeve said. Her demeanour in the classroom was stern but well-seasoned with kindness and sincere concern for all of her students. She was the only instructor who had been teaching for thirty years with no sight of retirement and was voted *Teacher of the Year* five years in a row. Well regarded and highly respected by her peers and students, Mrs. Cottcreeve always made it a point to meet with the parents of her students at PTA meetings and was well acquainted with Joy's mother, and she was always greatly impressed.

"This morning we'll continue our studies of South America. The last entry in your notebooks should be about a small island called 'Barbados'. Since we are moving further southward in our studies, today we'll begin our study of a country called 'The Republic of British Guyana'. Guyana means: 'The Land of Many Waters'.

"Can anybody tell me why? Nobody?"

"Guyana is called The Land of Many Waters because of the extensive number of rivers located within the country. Be sure to write that fact in your notebooks as you may see it included as a question in your final exam next week. Now...let's begin to read the chapter. Does everyone have the right page?"

"Yes, Mrs. Cottcreeve," the class answered in unison.

"Will you stand and begin reading, Joyce?"

Joy fumbled with her text until she found the right page. Rising slowly to her feet, she began to read but, her mind wasn't concentrating on the words in front of her. In the back end of her row, she could here Charles laughing and giggling...or was it just her imagination?

"Located in the northwest corner of South America, Guyana is a land rich in natural resources that...err..."

"Keep reading, Joyce," Mrs. Cottcreeve said with a look of concern on her face.

Joy couldn't stand it anymore. Slamming her book down on her desk, she bolted through the classroom door and down the hall. Knowing this display was out of character for Joy, Mrs. Cottcreeve instructed her teacher's aide to have the rest of the class continue reading and stepped into the hall. She found Joy standing by a water fountain three doors down. She was holding her hands to cover her face and sobbing uncontrollably.

"Now there, there, Joyce Ann. Would you like to talk about what has upset you so today? Won't you tell me what it all about?"

Joy grabbed her teacher around the waist and streams of tears stained Mrs. Cottcreeve's yellow silk blouse but, Mrs. Cottcreeve was more concerned about the child in her arms. Joy finally raised her head and looked into her compassionate eyes.

"Mom told me once that special changes would happen to my body as I grew older but…it scared me this morning when I saw my bed sheets and pajamas."

"I'll tell you what we'll do," Mrs. Cottcreeve said. "We'll walk to the nurse's office together and let her explain the whole matter to you so you'll better understand what occurred this morning. It's perfectly normal for girls your age. She has pamphlets that will be most informative too. Don't worry about a thing and we'll keep this between us girls," she said smiling.

They walked down the hall hand in hand. While they were on the way to the nurse's office, Mrs. Cottcreeve reminisced about meeting Joy's mother at a PTA meeting. She remembered Arvis' gentle concern expressed for her daughter's progress. Jasper was…a different story. During the meetings, he mumbled to himself instead of making informed statements and shuffled around like a caged animal. When Mrs. Cottcreeve learned of Arvis' sudden intermittent in the hospital, she realized Joy was not getting the academic and emotional support she needed and strongly suspected there was more going on in the home than neglect. Mrs. Cottcreeve was definitely alarmed when she noticed that Joy's grades were dangerously slipping from the high honor roll status that she'd always maintained.

"The proper authorities must definitely be called," Mrs. Cottcreeve vowed, silently walking down the empty halls to the nurse's office. Joy and her teacher never spoke to each other again about the incident again.

The school year was finished and the school bell rang for the last time. Children of all sizes poured through the front doors of Eatontown

GRANNY'S PLACE

Junior High School and ran north, south, east, and west to get home. They were a mass of promoted souls, screaming, yelling and waving and their report cards in the air. Mrs. Cottcreeve viewed the wiggling crowd of proud children from her third floor classroom window. Her favourite pupil of the year made a beautifully decorated handmade card and left it on her desk. After reading the note, her tears stained her yellow blouse.

"Dear Mrs. Cottcreeve,

Thank you for caring. Thank you for reminding me there are people like you who seem to understand everything. Thank you for all the wonderful things you've taught me especially those things that can't be found in textbooks. I'll never forget you.

Love,
Joyce Ann Bailey"

THE DREAM

"Goodbye, everybody and have a great summer," Joy shouted and waved to her classmates. She scurried through shortcuts in the rear of the apartment complex and through paths marked by worn grass. As she darted past row after row of apartment buildings and ran through backyard play grounds, she finally reached the back door labelled 572 Pine Brook Road. Jasper wasn't home yet. In fact, nobody was home yet. Three weeks earlier Petula ran off with a divorced drill sergeant who had the same one hundred proof alcoholic problems. Joy didn't care and was glad to have her own bedroom again. She unlocked the back door with the key that hung around her neck, ran upstairs, and flung open the bedroom door. They were still there. Her pink leather suitcase with her train ticket still rested on the foot of her bed just where she left them. Time couldn't go by fast enough as she anticipated the wonderfulness of the train ride that would take her to her to Suffolk and the two most precious people in the world.

"Please God," Joy prayed. "Don't let Dad be late getting home today of all days. Let him keep his promise to be here on time to take me to the train station…Amen."

She felt as if she were a visiting stranger. There had never been a father-daughter relationship. She felt that residing in Eatontown was merely tolerated. The sound of the front door creaking open brought her thoughts back. Jasper was home.

"Thank you, God!" Joy said, blowing a kiss towards the ceiling. She snatched her suitcase and ticket off the bed and hurried down the steps.

Joy had never engaged in any kind of conversation with her father but noticed that the past few weeks his actions and words to her had been a bit more pleasant. Nevertheless, she stayed out of his way and spent most of her time in her bedroom reading or drawing in her diary. She didn't want to risk angering her Dad for anything and jeopardizing her train trip to Suffolk for the summer.

GRANNY'S PLACE

Joy didn't know it but Jasper was nice for a different reason. Three weeks ago, about the same time she'd been comforted by Mrs. Cottcreeve and the school nurse, Jasper was called to his base office and reprimanded by his company commander who warned him about his actions. The commander had grandchildren Joy's age and related to Jasper the dire concerns that Joy's homeroom teacher, Mrs. Cottcreeve had reported to him. The commander stated that if corrections weren't made on the home front concerning Joy and if not properly supervised, a stiff monetary fine, possible dishonorable discharge and jail time would result. Jasper got the point.

"You ready?"

"Yes, Daddy," Joy answered humbly.

As they drove to the train depot, only one or two mundane sentences were spoken. Jasper sat behind the steering wheel of the Mercury with his hands locked in a ten o'clock position and stared straight ahead at the road. Sitting on the backseat, Joy could barely contain her excitement as the car made a right turn into the train station parking lot. In the past, Jasper would have been mean enough to dash her hopes of seeing Suffolk by turning the car around for home and grinning spitefully but…not this time. That special teacher and a terrific company commander were her comfort for the hour.

"What are you sitting there for?" Jasper said, slamming on the brakes. "Get your suitcase and get out. Tell your grandma, 'Evil Powerful' I said 'hello'!"

Joy complied and got out of the car. Jasper sped off without even looking back to make certain his daughter was inside the station. She picked up her heavily stuffed suitcase and walked into the station to the ticket window.

"That express train boards on track seven," the ticket agent said. "But hurry because your train leaves in ten minutes."

"Thank you sir," Joy said.

"Trai…umber…45…is now…oarding…for all…oints…South!"

"It's a good thing I checked with the ticket agent first. I couldn't understand a word from that gurgling loudspeaker," Joy said, dragging her suitcase on the marble black and white floor. Awkwardly descending the centuries old, iron steps to the platform, she managed to get in the line that was fast disappearing at track 45. Having gotten on board, she inched along the narrow aisle as fast as her suitcase would let her and the passengers ahead of her would allow.

"Seat 14A," Joy said, looking at her train ticket and seeing there was a match. Standing on her tiptoes, she struggled to put her suitcase in the overhead rack.

"Here, Miss. May I help you with that?" While the kind gentile stranger dressed in formal military attire put her suitcase overhead, Joy noticed the nametag on the man's briefcase.

"Benjamin O. Davis, Jr.," she thought, reading the tag and remembering the name from one of Mrs. Cottcreeve's history lessons. I wonder could this be the same man. Nah-h-h-h...it couldn't be the same man...or could it?"

"There you are, Miss," the officer said, tipping his officer's hat.

"Thank you very much, sir."

"It was my pleasure, Miss."

Everybody settled in their seats and relaxed for the non-stop trip. Joy could hear newspapers rattling and people digging into their snack bags. Joy had no snack but it didn't matter because being on the train for Suffolk was snack enough for her. She stretched out her legs and lay down. There was nobody sitting in 14B. A ticket agent made his way down the aisle checking and punching tickets and mounting the approved tickets in the metal rim about the seat. The ticket agent was a tall stately looking elderly man whose uniform was immaculate. Medals of service decorated his lapels to indicate forty years of service. The train started rolling with a jerk and a hiss of the engine.

"Ticket please, little lady?" the agent said.

"Here you are but excuse me, sir. May I ask you a question?" Joy handed him her ticket.

"Yes ma'am, you sure may."

"How long will it take to get to Suffolk?" Joy asked delighted by the grown-up attention she was getting.

"Well...since this is an express and we'll be only stopping along the way to pick up passengers once, we'll reach Suffolk in...oh, I'd say...in about six hours. We're scheduled to arrive at 7:40 pm so will that suite you? It's 10:45 a.m. now."

"Yes sir but may I ask you one more thing?"

"What do you have in mind, sugar?" the ticket agent patiently asked.

"If I should fall asleep, would you wake me when we get to the Suffolk station? I don't want to miss that stop because I'm on my way to visit my grandparents for the summer and they will be worried if I don't get off the train."

"Sure, don't fret yourself at all. I've got five grandbabies about your age and I hope someone would help them if they had to travel alone. Rest yourself and don't worry about a thing. I won't let Suffolk pass you by."

By the time the agent came back down the aisle, Joy was fast asleep. He smiled but before passing her seat, he covered her with a blanket from the storage compartment above her seat.

Joy began to dream in full color. She dreamed she and her Dad were hiking one afternoon. The air was fresh and filled with the scent of pine trees and wild flowers. The sky was cloudless and blue. Joy felt amazingly strong and full of energy as they climbed the narrow ridge of a rocky path. They reached a level space on the mountain and decided to sit down and rest. The view from the height on the mountain was of breath taking. Green meadows landscaped by innumerable massive trees of all kinds was outstanding. Suddenly, wind filled clouds began to gather and move rapidly across the sky. It seemed a storm was brewing. Jasper was sitting on a large flat rock and Joy was seated on the ground in front of him almost able to touch his feet. Then...from behind him...a rattlesnake angry at having been disturbed from his rest was erected to strike at Jasper's back. Jasper didn't hear the rattle of the snake's tail. Joy saw and heard it and was frozen with terror. Something wouldn't let her cry out to warn him about the impending danger. With lightning speed, the snack struck Jasper in the back of the neck. Joy watched as Jasper's body stiffened in agony and began to swell. Just as the snake bit Jasper, the train's whistle screamed and jolted Joy awake. She threw off the lightweight blanket and sat up in a cold sweat.

"Whew! It was only a dream," she said, wiping her face with a tissue from her jacket pocket. "Mom told me if you dream in color, them what you dreamed would come true!" For the moment...she put the horrible images out of her head and readied for the Suffolk stop.

"Good, you're up," the ticket agent said. "I was just coming to wake you before I made my train stop announcement."

GRANNY'S PLACE

"You mean we're already in Suffolk?" Joy asked.

"We sure are. You have a real nice summer visit with your grandparents, okay?"

"Thank you. I know I will."

"Suffolk! Suffolk! Next stop...Norfolk!" the agent bellowed.

The train hissed and came to a full stop. Passengers stood with their luggage and bags in hand ready to disembark. Joy was standing with them too. All she could think of was the sight of her grandmother's round face and warm cuddly body framed with a thick grey braid wrapped around her head like a crown. As the line of passengers slowly moved towards the coach exits, Joy saw the military gentleman again and waved...and he did the same.

"Watch your step. Take your time. Travel with us again," another train agent said, as he helped each passenger get down the train steps. As soon as Joy stepped onto the platform, she began to make her way through the crowd to the train lobby. Like a herd of buffalo, other passengers rushed to greet friends and family who came to the station to take them to one address or the other. Just as she was about to enter the train station lobby, Joy heard the call of a familiar voice.

"Joy, darling! Over here! Here I am!" Joy dropped her suitcase and ran towards her grandparents.

"Hey, baby! How's my brown sugar? Did you have a nice trip? Did anybody bother my little sugar pea?"

"Good gracious, Eva. Give the child a minute to get a word in edgewise," Pervis teased.

"Oh, be still, Pervis."

"Hey, Mr. Ellis," Joy said.

"Hello, Joy," Harvey answered. "Looks like you've done some growing these past few months."

Throughout the verbal exchange, Joy's arms locked around part of her grandmother's ample waist as tears rolled down Joy's cheek. She finally felt safe. If only she didn't have to leave Suffolk again.

"I can't get over how much that child looks like her mother. This could have been my little girl," Harvey thought as he placed Joy's suitcase in the cab's trunk. The resemblance was so strong that it seemed as if he was driving Arvis home...once again. A smile crept across his face.

GOOD OLD SUFFOLK

On October 31st, Joy was born in her grandparent's house, her most favourite place in the world. Judith Brown now retired and living in a nursing home, was Dr. Diggs' faithful right hand nurse in bringing Joy into the world. Together, the old timed but wise medical duo helped to increase the population of Suffolk no less than two-hundred and seventy-five times…give or take a few babies. Arvis had been in labour for eighteen hours. According to the decorative birth certificate made out by Dr. Diggs, if Joy was born one minute later she'd be a twelve-month baby. However…Dr. Diggs was gone now. He was the last of his breed of homebound country doctors. The new generation of patients went to the ultra-modern Obici Memorial Hospital or the local clinic named in Dr. Diggs honor. Joy was back in the town that embodied her security, fun and adventure. Above all, Eva's country cooking was always the major event.

Suffolk was a huge city and the largest city land wise. There were massive magnolia trees, blooming dogwood trees, whispering pines, behemoth evergreen trees, and ancient weeping willow trees. Miles of sweet honeysuckle vines, row upon row of corn and tobacco fields, cotton farms, and rambling meadows snugly encompassed majestic hillsides and were blanketed with lush green carpets of grass. It was also the home of The Planter's Peanuts factory. The Mr. Peanuts statue sat on a high edifice that could be seen over most of the city of Suffolk. The peanut factory was the main artery of employment for the majority of Black folks. Suffolk's citizens family roots traced back for hundreds of years. Tradition and beliefs were deeply embedded and hadn't altered their way of thinking. It was a city of staunch values. It weathered past storms of unwanted changes from hostile outsiders but its residents were well aware of the latest world events.

The city's many shopping veins were Main Street or uptown and it housed a menagerie of small businesses. There stood two bank buildings, The Suffolk News Harold office, county and city offices, hardware stores, soda shops, Sear & Roebuck, Woolworth Discount Store, the A&P Supermarket, Hoffheimer's Shoe Store, wholesale seafood and meat markets, the Five-'n-Dime Store, specialty boutiques, beauty salons and barber shops.

The city itself was divided into subdivisions and rural areas. East Suffolk was four blocks over and across the railroad tracks from South Suffolk. With a twenty-five cent fare on the city bus, another section of town was called Jericho were many dubious activities were held and was off limits to everyone on the east side of the tracks. Directions were given as "down yonder", "across the way" or "on the other side of the tracks". There was a section of Suffolk at the edge of the northern boundary line of the city shrouded in an atmosphere of mysticisms. The borderline suburb was called Portersville and folks had a story about the folks living there. The newest rumour heard about Portersville was the birth of a baby girl. Rumor had it that Portersville was populated by hundreds of mulatto descendants who were the biological products of long dead, lusty plantation owners who had played late night tiddly-winks with female field and house slaves. No one could fathom why the Portersville population still bred by interracial marriage and refused any outside intermingling with their populous. As a result, most all of the suburbs youth had to make regular trips to the eye doctor's office for unusually thick eyeglasses. Their longevity was on an average of fifty years. Despite all the scuttlebutt about the place, no tangible records have ever been found to prove the Portersville history. That didn't matter to Suffolkonians though. They relished keeping a good story going if there seemed to be some truth to it.

Another reason Joy loved Suffolk was because of the tall tales she'd hear her granddaddy's buddies talk about on their weekend visits early on a Saturday morning. After a hot cup of coffee from Eva, the men would sit in front of Pervis' workshop weaving stories of long ago adventures when Suffolk was only dense woods and dirt roads. It was their way of passing along family history, having a good time, teaching morals to their young folks, and scaring the daylights out of whoever was listening.

One such story involved the city's County Courthouse circulated by old timers for at least three decades. The appearance of the concrete structure lent imaginative truths to the tales the old timers spun. The old-fashioned relic was two stories high not including a basement used to store old records and furniture and such. The first floor consisted of a porch on which massive Byzantine style columns went around the entire building and supported a second floor that housed the vital statistics office, school board office and marriage license office. The first floor also housed the Mayor's Office, the Mayor's secretary's office, and town council members' offices, voting office, more vital record offices and the Justice of the Peace. A modern annex of jail cells had been added to the rear of the building to make room for the increase in population crime growth over the years.

As the rumor has it, many years ago when water fountains were labeled "white only" and "colored only", members of the illustrious town council held meetings to remodel the outside appearance of the courthouse but voted to completely tear down the old courthouse building and replace it with a new one further up the block. An agreement was reached. Bulldozers were in place, but something happened that brought a permanent halt to the plans. Each time a bulldozer came within ten feet of the building, blood curdling screams rose up from somewhere beneath the building. No construction company in town would address the situation. The council members were horrified yet perplexed but were determined to execute their plans.

One night while on duty cleaning, an old black janitor…who paid no mind to the rumors…found a brittle, yellowed parchment partially tucked behind a loose brick in the wall in a council member's office. The next morning, the janitor gave the parchment to the council member. As it turned out, the parchment was a record and diagram of where the graves of Buffalo Soldiers were buried under the foundation of the courthouse. Also written on the parchment was a blood thumbprint of each soldier buried representing a sworn seal that if the bodies were disturbed in any way…the soldiers would rise from their graves and wreak havoc on any Confederate descendants that disturbed their sleep and many Confederates resided and worked in Suffolk. The only changes made to the courthouse building from then on were a good spring-cleaning and a paint job whenever needed. That was the way it was in Suffolk. Things just seemed to work out.

ONCE AGAIN

Harvey, Joy, Eva, and Pervis chattered gleefully about their uptown shopping trip and about this and that as the taxi moved along Main Street. Joy inhaled the smell of fresh country air as it whipped back loose strands of her thick black bangs. Fresh air was a blessed relief compared to the smell of exhaust fumes of congested Suffolk uptown traffic. Familiar sights of old country homes, corner stores, the old Texaco station, one of two stations in the black section of town, which was Benjamin Boone's Garage and Towing Service, The Veteran's Meeting Hall for black veterans, and the Ice Plant with its rusty refrigerated delivery truck parked next to it. Joy always wondered how those big blocks of ice were made into squares and how a block of ice managed to survive a delivery in that broken down and bent up truck.

The taxi bumped and jolted as it crossed over the four railroad tracks that literally divided the city in half. They were the same train tracks that brought Joy to Suffolk. Travelers through the city would have to sit in the stifling heat and patiently wait until train cars lazily lumbered along the tracks. While sitting in the summer heat, folks fanned themselves and chitchatted about the latest news in town. In the winter, the same thing would happen on the narrow two-lane road except the car heaters ran instead.

"Oh look, Granny! There's the Mr. Peanut statue!" Joy shouted. Harvey, Eva and Pervis turned their heads towards the giant marquee while Joy stuck her arm out the cab window and waved as if the statue heard her. The statue was decorated by a white collar, black bow tie, a black top hat, and spats over patent leather shoes. A monocle was attached to a gold chain and the statue leaned on one leg and poised with a black cane. Whether it was summer, spring, fall or winter, Mr. Peanut was smiling.

As the taxi crossed the tracks, on the next block was the old Broadway Theatre. On a summer night, the entire block would be invaded by local black teens plagued by hormone surges. In the past the theater was one of Jasper's stomping grounds. In Eva's book, the place was taboo...end of story.

"Look, Granddaddy!" Joy shouted.

"What is it, sweetmeat?"

"There's Jamaal! There's Jamaal Wilson!" Pervis smiled when Joy saw the youngster and noticed her smile was different this time.

"My goodness child, the way you sound you'd think you'd never seen that boy before," Eva giggled. Pervis turned around in the front seat and winked at his wife.

"Hey Jamaal, it's me, Joy!" Jamaal waved back at Joy and faded from view as the taxi moved along.

Mr. Peanut

Joy laid her head on her forearm and squeezed her eyes shut with the excitement of being in Suffolk again. She listened to the three adults loudly debate about everything and anything. She wanted to forget images of New Jersey and Jasper.

Her thoughts were of her summertime friend Jamaal and the summer antics they'd had together. This summer it was his turn to discover a new path to travel or some forgotten road to cross.

One discovery during their last summer together was old Jericho Cemetery. It was a place for only Black folks funerals. It puzzled her that people could be so concerned where the dead were buried because... black or white...if you're dead, that's it. Nevertheless, Joy love to make charcoal tombstone rubbings while Jamaal examined tombs neglected or forgotten.

Joy especially loved Memorial Day. It seemed that every family in Suffolk wanted to honor someone on that day. The Tazell and the Wilson families would commence the day by cleaning and grooming the burial place of a family member. Arvis was remembered on that day too.

Joy remembered Jamaal's father said there were many former slaves buried in the Jericho Cemetery but where they were buried was a mystery because no records were recorded about them. They had bought their freedom from their slave masters and some managed to live inventive and productive lives. Decades of history lay silently beneath the earth. Joy suddenly remembered! That's where she'd seen the name. It was on a tombstone and read, "Benjamin O. Davis, Sr." She'd be sure to get a charcoal rubbing of that!

Joy began thinking of last year summer's bit of history about Jericho Cemetery which was told by one of her granddaddy's friends who as a lad, witnessed a lynching in the cemetery. The incident happened one wintry night, many years ago, when he and his parents were taking a shortcut through Jericho on their way home.

A youngster walking ahead of his parents, had a three-pound slab of fatback slung over his shoulder. He heard a commotion and instantly the family hid in nearby shrubbery. The noise was the lynching of a young fifteen-year-old Black boy who'd been accused of…heaven only knows what. The boy's limp body hung from the branch of an old oak tree almost all night. As morning hours drew near, the boy and his family waited until they were sure the White Supremacist were gone. They reverently buried the boy under the same oak tree. According to Pervis' friend, on a clear moonlit night, on the same night the lynching happened, you could see the lad sitting on the same tree limb where he'd been hung. He would just sit on the tree limb with one leg swinging and weaving a rope. In his own way, he was trying to tell anyone who passed by just what happened that night. If you were brave enough to hang around, you'd witness the ghoulish spectacle return to his grave until the same time next year. Suffolkonians knew well of the tale.

"Here we are," Harvey announced. He parked the taxi in front of the house, took Joy's suitcase out of the trunk, and placed it on the front porch. Eva offered Harvey the taxi fare but Harvey refused to take it.

"See you later, Harvey," Pervis said, as he waved to Harvey. "Don't be a stranger. Stop by for supper soon."

"You can count on that," Harvey replied smiling. As far as Harvey was concerned, nobody in all of Suffolk could spread a table like Eva.

139 SOUTH FOURTH STREET

Joy followed her grandparents up the whitewashed concrete steps that hugged on each side by huge snowball bushes. The blue and white flowers stood proudly as if welcoming the family home. The aroma of baking peach cobbler invaded Joy's nostrils as she mounted the stairs.

The house was a structural oddity with many added corners and turns. Her grandfather, born on the island of Barbados, was a man who held to strict traditions of the past. He used his expertise as a carpenter to build all around the house enlarging the structure. He made up his mind to do so when one day Eva was waxing the wooden living room floor and noticed a perfectly round circle, about the size of a saucer. It was damp, dark and sweaty. It looked like someone set a wet plate on the floor. Pervis went under the house to see if a small animal was dead and decomposing. Finding nothing, he sanded the floor to remove the spot but it returned exactly as it was a few days later. Both he and Eva were perplexed and resolved to take other measures to deal with the situation. Pervis made a call to his brother who was living in New York. His brother told him the ingredients of a long forgotten recipe that so poisonous that if tasted it could kill five elephants…at one time!

Pervis instructions were to go back under the house and pour the slimy black liquid exactly under the sweating spot. Not only did he have to follow those instructions exactly, but he had to construct something…anything…around the house. He decided to enlarge the structure in a useful manner for Eva. That's why there's an upstairs and downstairs back porch. Never again did he and Eva have to deal with the mysterious spot again.

With the delicious scent of peach cobbler invading her nostrils, Joy walked across the linoleum covered front porch and through the heavy opened front door of the house. Each year Pervis had the linoleum replaced. This year it was a light grey with a faint white azalea design. At the left far end of the rectangular porch was an old-fashioned light green swinging glider. The glider sat beside the living room windows. Against one of the windows and glider sat Eva's metal rocker. Pervis' matching metal rocker sat on the opposite side of the house main door and the right of the porch.

The doorway of the house attached itself to the beginning of the upstairs banister leading to the second floor. Once past the front door downstairs, a narrow hallway led to a telephone nook built by Pervis under the upstairs steps. Next to the telephone nook was an under-the-stairs small closet for storage. A few steps more and you were in a small room filled with encyclopaedias and all sorts of educational books where Arvis and Barbara use to study. A small window graced the tiny but significant room.

Joy followed her grandparents upstairs. The metal knee hinge of Pervis' wooden artificial leg squeaked as the three mounted the stairs. The banister creaked as Eva used it to support herself to go up the narrow staircase. An antique, seven-foot high, cedar wardrobe faced them at the top of the stairs. In it hung Pervis' best suits, dress shirts, his half-length summer choir robe and a long burgundy robe for the winter. A shelf at the top of the wardrobe housed three wide brimmed dress hats. At the bottom rested four pair of black and neatly polished wing-tipped shoes.

"Blasted arthritis," Eva said. " It's going to rain this afternoon. My aching knees are talking to me." If her knees ached…rain clouds were someplace nearby.

The upstairs ran north and south of the entire house. Over the downstairs front porch was another storage room. To the right of that storage room was a guest bedroom, once Barbara's room, and then a bit of wall space that was accented by a leather antique stagecoach trunk next to Eva and Pervis' bedroom. Next to Eva and Pervis bedroom, more hallway space and then another extra-large bedroom and across the hall from the last bedroom was another bedroom that was deemed as Joy's room and had been Arvis' old bedroom. Coming back towards the stairs, there was the Caribbean designed bathroom. The wooden square tiles around a tub that sat on four ornate legs were painted bright greens, yellows and pastel blues. The outside of the bathtub was painted a bright green too. From the bathroom was a bit of hall space and then Pervis' wardrobe and back to the top of the stairs.

GRANNY'S PLACE

The back windows in back bedrooms at one time emptied into a view of the backyard. The porch was used to store household paraphernalia, racks of clothes and book wooden storage cabinets. Some clothes were Eva's and too small in size and some new outfits. Other garment bags stored Arvis' clothes. Huge cardboard boxes of various items contained clothes, from years gone by, were stacked up to the ceiling in right porch corner. In the between two large windows hung a huge industrial fan. The fan used to be hanging in an industrial room of the shipyard. Every three years a new fan was bought. Pervis did a complicated private electrical wiring job for his supervisor. He asked Pervis what he wanted for the work. Pervis said he wanted the fan.

Sitting against a wall to the left of the fan, was an antique shelf with six glass doors that opened by lifting the door up and sliding it back. Except in the summer, Eva kept the porch door propped open with a brick. The forceful draft created by the fan, air-cooled all the upstairs rooms. The downstairs rooms were cooled off the same way with a smaller air conditioner in the dining room, but it strained to change the air temperature because some days were so hot. It was always set on maximum but only managed to cool off the dining room and part of the living room.

Joy's bedroom was the last room on the east side of the house and a floor to ceiling window opened to the spacious, green grass yard. A rocky path joined Pervis' workshop to the side of the house down to the front gate. In the center of the spacious yard, a magnolia tree stood taller than the house. Eva had planted it when Arvis and Barbara were born. It was a living family monument. The scent of its white blooms perfumed up half South Fourth Street. On either side of the magnolia tree were two peach trees. On the other side of the yard, sitting right beside the chain link fence, was Big Mama's house. Big Mama was deemed as South Fourth Street's news carrier.

The end of Fourth Street was incomplete, so the house sat on a hill. Foliage sprouted into a beautiful forest scene all the way to the bottom of the hill…and that was that.

The massive window in the bedroom across from Joy's room was a view of down the steep hill and a rippling creek that was part of Dismal Swamp. On the other side of the creek were tall trees overrun with

Devil's Shoestrings. The design of the house had always been a curiosity to Joy but she didn't care. The Tazell home was her haven of safety.

"...surprise!" Joy's grandparents hollered as they walked into her bedroom. Eva had redecorated the bedroom windows with double tiered, peach colored, ruffled, Cape Cod curtains. Starched and ironed curly edged crocheted white doilies adorned the top of the Victorian styled, five-drawer dresser sitting at an end wall and opposite the foot of a single bed. Eva crocheted the scarves three months before Barbara was born. A huge brown teddy bear wearing a velvet red bow tie sat on the ruffled bed pillows that matched the comforter. Arvis named the bear "Timothy" and had won the fuzzy animal at a July 4th county fair when she was a thirteen-year-old teenager...just like Joy.

"How do you like it, Joy?" Eva asked. Pervis already knew what her answer would be by the expression on Joy's face.

"Everything looks so beautiful," Joy replied teary eyed.

"We're so pleased you like it, Joy," Pervis said. "We'll leave you to unpack. When you've finished, come on down to the kitchen and have a dish of peach cobbler and homemade ice cream," Pervis said.

Joy flopped down on top of the summer comforter that draped over her twin bed and rubbed her hand over the delicately raised pattern of peach blossoms and mint green leaves. Not wanting to soil or snag it, Joy placed her suitcase on the stool to the vanity dresser that sat against the wall and next to the bed. She opened her suitcase and began to unpack. She put away a pair of navy blue sneakers, a light blue pair of shorts, a pair of blue jeans, a tan windbreaker jacket, and a sweatshirt with the Eatontown Junior High School emblem printed on the front. Next, she reached in the suitcase to hang up a sleeveless white cotton blouse, four pair of white bobby socks, a comb and brush set her Mom gave her two Christmas' ago, a few modest toiletries, her eight by nine inch drawing paper, a box of charcoal bricks and sticks and a set of color pencils. Thinking of the peach cobbler and ice cream and listening to her stomach grumble, Joy was ready to go downstairs. Just before leaving her room, she noticed the small black and white photo stuck in the upper right corner of her vanity mirror's wooden frame. She gently touched the photo. It was a photo of Arvis. She had a feeling her grandparents put the photo there for her.

"All done," Joy said to herself, closing her suitcase and placing it under the bottom of the small wardrobe sitting next to the dresser. She took off her Sunday patent black shoes and plain cotton socks she was wearing and decided to change into a jump suit instead. Wiggling her toes and letting the cool air slip between them, she put on her rubber flip-flops and ran downstairs shouting, "Suffolk! I'm in good old Suffolk!"

"Have another helping if you want, sweetmeat," Pervis said.

"No thanks, Granddaddy," Joy said, rubbing her full stomach. She'd have to get use to her grandmother's rich country cooking again. It was a far cry from a constant diet of cornflakes, cheerio's, cheese sandwiches and Petula's mystery meals.

BEEP! BEEP! BEEP! BEEP!

"That's Harvey beeping the taxi horn in the front yard, Eva," Pervis said, scooping up the last spoon of ice cream off his plate. "I'll see you two ladies later."

"All right, Pervis. Take care," Eva said.

"Granny…?"

"Yes, darling?"

"Why does Granddaddy have to go to work now…I mean today?"

"He traded shifts with another co-worker so he could be home with me to meet you at the train station."

"Gee…I'm glad he did."

"Why don't you go out on the porch and relax yourself on the glider. You know that's your favorite place to sit. You took a mighty long trip today. Aren't you tired?"

"Oh no, Granny," I slept on the train. Anyway, I want to help you in the kitchen."

"Okay…suit yourself. You wash the dishes while I clean off the table."

"Sure, Granny," Joy said, as she ran the warm water, poured in the dishwasher liquid and began to wash a small bowl. Eva noticed the frowning expression on Joy's face.

"Is the water to hot, Joy?"

"No, Granny. It's just that sometimes the sight of dishwater makes my stomach turn sour."

"Makes your stomach 'sour'? Maybe you ate too much ice cream. It was rich, you know," Eva said.

"No...that's not it."

"Well...what is it, baby? Tell Granny what's bothering you."

Jasper's constant warnings of not speaking of the happenings in New Jersey still gripped her with fear. However, this time...she managed to conjure up enough courage to speak up.

"You see, Granny...it's like this. Once, when I had to do the dishes back home, Petula tried to cook scrambled eggs. Some of the eggs stuck to the iron skillet. Since it was always my job to clean up the kitchen before going to school, I poured some dishwater in the pan to loosen the dried eggs so the pan would be easier to wash. Just as I did, Daddy came in the kitchen and saw the soaking skillet on the cabinet. He asked me if I was the one who left all that egg in the pan. Before he let me explain that Petula was the one who cooked the eggs, he poured out the dishwater and got a spoon. He told me to take the spoon and... well...I got sick to my stomach after the last mouthful."

"Wait a minute, Joy. Let me get this straight. You mean to tell me that he made you eat that mess?" Eva asked.

Joy's body trembled and she began to sob. Describing that awful moment was painful but it was a relief to get it off her chest. She'd finally had the chance to unload a bit of the gunk she'd been harboring to her grandmother. Eva embraced the crying child. With the corner of her apron, Eva wiped away the tears on Joy's cheeks.

"Hush now. Let me finish the dishes. You go and rest on the front porch on the glider and stretch yourself out if you want to."

"All right, Granny," Joy sniffed.

"That Jasper is one sick puppy. Pervis will have a fit when I tell him this monstrous titbit of news," Eva said to herself, as she stacked the last dessert dish on the cabinet shelf.

THE FRONT PORCH

During the summer, the front porch was the place where matters of importance were discussed. New neighbors, friends and strangers greeted each other there. Folks could just relax and escape into their own thoughts. In the winter, the kitchen became the conference room. Tonight, porches were darkened, but faces could be seen anyway. Eva and Pervis always listen attentively to all matters.

    Joy made herself comfortable on the swinging glider. It was made of wrought iron but was fashioned in a way to look like lace. Rusty impressions in the linoleum flooring left tale-tell marks that the glider sat in the same position at the far end of the porch for some time even though Pervis recently replaced the porch linoleum. At Eva's request, Pervis had the stoic artefact painted dark green to blend in with the linoleum. Many paintings and dozens of brush strokes had clogged a few of the tiny holes of the glider's intricate design.

    With one foot dangling off the glider and dragging on the linoleum, Joy gave the glider a push with her big toe. The glider quietly squeaked and squawked with each swinging movement. Pervis had forgotten to oil the hinges but the swinging created a gentle breeze that caressed Joy's body.

    A sudden burst of warm summer air aroused the fragrance of nearby honeysuckle vines. Joy managed a smile as she recalled images of her and Jamaal picking blossoms from the vine and chewing the small white petals to taste the sweet nectar that was hiding inside the petals. Since last summer, the vines had overrun the chain link fence bordering a small plot of grass only a few feet from the front porch steps. The honeysuckle-covered fence ran all the way down the hill and ended at the edge of the soft muddy riverbank at the bottom. Pervis added to the mystic of the river by telling Joy that if you followed the river until it ran out, you'd find yourself in the Florida Everglades. Sometimes, a bobcat or a stranded bear cub would wonder along the river's banks. Sniffing the scent, neighbourhood dogs would bark and chase the confused animal well into the woods and create a splashing ruckus resulting in the dogs yelping and running back defeated and out of breath.

Back home in Eatontown, Joy felt trapped between the walls of the small two-bedroom apartment. Her summer vacation to Suffolk was a welcomed relief from the constant weekend racket of Jasper's noisy card parties and giggling "anything goes" women. Giving the glider another push, Joy's eyes filled with tears once again.

As Eva made her way down the hall to the front porch, the telephone rang.

"Hello? Oh! Hello, Big Mama. Yes, I'm fine and how about yourself? Yes indeed. Pervis and I picked her up from the station only earlier this morning. Yes. She'll be spending the summer with us again. Pies... sure I can. How many sweet potato pies do you need by tomorrow? Three pies...uh-huh. They should be ready about two o'clock tomorrow afternoom. All right then. See you tomorrow, Big Mama. Bye now and thanks for your order."

Eva reached into the phone bookstand and pulled out her bakery order book. She filled in all the necessary information and placed the book back. She'd been keeping the book for years as was evident by the tattered pages. After the phone call, she continued down the hall to the front porch where she plopped down in her rocker wiping the perspiration from her brow with the corner of her terrycloth apron that she had made years ago.

"Well...weekend orders have started already."

"Can I help, Granny?" Joy asked, remembering her favourite cooking pastime of licking the bowl and spatula used to whip the cake batter.

"Sure, baby, I'll enjoy you for company but are you certain to get up that early? You know I get up at dawn. Are you feeling better now?"

"Yes, Granny," Joy answered sheepishly.

"My goodness," Eva remarked.

"What is it, Granny?"

"I forgot to take those sheets off the line and gather the eggs I need from the hen house. I need those eggs for tomorrow." With that...Eva was off down the hall again.

GRANNY'S PLACE

Folks all over town knew of Eva's cakes and pies. Even folks from "uptown" have tasted her culinary skills and had their limo-drivers pick up regular orders. Pervis always suggested that she open a bakery shop but Eva always resisted for reasons of her own. As it was, years of standing and cooking for her family and others had taken a toll on her knees. Years ago, just before she and Pervis made their move to Suffolk, she swore that the only meals she'd prepare would be for her own family members but, her weekend baking orders were a pride and joy to her and an opportunity to try new recipes.

"Joy!" Eva called.

"Yes, Granny!" Joy yelled back.

"Come to the backyard for a minute. I want to show you something."

"I'm coming, Granny," Joy said. She sat up on the glider, slipped on her rubber flip-flops and flip-flapped down the hall to the kitchen and outside into the back yard.

The clotheslines shuttered in the wind as, white sheets held tightly by clothes pins, fluttered and flapped. Sitting at the end of the backyard, Pervis' workshop and combination tool shed was an arm throw away from the back of the house. Attached to the side of the workshop was a chicken-coup Pervis had built a year after he and Eva moved into the house. Twenty-five white feathered chickens pranced around in the small enclosure in the front of the hen house like vain ladies in waiting. In the midst of them, proud and stepping high while overseeing his domain, was Old Colonel…the rooster. He was the chicken coup chief but a pitiful sight to behold. Most of his plumage had fallen out because of several fights with stubborn hens and the tip if his beak was chipped off but, he was the protector of his realm, nonetheless. Joy opened the small wire gate and entered the coup. Chickens clicked and scattered everywhere…including Old Colonel.

"Look over here, Joy," Eva said, pointing to something just inside the door of the hen house. Huddled together in a cosy nest of straw and feathers were six fuzzy yellow baby chicks.

"Aw-w-w look at them," Joy squealed. "Is it okay if I pick up one of them, Granny?"

"Sure!"

Joy rubbed the soft chick against her cheek.

"Go ahead. Isn't it grand how nature gives everything a fresh new start?"

"Ouch! The little rascal pecked my ear," Joy giggled.

Eva and Joy left the chicken coup, secured the gate, and began to fold up a load of sheets and towels she'd hung to dry earlier in the morning. Pervis had rigged a clothesline by stringing a thin steel cable between the back corner of the downstairs back porch and beside the workshop's door jam. A long pine eight-foot wood plank propped the middle of the clothesline to give it extra support.

"Joy, would you collect the eggs from the chicken coup nests? Take that basket over there to put them in. I'm going to finish folding these towels."

"Sure Granny, are you sure the hens won't mind?"

"Don't worry, honey. The hens wouldn't give you a problem."

"What about him?" Joy asked, pointing to Old Colonel.

"Ha! Ha! Old Colonel is just a lot of hot air with feathers."

Ten minutes later, Joy exited the chicken coup after collecting nineteen eggs from the nests. Propped on the top of the hen house, Old Colonel eyed Joy suspiciously, as she made her way through the chicken coup yard and out of the gate.

"Here you are, Granny," Joy said, showing her grandmother the basket. "That was the first time I did that. May I collect eggs for you again?"

"Sure you can, baby. You were too young before but now you can be the official egg collector. Now…go and play and soak up some of the rest of this sunshine and good clean country air."

Joy looked down the hill where Granny carried the trash each evening. She carried it down the hill because Pervis wasn't able to do so because of his wooden leg. Joy viewed the hill at the top and, with her imagination, had transformed the slanted hill into a miniature ski slope covered with glistening snow.

"Be careful, sweetness. Don't go down that hill too fast or you'll fall and start rolling," Eva hollered outside the back porch door. "I'm going to take these sheets and towels inside and start putting them away."

"Granny, before you go in…what's that stuff covering those trees over there across the creek?"

"That's called Devil's Shoestring."

"Devil's what?"

"Devil's Shoestring, it's a wild vine known in these parts and it's as strong as a new rope."

"Why is it called Devil's Shoestring?"

"Because it will eventually choke the life out of most anything it wraps itself around. Folks say it grows so fast that if you take your eyes of it for five minutes, it will have grown a full inch."

Joy looked at the mass of vines that weighed down branches of a maple tree. That was enough gardening information for her today.

BEST FRIENDS

Harvey was glad for the drive with Pervis to Norfolk's shipyard. He was glad for the drive because it gave him time to relax with his best friend and the two could catch up with talk about whatever they felt important to discuss.

Pervis had been working at the shipyard for twenty-six years. He'd started work as a laborer and worked his way up to a supervisory position and he was well liked by everyone at the plant. They admired his stick-to-it attitude for getting any assignment done and his years of dedication and everyday punctuality.

He was a thin man whose six foot four height gave him the appearance of an African warrior. His soft peppered grey hair was always cut in a short style and combed neatly with a part in the side. His right leg was severed just above the knee because of a truck accident while he and Eva lived in Long Island, New York. Fifty-nine years ago, Pervis was born on the island of Barbados and was raised to believe that a man who didn't take care of his family, he wasn't worth the dirt he was made from.

Pervis had met Eva through his brother Rupert while Pervis was visiting in New York. He always had a good eye for a woman of the highest quality. Rupert is now a retired merchant seaman now living in Florida.

In 1924 while visiting Pervis with a shore leave pass, Rupert's attention was drawn to a lovely brown skinned damsel shopping at a vegetable market on a bustling New York street. Her lavish black hair cascaded to her waist in a long, thick braid. Rupert walked over to her, started a conversation, and carried her loaded shopping bags. Walking her home, Rupert found her to be intelligent and sociable. With the next breath, he invited her on a double date with Pervis and young damsel that took Rupert's breath away too. The couples enjoyed an evening of chatting, giggling and dancing. By the end of the evening,

Rupert had fallen in love with Pervis' chattering date and Pervis has fallen in love with Eva. The rest is history.

Harvey was an inch shorter with a medium build and a powerful muscular frame he kept fit with exercise each day in his home gum equipped with two sets of barbells and other equipment. Both men were mild mannered by nature and both had the strength of a mules kick. The age difference didn't seem to matter. When the two had an arm wrestling match…it would end in a draw.

"How are things on the home front, Pervis?"

"Just fine, Harvey," Pervis replied as they sped along. "Eva is tickled that she has company for the summer and especially that it's Joy."

"That's a sweet little girl," Harvey said.

"Mind if I ask you something, Harvey?"

"What's that, Pervis?"

"Why didn't you go after Arvis?"

"What do you mean, Pervis?"

"Come on, Harvey. You know what I mean. Why didn't you come forward and peruse Arvis? Eva and I would have loved to have had you for a son-in-law."

"But how did you…I mean how could you…"

"How did we know how you felt? Arvis told us. She even told us how she felt about you. We just knew you'd be the one. Your grabbing her first would have stopped that blasted Jasper dead in his tracks."

Harvey could hardly believe what he was hearing.

"Hey!" Pervis shouted. "Get back on the road, boy," Pervis smiled. Harvey made no reply but smiled too.

THE BISCUITS

Joy cherished each day with her grandmother. She had her attention all to herself.

It was one o'clock in the afternoon and Pervis would be getting of the work van at six o'clock. The van transported seven other shipyard workers to Norfolk too. The van driver always dropped Pervis off at the top of Fourth Street. Day after day, no matter what the season or if he had to work extra hours, Pervis was satisfied to walk down the street greeting neighbours and swing his black metal lunch box. Most of the time he was whistling a tune or two. He had a whistle that was unique because it sounded like three people whistling in at the same time.

Joy helped Eva finish putting away blankets and crocheted scarves in the upstairs hall trunk. Since the evening's supper menu consisted of yesterday's warmed leftovers of smoked ham, homemade potato salad, candied yams and collard greens, Eva got a head start on the homemade rolls she'd made and put one batch of dough in a large freezer bag for Sunday morning breakfast. She never believed in the new-boxed stuff that cooked in an instance and polluted the supermarket shelves. Eva always believed anything that went into her oven was from scratch. Joy waited patiently in the kitchen to help her grandmother in anyway but most of all…so she could lick the batter left in the Pyrex dish.

"Granny," Joy said.

"Yes, baby?"

"How did you learn to cook so many yummy dishes?"

"Well…my Mamma passed down lots of her favourite recipes and little cooking secrets to me. I use to help her set up family meals and would always as her questions just as you're doing now. The only difference between then and now was that my Mamma didn't have all these modern-day appliances like that Sunbeam electric mixer over there." She chuckled to herself.

"When I married Pervis, I had learned enough about cooking to keep him coming back for more. "

"Really Granny," Joy said, smacking her lips on a piece of bread dough.

"Uh-huh. It wasn't until I'd started cooking for a family in Long Island, New York that I really learned my way around the kitchen."

"By the way Granny, wasn't Mom born in Long Island, New York?"

"Yep, she was, honey."

"Aunt Barbara was born there too?"

"Yes again, darling."

"What was it like for you and Granddaddy back then? Did you live in a house like the one we live in now?"

"Oh no, child, we lived in a two room flat on the fourth floor of a five-story apartment building. Actually, we lived in two large storage rooms. And…we were fortunate enough to have a small bathroom too."

Eva finished making the dough for the bread rolls and put the last batch away in the freezer. Then she took out all the cooking ingredients for making her famous coconut cake and lemon meringue pies and sat them on the table. Joy's eyes widened as big as silver dollars.

"Gosh, what was that like for you, Granny?"

"Oh…I didn't think it was so bad. In those days, it wasn't easy for black folks to find a place to live in that neighborhood. Your grandfather was a truck driver. Of course, your Mamma and Aunt Barbara were babies then."

"Gee, why didn't you stay in New York?"

"Pervis and I talked about that very thing one night. We decided that the city wasn't the place we wanted to raise our daughters so we decided to make a move and we decided to go south."

"Why did you move south, Granny?"

"Being from a place where you wake up to sounds of sea waves and feel the warm breeze as palm trees waved back and forth, Pervis felt closed in by living in the city like we did, Joy. Crumbling brick buildings crammed together in blocks separated by asphalt streets were getting on your grandfather's nerves."

"Granddaddy was born in Barbados, right? See? I remembered from the last time you told me, Granny."

"Right, sugar…Barbados."

"We studied about Barbados and Guyana in my Social Studies class. I'd like to visit those places someday."

"You help yourself, child because you never know. Life has a way of turning things this way and that way to see your dreams come true."

Eva handed Joy the empty cake bowl and spatula. She smiled to herself as she watched Joy lick the bowl. She deliberately left some extra batter inside too.

"You're going to bake rolls now even though it's not Sunday morning?"

"Yes, honey. I thought cooking them would be a good idea and… I'm cooking them just for you."

Joy was about finished licking the bowl and spatula of lemon cake batter.

"If you lick anymore, I won't have to wash that bowl and spatula," Eva laughed.

Joy handed her the cooking utensils and Eva took them to the sink. She placed the cloth covered rolls on the narrow top of the cabinets. The heat from her kitchen cooking rose to the top and the yeast in the rolls had to raise first….and rise they did.

"That should do it. Let's go sit on the front porch and wait for Pervis to come home."

"All right, Granny. Can we finish the Long Island story later?"

"Sure."

The two generations giggled as they walked towards the cool early evening air drifting through the fine mesh screen that enclosed the front porch. Eva plopped down in her rocker and Joy made a beeline for the glider. No sooner had they taken their seats that they both heard a familiar whistle. Joy recognized the sound and remembered the source. She made sure her flip-flops were securely on her feet, jumped all the way to the bottom of the concrete front steps and ran up the street as fast as she could.

"Hello there, sweetmeat," Pervis said with a cheerful grin on his face. "How's my girl enjoying her first day of summer vacation?"

"I've had a ball, Granddaddy," Joy said, insisting on carrying his lunch box.

"Granny and I did lots of things together today. I picked up a baby chick, collected eggs from the hen house, watched a Devil's

Shoestring grow...I think...and I helped bake a cake, and licked the bowl and spatula."

"Hah-shoo, baby! Seems like you two had a busy day," Pervis said.

"We sure did and then Granny filled me in on some details about the time you and she lived in Long Island. Um...does your leg still hurt, Granddaddy? I mean...since the truck accident and all."

"Well, sweetmeat," Pervis began, as he rubbed his chin pretending to ponder deeply. Sometimes my toe itches."

"Really Granddaddy?" Joy asked sympathetically.

"Gotcha," Pervis howled with laughter. He loved playing that joke on folks who asked him about his leg.

The two chuckled heartily and continued to babble until they reached the front yard gate. They continued to walk along the side of the house until they came to the same small porch that Eva and Joy had used earlier in the day. Two concrete steps led up to an enclosed back porch that Pervis had built. There was also a door at the right side from the entryway that led into the downstairs back porch. The washer, dryer, numerous canned goods and boxed of new canning jars, tools, bicycles and other household items were stored there. To the other side of the porch were two large freezers. The back of the refrigerator was set in an opening with the front of the refrigerator in the kitchen.

Peeping in the oven, Eva checked on her rolls to see if the yeast had done its job proper. The table had been set and everything was ready for supper. Pervis kissed his wife, washed his hands, sat down and blessed the table. He was anxious to satisfy his appetite by enjoying his wife's cooking.

The family talked about some special something that happened during the day. Joy did most of the talking.

"Don't get up, Granny. I'll clear the table for you."

"Why thank you, sweetie."

"The dishwater won't bother me anymore."

"Are you sure?"

"I'm sure," Joy reassured her with a smile.

Pervis had a puzzled look on his face but he knew Eva would explain it in time.

"I'll see you ladies on the front porch. I want to read the newspaper before it gets to dark," Pervis said, carrying the evening edition of

GRANNY'S PLACE

the Suffolk News Herald. The hinge if his artificial knee creaked as he lowered himself into his rocker.

The kitchen clean up routine was quick and orderly. Chrome appliances glistened as they sat on wiped marble counter tops while six perfectly browned cake layers cooled on the long section of the L-shaped counter tops. The clock on the top of the stove faithfully kept a vigil over the time as if anxiously waiting to be set for another cooking feat…more homemade rolls.

Eva and Joy finally came onto the porch too. Eva plopped down and let out her usual "oomph" and "Thank you, Jesus". The early evening sky began to attire itself with soft hues of violet, pink and orange reflections of a setting sun. Joy relished each bit if family history her grandparents shared while on the porch. Her picture diary was steadily growing with sketches of visual interpretations of irreplaceable memories. Tonight…the image of a fuzzy baby chick would be added.

"I got orders for three sweet potato pies and four cakes, Pervis," Eva said.

"Sounds like a winner to me, Eva. Then again…you wouldn't be happy unless you were making music with those pots and pans of yours."

"Oh gwan, Pervis, you sure love to tease."

"Granny," Joy interrupted. "Would you finish your story about Long Island?"

"Sure, sugar."

Eva began by refreshing Pervis' memory to where she'd left off earlier. He nodded his head in acknowledgement of his wife's statements thus far. Then he folded the newspaper, placed it on the porch stoop near him, slouched down in his rocker, stretched out his wooden leg and leaned his head on the back of his chair. It had been the umpteenth time he'd heard Eva tell the saga of Long Island, New York but he enjoyed listening each time anyway.

"Let me see now. Where did we stop, Joy?"

"You were telling me about the cold water flat and the cooking job you were going to take."

"Cooking job?" Eva said as she pondered the statement. "Joy, I don't remember getting to that part yet."

"Yes…you did, Granny."

GRANNY'S PLACE

Eva was more puzzled than ever by Joy's prediction of an event that she hadn't lived long enough to know about. Eva decided to resolve the matter by reminding herself that Joy was a ten-month baby that was born with that special gift. With his eyes closed in pretended rest, Pervis heard it too.

"You're right, honey. I'd found work as the head cook for a rich White family whose had the last name of 'Lewis' who always hired two cooks…the main cook or planner and an assistant cook. The assistant to their current planner quit so I was recommended by the planner and got the job."

"Did you already know the head cook, Granny?"

"No, but black folks really stuck together back then because when the head cook knew she was going to quit, she put out her feelers around the neighbourhood and I got the job."

"Go on, Granny. Go on," Joy prodded.

"Well…I have to admit first that the head cook was the prettiest black woman I had ever seen."

"Not in my book," Pervis interrupted.

"Shush, Pervis. Let me go on with the story. Anyway Joy, Nancy Greene was her name. She became the most famous smiling, bandana wearing women in town."

"You mean to say that she was 'Aunt Jemima' on the pancake box?"

"The very same one, Joy," Eva said.

"Wow! That makes you famous too!"

Pervis smiled to himself. It always tickled him whenever he heard Eva slip in the fact that she worked with a celebrity.

"Aunt Jemima on the pancake box," Joy sang.

"I'll tell you something else. That woman on the pancake box at the time was a white woman."

"What? A white woman, you've got to be kidding, Granny!"

"Nope, Black people were played by whites by painting on black faces because of racism. When Amos 'n Andy first came on the radio… they were played by white actors."

"Gosh Granny, I never knew that and, I bet most blacks today don't know that either. You should have been a history teacher instead. Anyway, what happened while you were cooking for the Lewis family?"

"After eight months working in the kitchen, Nancy secretly told me that she'd be giving up her job with the Lewis clan and was going to recommend me for her position. It would mean only ten dollars more for me but, I kept moving the family to the south on my mind. I had to stay focused because that family was the meanest bunch of folks you'd ever seen but, they agreed to give me the job as head cook when Nancy left."

Joy looked and listened to her grandmother intently while in her mind translated every one of her words into images for her picture diary.

"Nancy," Eva continued, "asked me if I could work a few hours early for the next month. I agreed and she and I went over the meal plans since the next month was only a week away."

"What time would you have to be at work then, Granny," Joy asked, thinking about all her own mad dashes to get to school on time.

"That's a good question, Joy. I'd have to find a different babysitter I could trust and one that could deal with my babies at four in the morning. Bless God...I found one...and right in the same apartment building."

"Was she a caring sitter, Granny?" Joy asked thinking of Petula and all her weirdness.

"Yes, she certainly was, Joy. Her name was Ruth Steinberg. She was a German woman who lived below us. From time to time in the past, Ruth and I had shared a hot cup of tea after Pervis got home and could watch the babies for me. That's when I told her about the new job and that I was looking for a good sitter. As it turned out, Ruth became my sitter. She didn't even mind that I'd have to bring the girls down so early each morning."

"Boy! Four o'clock was so early, Granny."

"I know but I had to catch three buses to get to work by five thirty to be at my job by seven o'clock."

"Golly! If I had to get up that early every morning...I'd never be able to keep my eyes open."

"Ruth was more than true to her word. Arvis and Barbara were the best acting little girls even early in the morning. She was up and perky to receive my girls each morning. One morning, she wanted to dress and feed the girls so she came upstairs. I suspect she was a lonely

GRANNY'S PLACE

kind of person and it did her heart good when she had her hands full with something to do. I'd already had a steaming pot of cream-o-wheat on the stove. Downstairs, in her apartment, Barbara and Arvis' favorite part of the day was playing with her basket of scrap yarn. Ruth used to make the finest shawls and sweaters from her crochet patterns. She made the cutest caps and sweater set for my babies. However…Arvis and Barbara's favorite part of the day was when Ruth read them a story. I declare…I'd never seen as many books as that woman had. It was as if she had her own library. Ruth loved children no matter what color they were.

"Didn't she have family and a husband too, Granny?"

"Yes, Ruth had a husband who was killed during World War I. Ruth showed me a picture of a baby boy only five years old. He was the cutest blond curly-topped little fellow you ever saw. I could tell by the expression on her face that it was painful to speak of him."

"That's sad, Granny. Was her husband a soldier too?"

"No. I remember Ruth telling me he was a jeweler and everything in the shop was confiscated and they were forced to live in another location called the ghetto quarter. They had suffered all because they were Jewish. They escaped from Nazi occupation and were smuggled to another German village to catch a cargo ship to America. Somehow, Ruth and her husband got separated. She learned later that he was killed."

"We studied about *The Diary of Anne Frank* in English class. She was thirteen…just like me," Joy said proudly.

"Anyway…Nancy was an incredible teacher and I learned everything from preparing the simplest gourmet recipes to carving the fanciest meats. My Mamma's recipes had given me plenty of practice beforehand but, this job added to my kitchen activities. She assured me that I'd do fine because I seemed to have a natural touch when it came to cooking.

Nancy's last day arrived and boy did I hate that she was leaving. She'd given the Lewis family twelve years of her life without missing a single day but the decrepit couple didn't give a hoot about that. Old man Lewis just scoffed and reminded Nancy…and everybody else in earshot…that if it weren't for the generosity of some white folks, colored folks wouldn't be able to enjoy buying a new pair of shoes. When he was done with his warped farewell speech, my blood began to boil but I held my peace and thought of the move south. Nancy warned me not to let the narrow-minded bigotry of the Lewis family get under my skin and to always be reminded that all kinds of folks make up this world."

"Mrs. Cottcreeve said that some people can only feel good about themselves unless they find somebody else to pick on for no reason."

"She was right child, and they sure got what was stored up for them."

"How so, Granny?" Joy asked.

"Mr. Lewis found out some weeks later that Nancy had moved to Chicago to cook for another rich and kind white family by the name of Hudson who had more social influence than the Lewis family. The head of the Hudson family was a retired judge named Henry Hudson who also owned R.T. Davis Milling Company. Nancy had taken a real liking to that family and the family took a liking to her too. I believe that she was fifty-nine at the time."

"How did her picture wind up on the pancake box?"

"Let me see now. Oh, I remember! Back in 1889, two white men had bought a business called the *Pearl Milling Company*. Around 1894, the men discovered the formula for producing a powered pancake mix. They'd even made up a tune for a commercial too. When the men fell on hard times, they sold the pancake formula and the tune to another business named *R.T. Davis Milling Company*. One day, Judge Hudson somehow heard the tune and liked the song so much that he called the pancake mix by the name of the tune."

"But how did Nancy's face get on the box?"

"When the Judge Hudson was trying to think of a gimmick to sell the product, he remembered Nancy and he got the idea that using her face would sell millions of boxes of the mix…especially to Black folk. He got the idea to use her face because she always cooked pancakes on Saturday for the Judge's breakfast and he loved them."

"Well isn't that something," Joy remarked in awe.

"You can say that again, sugar. Before Judge Hudson retired, he was invited to put on a big splash at the *World's Colombian Exposition* of Chicago, Illinois. As part of the display, Nancy would stand on a barrel in front of a stove and flip pancakes as she had done for the Judge's family each Saturday morning. She draw a huge crowd tasted samples of her pancakes and profits got good. She was nicknamed *The Pancake Queen*. Not only did Nancy prosper from the company, she toured the country and giant billboards spread her picture over forty-eight states. The company was rolling in money not only for the secret pancake formula made only by Nancy but because of her bright smile on the front of each box. You know…kind of like Uncle Ben's Rice."

"That's fascinating, Granny. To actually sit here beside someone who was a friend of Aunt Jemima leaves me breathless," Joy said. She gave her grandmother with a look of admiration. "What's Miss Nancy doing now?"

"Pervis and I got a telegram from Chicago one day…before we made our move south. The telegram read that during one of her tours, Nancy was killed by a hit and run driver." Eva paused for a long moment and wiped her eyes. Pervis was looking at her now because he knew how much she loved Nancy.

"The last letter we had gotten from Nancy was her telling us to follow our dreams and move south safely," Pervis added.

"Did you work long for Mr. Lewis after that, Granny?"

Having composed herself, Eva replied to Joy's question.

"Sometimes you do what you have to do, no matter what, and at the time of the news about Nancy, I had become thick-skinned to the Lewis' arrogant insults. I kept the thought of moving south on my mind because there was no quitting for me. Err…it's getting late, Joy."

"Please go on, Granny. I'll wake up whenever you want to," Joy said.

"All right then, Joy. I'll hurry up and finish the story."

Pervis was snoring…again. He was snoring because of a combination of relaxing from a hard day's work and enjoying the cool breeze of the evening. It was a habit he'd repeated since moving to South Fourth Street. Glancing at her husband, Eva smiled and continued with her saga.

"There's one incident that I'll never forget to this day. A Black girl named Millie Bowers was hired as my assistant since I had been moved up to Nancy's position. That child had many duties to finish by the end of the day. She had to assist with meal preparation, serve the meals, help clean the kitchen, make certain that all the pots and pans were spit-shined, and…help the two upstairs house cleaners finish their chores.

The Lewises were as sloppy as pigs too. That high-minded Mrs. Lewis' reason for assigning Millie all that work was to try to break the strong character Millie had. It seemed to bother the dickens out of Mrs. Lewis. However…Millie wasn't anybody's fool and knew from the look on Mrs. Lewis' face meant that trouble was coming soon. So…one a Friday afternoon it was unusually hot and I was preparing supper. The kitchen was separated from the huge and spacious dining room by a heavy wooden door that swung open on its hinges. A whirling ceiling fan in the kitchen was little relief from the heat of two heated ovens and folks scurrying around all over the place.

The dining room had six floor-to-ceiling windows that cooled off the rest of the downstairs. Millie served a hot cucumber soup instead of a cool Caesar salad because I knew it would make those greedy, big gut, heavy eaters sweat. While the family waited for the next entrée, Mr. and Mrs. Lewis were talking a bunch of nonsense about how they were proud of the fact that they were born into a long line of descendants of Georgian plantation owners and blah…blah…blah. Mr. Buford Lewis, with his thumbs tucked behind his suspenders, sat at the head of the long, clunky antique, maple dining room table in an oversized and over designed hi-backed chair inherited from some kinfolk who probably didn't want the ugly furniture anyway. He had on his coke-bottle thick, black framed glasses and his hair was gone on top of his pointed head except for a few greasy strands he managed to comb over his baldness. To add to the mess, he wore a light blue seersucker suit and big circles of sweat stained the armpits of his crumpled suit jacket.

In the meantime, the eating family didn't notice Millie propping open the swinging door a few inches to try and take advantage of the cool air in the dining room. It was then that we all heard old man Lewis say that Abe Lincoln was a son of the devil and he had no right to try to help those dirty coloreds and that he and all the Lewis family intended to embrace the pride of the south. The whole clan held up their glasses and made a toast to the insulting statement."

"That family sounds like they were awfully mean, Granny."

"Yes, indeed they were, honey."

Sally Buford sat at the other end of the table listening to the orations of loudmouthed Buford. Her arched eyebrows were penciled over with two crooked strokes because she had plucked the eyebrow hairs out for so long until they wouldn't grow back anymore. She had on bright red lipstick that left hard to clean off smudges on the silverware. Her face was heavily powdered to try to hide deep wrinkles while the rouge on her cheeks made her look like a circus clown. Her stringy, thin hair pulled up on top of her head was wrapped around a fake bun."

"Did they have any children, Granny?"

"Yes…Lord, have mercy because that was the worst of all."

Pervis chuckled quietly.

"Buford, Jr. and Alfred were fifteen year old twins and were the worst behaved urchins this side of Jerusalem. They sat across from each other on either side of the table. As the boys pretended to sword fight across the table, Millie overheard something else after everyone in the kitchen heard the Abe Lincoln comment made. We all looked at each other in shock."

"What was it, Granny? What?" Joy asked, from the edge of the glider seat.

"Well…we all heard Mr. Lewis say: 'Integration eh?' Forget that junk and nonsense. There's no way my wonderful boys are going to go to school with those blasted coloreds. It's like putting pigs in a pasture! God made white folks to run His creation. No-sir-re, I'll never agree to educate coloreds with my boys!"

Pervis sat up now and was still chuckling because he knew the next happening of his wife's saga to well.

"Millie and I and all the rest of the kitchen staff stared at each other as silent rage for the pitiful family rose up to boiling," Eva continued. "Then…a devilish smile began to form on Millie's attractive brown face. In the back of all our minds, we knew we needed our jobs for some purpose but…today…we needed a good dose of sweet revenge."

"Come on, Granny. Tell me what you and the others did."

"Honey child, I'm not proud of what I let happen but, I'll never forget it as long as I live. Millie turned around from the swing door, sat the serving tray down on the counter next to me, walked over to the bowl where I was mixing up some biscuit dough and placed her hands on the side of the bowl. We all thought she was going to cry or something but then we heard it…a low guttural sound rose up from her belly to her throat. She bent her head further down in the bowl and… SPLAT! 'Let's see how they mix with colored folk now'," she said.

"Ugh-h-h-h," Joy squinted, squirmed, and laughed. "Now that was nasty, Granny. What did you do next?"

"Me? Why I mixed up that dough, cooked the biscuits and watched Millie serve the family. I only wish to this day, I had a photo of Millie carrying that platter of biscuits into the dining room with her head bowed in mock servitude. That girl was something else. The other staff and I were holding our sizes from muffled laughter and tears rolled down our cheeks.

"You mean the Lewis actually ate those biscuits?"

"Yep, those greedy folks gobbled them up as if they were the last thing they had to eat. We laughed even more at Mr. Lewis' comment."

"What did he say?"

"Lord! He said the biscuits were dog gone delicious and washed down the last biscuit with a mouthful of lemonade. Boy! What a satisfying day that was. Some weeks later, Millie and I decided that enough was enough of working for the Lewis family. Me, Millie and the rest of the staff didn't show up for work the next day. Luckily, the day before we made out move was payday. Anyway…a week later…Pervis and I made our move to Suffolk and we've been in here ever since."

Pervis thought of the time when Eva had told their daughters of the biscuit saga when they were a young age and to anyone else who had the time to listen. He didn't mind at all because he knew the facts she told were part of the Tazell family roots.

Lying back on the glider, Joy thought of the frying-pan-and-scrambled-eggs-incident and knew that it would definitely be a part of her picture diary.

The night sky covered everything with deep blue shadows. The miniature grandfather clock sitting on top of the television near the front porch window tolled nine-thirty. Crickets and bullfrogs continued their evening lullaby of chirping and croaking. Fireflies bobbed around the azalea bushes and lit up like tiny night watchman. A critter splashed about in the creek down the hill while Eva rocked in silence and Pervis whistled softly. Satisfied at having heard another piece of family history, Joy set the glider in motion one last time.

"Well…another day well spent," Pervis, yawned as he rose from his chair. "I feel my nice soft bed calling me now."

"I've got lots of baking orders to get out tomorrow and I'll have to get up early to finish them up," Eva said, stretching and rising from her seat too.

"…and I've got to get up early and help you with your baking, Granny."

Hugs and kissed were exchanged, doors were checked and locked by Pervis and all the downstairs lights were turned off. Eva read Psalm 91 and peaceful slumber enshrouded the Tazell home.

T.J. JONES

Saturday's morning sky was crystal blue, but the air was heavy and muggy. The pulsating heat of the rising sun absorbed the last beads of early morning dewdrops. The sounds of Saturday morning activities came through Joy's bedroom window and invaded her sleep. She opened her eyes abruptly when she heard noisy squawking coming from the chicken coup and Old Colonel's late waking crowing.

Eva and Pervis had been up with the rising sun. Two sweet potato pies, two three-layer coconut cakes and three two-layer devil's food cakes were ready and waiting for pick up were sitting on top of the freezer chest on the back porch. Eva was busily kneading a batch of her dough for homemade rolls.

Pervis sat in front of his workshop putting the final additions on his saw sharpening chores for farmers and do-it-yourself handy men. He always sat in front of his workshop to take advantage of the early morning shade that slowly disappeared as the sun rose higher in the summer sky.

Joy kicked off her summer comforter, stretched herself as hard as she could and flopped back on her pillow for a few moments more of rest. Staring at the ceiling, she contemplated the wonderfulness of not having to worry about an alarm clock ringing at a certain time, getting whips marks on her legs that showed when she changed for gym in school, and having to eat the results of Petula's terrible cooking or the smell the odour of her awful liquor smelling breath. There were many other incidents of cruelty she wanted to tell her grandparents but the reality of holding her tongue because of the fear of Jasper finding out gripped her. Shaking away those thoughts, she got up off the bed and sat down at her vanity table, propped her elbows on the glass shelve, held her chin in her hands and studied her facial features with scrutiny. Upon examination, she found that the image looking back at her was a bit more grown up looking. Her trim and smooth brown skinned face was in perfect proportion and downright pretty. Thick eyebrows framed large round eyes and thick long lashes. Her hair cascaded beneath her shoulders and reached the middle of her back. Her nose was full but petite at the same time and her lips were defined by a natural outline. Satisfied with what she saw, her eyes were drawn to the tiny black and white photo of her Mom. It was the last pictures she had taken. Her hair was piled on top of her head in a mass of shiny black curls. A sweet smile graced her lips. It could have been a photo of Joy. The two looked so much alike.

"It's almost like she's looking right back at me," Joy whispered to herself. "I wonder if she can still see me."

"That child certainly must be tired," Eva thought while placing her first batch of bread dough on top of the kitchen cabinets to rise. She returned to her floured kitchen table and punched the second batch of bread dough down with her fist.

"To bad this dough isn't Jasper's jaw," Eva mumbled. She wiped her hands with her apron and proceeded to climb the stairs to check on her granddaughter.

"Here now. What is it, child?"

"Nothing Granny, I'll be okay in a little bit," Joy said trying to stop crying.

"Nothing you say? It's not ordinary to cry for nothing. You can't fool your grandmother either. Now…tell me what's bothering you."

"I can't, Granny. I just can't."

Eva sensed something had a chokehold on her granddaughter. Never before had her grandchild been unable to tell her or Pervis anything no matter how horrible it was. She also sensed that the chokehold had to do with Jasper.

"All right, baby. I won't press you anymore but this thing has to come to a head. You understand that don't you?"

"Yes, Granny. I want to tell you everything but…I'm afraid of making a lot of trouble for you and Granddaddy."

"What kind of trouble?" Joy started crying even more.

"There, there. Let's forget about this mess for now."

Sitting on the edge of Joy's bed, Eva consoled Joy and cradled her in her arms while rocking her gently. Joy's sobs turned to sniffles. Eva was sure of one thing and one thing only and it had to do with Suffolk's unwritten law.

"Granny...do you think I'm pretty?"

"For goodness sakes, child, of course I do."

"Thanks, Granny. That means a lot to me to hear you say that," Joy said with a timid smile on her face.

"What a curious thing to ask," Eva thought.

However, one thing was for sure. She and Pervis had lost Arvis because of Jasper's maliciousness but there was no way he was going to rob them of the only living remembrance of their daughter. This was the second time she had seen Joy upset behind the goings on in New Jersey.

"It's time for Pervis to hear about this...today," Eva mumbled.

"What did you say, Granny?"

"Never mind, baby, just get dressed and come on down to the kitchen for a bite of breakfast. You can help me with more cooking too...if you like. I knew you wouldn't be able to get up with the crack of dawn so I put aside a frosty glass of orange juice and some hot buttered biscuits for your breakfast. How does that sound?"

"Granny?"

"What is it, honey?"

"Would you comb my hair when you have the time?"

"Sure, baby. I'm never too busy where you're concerned...understand?"

Eva left Joy's bedroom and went back downstairs to her kitchen and to her baking. She prepared a plate setting on the table for Joy. Joy's tears emotionally touched her and this time her own tears blurred her vision as a prayer rose up in her heart.

"Dear God, please lend me your ear for a minute. Something is bothering my grandchild...the one you gave me and saw fit to bless. Show us what to do to get to the bottom of this mess. Please give us direction and be in our every word and action. In Jesus' Name I pray...Amen."

Feeling relief from her grandmother's soothing words, Joy got dressed while thinking of a hairstyle. The idea of Granny combing her hair and not having the plain ponytail she usually wore was like Christmas in July. With one last glace at the tiny photo of her Mom, she blew a kiss in the direction of her vanity mirror and sprang downstairs to the kitchen.

"Look in the refrigerator and get your glass of orange juice, Joy."

GRANNY'S PLACE

Joy took out the glass of juice, sat down at the end of the table and crammed a bite of a buttered biscuit into her mouth. From where she was sitting at the table, she could look out the back door. The branches of the peach trees and the magnolia tree swayed gently in the summer breeze.

"Granny, how old is that magnolia tree?"

"It's twenty-six years old, Joy. Your Mamma and Aunt Barbara were only four years old when your grandfather planted it."

"Good morning, Mr. Tazell," a voice interrupted.

"Hey, young fellow, watcha know that's good?" Pervis asked.

"Oh, nothing much but, is Miss Eva home? I'm going to help with the peach picking today."

"Go right in, son. She's in the kitchen," Pervis said.

"Hi, Jamaal," Joy said grinning from ear to ear.

"Hey, Joy! How's it going?"

"Come on in, Jamaal," Eva said. "How're your folks doing?"

"They're fine, Miss Eva. By the way, ma'am, Mom says to tell you she might be about a half hour late this morning. She had to stop by the Emmett's place again."

"What, Jamaal? What number does this baby make?"

"It's her seventh and it was a boy, Miss Eva."

"O-o-o-w-e-e! Her husband sure keeps her busy," Eva chuckled. "That will be fine if she's late because the rest of the ladies won't be here until later either and besides, we have the whole day set aside for our peach peeling and canning." "Would you mind if Joy helped pick Peaches too? This will be her first time so you can give her a few tips."

"No ma'am. That'll be fine with me. Come on, Joy. Let's hop to it. We have a lot of peaches to pick."

Joy downed her last bit of orange juice with one gulp, jumped off the back porch stairs and joined Jamaal. As he watched them, Pervis paused from his sharpening chores, sipped from a jar of ice water sitting on the ground beside him and smiled as he watched the two youths. Eva was watching from behind the screen door too.

"Now that you understand what I showed you, Joy, you start picking up the peaches that have fallen to the ground. I'll give you a holler when it's time to for you to empty my sack into that number two tub over there. Okay?"

Like Joy, he was only thirteen years old but, Jamaal knew how to do a job and get it done well. For him, picking peaches was more fun than a chore. As they picked, he and Joy talked about happenings of the past school year and about Jericho Cemetery. Before long, they'd filled two metal number two tubs to the brim with unblemished juicy peaches.

"Whoa thar Josie, whoa thar, girl," TJ hollered."

All peach picking came to an abrupt halt as Joy and Jamaal caught sight of the strange looking being who was at the front gate. He came on through the gate parked his cart of straw in front of Pervis' workshop.

"Hello, TJ old boy," Pervis yelled, putting aside his last perfectly sharpened saw.

"Hey thar, Mesta Pervis," TJ responded with a wave of his hand.

"What've you been up to these days?" Pervis asked as TJ patted Josie's nose. He led his faithful mule, wearing a cut-out-for-the-ears hat, and pulled the flatbed wagon up nearer to Pervis.

TJ and Josie were inseparable and seemed to have a special language all their own. Folks said if you spotted the faint glow of an oil lamp right out in the middle of nowhere, it was probably TJ sitting by a campfire enjoying a late evening meal with Josie. A meal to those two characters would most likely be fatback and cornbread bought after a day's wages and of course, Josie would enjoy a succulent bucket of oats.

Joy was dumbfounded and a wide-eyed. Jamaal stood with his mouth hanging open. TJ knew that he was a new sensation for Joy and Jamaal. As he walked past the peach trees where the two living statues stood gawking, a sudden breeze swayed the tree limbs and flung the rest of the peaches from the branches, but not one peach was bruised from the fall.

Snaggletooth TJ Jones folks called him and snaggletooth he was. All of his teeth were missing except for six in the bottom jaw at the side of his mouth. The remaining teeth were pearly white and TJ hadn't seen a dentist in eons if at all. His clothes were old, worn and too big for his gangly frame. Old patches needed new patches. His eyes looked like large black jewels in a pool of milk. They sparkled like new marbles from the uptown Five-'n-Dime store and were set within weather beaten dark skin aged by years of travel along some lonesome country road. Nobody really knew how old he was or where he was from. Life was simple for TJ and he was content to pick up an odd job here and there like the one he was doing for Pervis today. No one could figure out how he lived in inclement weather or with the few dollars he'd earned but, today he'd come to the Tazells to deliver one hundred pounds of feed for Eva's chickens and twenty planks of lumber for Pervis.

Joy looked at Jamaal and Jamaal looked at Joy. To them it seemed like TJ was pulled from the pages of a story about Uncle Tom's Cabin and got stuck in the here and now. He had been known to townsfolk to be a fixture that had managed to live beyond Suffolk's historical past. Pervis chuckled to himself as he observed the expression of puzzlement on the youngster's faces.

Josie stood motionless in the hot sun as if the heat didn't bother her one bit. Joy and Jamaal started picking up the peaches that had fallen and had almost filled another number two tub but they could hardly take their eyes off the ancient looking figure.

"Boy! That's the strangest looking sight if ever I saw one," Jamaal said.

He and Joy weren't afraid but terribly curious. TJ was use to people staring at him. He knew he stood out like a fish out of water and made the same impression on many new folks he'd met. He retrieved the hundred pound feed sack off the wagon with little effort. Propping the sack on his shoulder, he walked past the peach pickers and gave them a toothless grin and a twinkling wink.

"Well my, my, my, TJ it's so good to see you again," Eva remarked as she swung open the kitchen screen door and stepped outside.

"Aftanoon, Miss Eva. Somtin' in dat kitchen sho' nuff smellin' real good," TJ said.

"You know you're more than welcomed to have lunch with us. I was putting the final touch on some turkey sandwiches. Won't you have a couple too?"

"Dat sounds powerful tasty, Miss Eva. Don't mind if I do, ma'am."

Another tub was filled to the brim with plump juicy peaches... and not a bruise on any.

"You and Jamaal did a mighty good job and so fast too, Joy. Leave the tubs where they are. Pervis and TJ will put them inside the house for me. You two wash up at that outside facet and don't forget to rinse off your faces too. I'll be out with lunch as soon as I sweetened the ice tea," Eva said as she went back inside the house.

Joy and Jamaal washed at the facet playfully giggling and splashing water on each other. They then took refuge from the hot sun at a picnic table shaded by the magnolia tree. From their vantage point, they were sitting within full sight of the hypnotizing and beguiling vision busily assisting Pervis unload the last of his planks of pine lumber.

"Have you ever seen TJ before, Jamaal," Joy asked without taking her eyes off TJ.

"Never Joy," Jamaal said softly. Neither noticed Eva approaching the picnic table carrying a large round tray of turkey, cheese, lettuce and tomato sandwiches surrounding a large pitcher of ice tea.

"I know TJ looks a bit odd, but he won't bite," Eva said, startling the fascinated twosome.

"Granny, you want to know something?"

"What, Joy?"

"Even though TJ looks like a walking fairy tale character, there's a sort of quiet kindness about him. In fact, I actually feel like I've known him for a long time."

"Oh brother," Jamaal laughed. "Earth to Joy, earth to Joy," Jamaal teased again.

"Oh hush, Jamaal. It's hard to explain what I mean."

Eva listened to the two while spreading out a tablecloth and arranging the food. She went back to the kitchen for more goodies... especially the ones TJ liked. When she returned, Joy asked, "Have you and Granddaddy known TJ for long?"

"We first met TJ when Harvey started up his taxicab business. TJ seemed to come out of nowhere when we three were sitting on the porch one night," Eva replied as Joy and Jamaal helped her with the picnic table. "On the other hand, we just enjoy his company whenever he decides to come around...and you're perfectly right Joy, there is a kindness about that man. Yes indeed...something special. I don't know just what it is but I know there's something about the man. Pervis feels the same way too."

TJ unloaded the last of the pine wood lumber planks from his wagon. After five trips carrying wood on his shoulder, Eva admonished the men to wash up and get out of the blazing sun. Pervis said, "Good, gracious! It sure is a hot one today," as he wiped his face with his blue and white bandana handkerchief. Having splashed water on his face, TJ joined Pervis at the picnic table.

"Whew!" Pervis breathed. "Old man sun means business today."

"That's exactly why I called the two of you to get out of the sun. You're not getting any younger Pervis Tazell," Eva said.

"How old are you, TJ?" Joy blurted.

"Joy!" Eva shouted with sternness. "You never ask a grown-up that kind of personal question."

"Dat's okay, Miss Eva. Dis is dah first time chilins' has asked me anything 'bout myself. It don't botha me none."

"What's on your mind, Joy?" Eva asked.

"Well…err…how old are you, sir," Joy asked again sheepishly.

"I's as old as time, little lady," TJ chuckled. "Folk often wonder 'bout dat."

"I hate to be the one to change the subject but those sandwiches look mighty tasty," Jamaal said as he licked his lips.

Heads bowed as Pervis blessed the table and then undivided attention was given to the platter of sandwiches and other goodies. The fragrance of magnolia blossoms filled the whole yard around them as a hummingbird jetted back and forth collecting precious sweet nectar deep within the large white petals of the magnolia flowers.

"After a thirst quenching gulp of ice tea, Pervis asked, "TJ, how in blazes can you stand that flannel shirt and wool jacket in this heat…if you don't mind my asking?"

"I declare, Pervis. I don't know whose worse…you or Joy," Eva said.

"The heat don't botha me none, Mr. Pervis. Josie and me just plain don't pay da wetha no mind."

Joy stole a few glances now and the when she could and decided right away that a drawing of TJ would be excellent for her picture diary. The adults sat under the magnolia tree and chatted about the latest events that happened around town while Joy and Jamaal removed their shoes and socks and romped around on the thick grass of the spacious back yard.

"Well…time for me to get back to my sharpening chores," Pervis said as he patted his stomach.

Eva served TJ another tall glass of ice tea and handed him a large slice of homemade peach pie and a large brown sack filled with home cooked goodies. TJ smile and nodded a thank you as he gobbled up the pie. Following Pervis back to the wagon, TJ paused, looked back over his shoulder and caught Joy's eye.

"Youse gonna be a mighty fine artist someday, Miss Joy. Folks all around gonna know yo name."

The two locked eyes for several minutes. "Granny, did you hear what he said," Joy asked her grandmother.

"I sure did, honey."

"How'd he know I could draw, Granny?"

"I haven't the slightest idea. Sometimes that man says some of the strangest things. He seems to know about most everything and shows up at the darnedest times. When he does…well, I don't know how else to put it but whatever the situation…things just seem to work out and get better." Suddenly, a shiver ran down her spine and a proverb came to mind. *"Be careful how you entreat strangers because you might be entertaining angels unaware."* Shaking her head, she dismissed the thought, cleared away the remnants of lunch at the picnic table and went back into her kitchen. Just as she did, the telephone rang.

"Yes," Eva said. "Hello, Mrs. Bremond. How are you? You and the other women are on the way to help with the peach picking chores? That will be just fine. I'm just getting ready for everybody here. Yes indeed, your helping hands will be a delight. That's for calling. Bye."

Canning fruit and vegetables was another of Eva's favorite things to do and she did a professional bang-up job. The kitchen was about to be filled with all sorts of stories and tales and titbits of news of this or that or the other. TJ would be included today.

In the meantime, Jamaal had conjured up enough nerve to approach TJ, before he and Josie left the yard, and asked him question after question. Jamaal liked to investigate new encounters. This encounter he wanted to investigate and for unexplained reason…he liked TJ.

Joy relaxed on the grass under the green canopy created by the magnolia tree leaves and let her artist's mind have its way. She imagined the sunlight flickering through the tree limbs were golden fairies darting here and there as they whispered magical secrets to one another.

She stared at TJ as he and Josie left the front yard. His grease stained, wide-brimmed cowboy hat was perched on top of thick, woolly snow-white hair. A bushy white moustache covered his top lip. Joy rehearsed his last comment repeatedly in her head. "I wonder how he knew I had a love for drawing and better yet…how did he know I wanted a job involving art? He's never seen me before…so how did he know?" She then decided to trade the grass for the glider.

The peach peelers arrived and were in the kitchen tee-hee-hawing about left over news of the last Wednesday night's prayer service. Pervis had secretly given TJ a monetary handshake. Pulling out an old dented harmonica from his patched jacket pocket, TJ began to play a soothing tune as Josie lazily pulled the two out of the gate to who knows where. The mule's gait kept in time to the rhythmic melody played. Joy listened intently as she swung the glider with her big toe. Without warning, a gust of cool breeze pushed back the sultry curtain of humid air. Pervis remained standing at the yard gate until the old timer and his wagon and the sound of his harmonica had gone up the street and out of sight. Mysteriously, the breeze stopped at the exact time TJ and Josie disappeared from view. Once again, the afternoon stratosphere put on its muggy heaviness. Pervis smiled as he turned back to his workshop to lock the door.

"Joy! Joy! Where are you?" Jamaal shouted.

"I'm on the front porch, Jamaal," Joy shouted back. Jamaal scurried past Pervis as if the devil himself was behind him. He leaped up the front porch steps lickety-split.

"What's got you so worked up, Jamaal?"

"You aren't going to believe this, Joy."

"What? What, Jamaal?"

"TJ is going to take us on a ride on his wagon."

"That sounds great, Jamaal. Where will we be going?"

"Err…I forgot to ask where but a surprise ride won't hurt us any. But anyway, a ride with him will give us a chance to find out more about him. You know…where he comes from and all. Don't you think that's a swell idea for our fist summertime adventure?"

Hesitating for a moment as if trying to figure out a complicated mathematical equation, Joy said, "But that's just the point."

"What in the world are you talking about, Joy. You got all your marbles?" Jamaal said with frustration.

"I mean…nobody knows anything about TJ and suppose he turns out to be some kind of kook, Jamaal."

"Give me a break, Joy. Why are you talking so uppity? Since when does it matter what a person looks like to you. New Jersey's got you acting so crazy?"

"No way Jamaal, I'm sorry I said that and don't know why I did. A lot's been on my mind lately."

"Well then, what better way to take your mind off things than an outing with TJ? It will be our first adventure for the summer."

"I guess you're right, Jamaal. I'll ask my grandparents. It should be okay."

"Beat you to it because I've already asked them and they said it would be fine. I'll ask my parents too. I'm sure they'll say yes. Check you later." In a dash, Jamaal was up the street.

It was now early evening. The peach canning was over for another season and the last of the W.B.F.C. was out of door. As she did many times before, Eva not only thanked them all for their help but gave each woman a jar of brandied peaches. After all good-byes were said, Eva retreated to the kitchen once again to do a last minute check and make certain all ingredients and preparations were ready for Sunday morning's breakfast. The delightful scent of cinnamon followed Eva down the hallway to the porch where she flopped down in her rocker after another satisfactory day in the kitchen.

Joy was asleep on the glider and Pervis, having closed up his workshop, joined them too. Both he and Eva watched their granddaughter sleeping. Her hair had fallen across her face in a tangled mess.

"Oh, Pervis," Eva said softly so as not to wake Joy. "I forgot the child asked me to comb her hair today but with my canning peaches and baking today, it completely slipped my mind."

"Don't worry yourself, Eva. I'm sure Joy realized you were too busy today."

"I know Pervis but I had no intentions of letting her down. She had nothing but disappointments especially since her mother passed and I didn't want to add to her upset. I know there was a deeper reason she asked me to do her hair in the first place."

With that, Eva told Pervis of the "dishwater and eggs" incident. By the time she finished, Pervis' jaw was rippling, and his fists were clinched tight. He was livid.

"I don't know how but that little army weasel is going to be dealt with and I mean dealt with good," Pervis said.

It was dusk now and all of nature became a shadow of what was once before. The sun made its exit from the sky and was replaced by a bright full moon. Joy woke up stretching, greeted her grandparents with a loud yawn, and put the glider into motion again with her big toe.

Pervis slumped in his rocker to hide in the evening shadows not wanting his granddaughter to see the angry expression. He whistled softly in his usual way to calm himself down but, the words Eva had spoken careened through his mind like a bulldozer through dirt. It was like elevator music playing the same songs over and over. Finally, he was able to put the information on a back shelf of his head with the rest of his mental library labelled "Jasper".

Bugs began a strange dance in a circle around a dull street lamp light bulb. The evening wore a shroud of darkness turning all it touched into silhouetted images against the sky. Joy loved the ritual end of the day as feelings of serenity of the family gatherings on the front porch embraced her soul. She didn't care if she wasn't included in the ongoing conversation or not but just being with her grandparents was enough.

"By the way Eva, TJ promised to give the kids a ride on his wagon and I told him it was okay if it was alright with you."

"I don't know, Pervis. We really don't know much about the man and he is indeed a strange looking creature."

"Why would you say that? Has he done something that I don't know about?"

"No, Pervis but let's just say he's odd…that's all."

"Well, if that all that's bothering you then I don't see why not." A hayride with TJ would be great."

"You haven't told me what you really feel about TJ, Pervis."

"If you ask me…there's more to the man than meets the eye. I can't put it all together yet but, I have a feeling we're going to be seeing a lot more of TJ in the days to come."

"I don't know, Pervis. Today, TJ said something that made chills run up and down my spine because he's never met Joy to know anything about her."

"What did he say?" Pervis asked his wife frowning with concern.

"He told Joy that she would not have to worry about making a trip to a foreign land and that she'd make a fine artist someday."

"I see what you mean, Eva. I can't explain what I feel about the man but I believe TJ doesn't have a mean bone in his body. If I did, Joy, Jamaal or anybody else would've notice it and wouldn't ride with the man at all. Children can sense something about a person right away and Jamaal can't wait to be around the man again. You know Jamaal. Eva. He's never been the kind of boy who would accept anything if all angles didn't fit."

"I suppose you're right, Pervis."

"I'll tell you something else I've been thinking about, Eva. Folks seem to fear what they can't or won't understand even though the facts are right before their eyes. That's true about us too because when we first met him and we were on the porch talking with Harvey one night, we though he was a strange fellow then. Remember?"

"I remember that night, Pervis. I remember it as clear as day. It was when Harvey was having all that trouble with his wife and as we were sitting and talking. We heard that harmonica music and felt a strange breeze come up all of a sudden. It was only a few days before Harvey started his own cab business."

Eva and Pervis listened to the sounds of night while they thought deeply about the words they had just exchanged. A full moon hung in a satin black night sky. Millions of tiny stars flickered like candles that had been lit by some giant unseen hand.

"Well, tomorrow is another Sunday. How about we call it a night, Eva?"

"That sounds about right to me. How about you, Joy? You ready?"

"You couldn't even see my face, Granny," Joy chuckled. "How did you know I was wake?"

"Oh, a little birdie told me," Eva joked back.

Sundays always held a full agenda of Sunday school, long church sermons but best of all, a table full of Eva's excellent dishes. It also meant Eva scurrying around in her steamy kitchen fussing over the preparations of the day and cooking a wholesome breakfast.

The two generations went upstairs after Pervis did his nightly lock check. Each entered their domains of slumber to lie down on freshly dried sheets stretched over firm mattresses. Joy curled up in a fatal position and immediately slipped into untroubled dreams under her ruffle edged comforter. Pervis started snoring after only fifteen minutes as Eva finished reading Psalm 91 which was part of her nightly prayers. As a soft blanket of peaceful quietness draped itself throughout the house, the faint sound of harmonica music could be heard in the distance.

BRAIDS AND BEADS

Sundays always held a full agenda of Sunday school, long church sermons but best of all, a table full of Eva's excellent dishes. It also meant Eva scurrying around in her steamy kitchen fussing over the preparations of the day and cooking a wholesome breakfast.

Old Colonel was perched on top of the wire fence crowning his head off even though the sun had risen four hours ago. Eva was out of bed as usual and set the upstairs back porch fan on high speed to take advantage of early morning cool air.

Bedroom curtains fluttered to the air current and the familiar sounds of early morning could be heard. While Eva hummed along to a gospel tune played on the Old Time Gospel Show, she took out her fourth oblong pan of perfectly browned rolls from the oven. She sat it next to the other pans on a space she always made on top of the ceramic kitchen counter Pervis made for her and rubbed each roll with a stick of country butter. She went to the stove to finish scooping out the extra cheese and egg onto a large waiting platter that was already blessed with sausage patties and bacon. The radio announcer made a special announcement stating that the thermometer would rise to a whopping 100 degrees in the shade.

Pervis ate an early morning breakfast of poached eggs, sausage, a few strips of bacon, ice tea and a good conversation with his wife who did the same except she had a hot cup of coffee instead of ice tea. He was upstairs putting the final changes on his Sunday best. Last but not least, he splashed on a palm full of Old Spice cologne.

During June, July and August, he and the other deacons were responsible for getting to Tabernacle Christian Church early to perform assigned tasks. This Sunday it was he and Dave who had the early church duty. He'd gone back into the kitchen for another glass of ice tea when he heard Dave blowing the horn in his car.

"Got to run, honey. Everything was delicious as usual," he said kissing his wife's full brown lips. "See you and Joy at church later."

GRANNY'S PLACE

Upon arrival at Tabernacle where he and Eva had been members for twenty years, he and Dave began to place hymnals in the book holders at the back of each pew. Once done, Pervis turned on the tall front fan that stood near the altar and Dave turned on an identical fan that stood in the corner in the back of the last church pew to create a cross current of air and opened the doors leading to the foyer too. Pervis went into the church office to get the stack of newly printed programs of the day and placed them at on a special table in the foyer of the church for other deacons to hand out to church goers as they entered.

"I sure hope Reverend Leyton makes his sermon brief today, Pervis. Did you hear the weather report for today?"

"I sure did, Dave. It's going to be a hot one and I can only hope that Reverend Leyton knows that too," Pervis chuckled.

"Now that everything is set up, how about we make a fast retreat to the annex and join me in a cool soda from the coke machine?" Dave said.

"That sounds good to me, Dave."

TJ was the topic of discussion as they drank their sodas.

"You're right, Pervis. TJ is a very peculiar kind of person. I remember one night just a month ago. I was driving a few W.B.F.C. members home from a social event when my car stalled as I crossed over the train tracks. It was dark and the only light came from a streetlamp a block down the road. I asked the women to get out and stand off the tracks for their safety. I lifted the hood to try to find the problem but, when the women heard the train whistle in the distance, they near panicked. As the sound of the train whistle got louder, the women started squealing. Then if the oncoming train wasn't enough, two shadows began to materialize out of the darkness. The women froze with terror and so did I. Those forms turned out to be TJ and Josie. I was relieved tremendously. One of the women started crying and confessing all her sins.

Well…TJ fixed the car problem, calmed the women and we all were safely off the tracks. The train sped by within the next ten minutes. TJ refused any payment but, said that helping to fill Josie's feed bucket and hanging it around her ears was enough payment for him.

As it turned out, the next day I took my car to Ben Boone's shop to have him check over the engine. While scratching his head, he asked me when did I get a new engine put in and why did I feel the car needed a check-up. I was shocked to say the least. The engine was sparkling and sure enough…brand new. All I could think about was the incident with TJ."

Both decided Dave's tale warranted another soda. More than anyone, Pervis had a feeling that Suffolk was about to become the location of yet another tale to be pasted on from generation to generation.

Back at home on South Fourth Street, the strong current of air created by the back porch fan drew the fantastic aromas of Eva's kitchen into Joy's bedroom and the smell of Pervis' Old Spice cologne lingered too. Joy sat up on the edge of her bed and according to the witness of her vanity mirror; her hair was all over her head in a tangled mopped topped mess.

"Please have time to comb my hair, Granny," she said with her eyes squeezed shut and her fingers crossed. "I hope I grown up to looked just like Mom," she thought as she looked at the small photo attached to her vanity mirror.

The rising temperature of the morning didn't slow Eva's pace in the kitchen one bit as she put the finishing touches on the bowls and platters of food for the Sunday supper. It had been her habit every Sunday to cook plenty of extra helpings of everything for unexpected guests who always seemed to find one reason or another to visit the Tazell home where they knew they'd be offered an example of her culinary delights. Without a doubt, two of the guests would be Reverend and Mrs. Leyton who came like clockwork for as long as she and Pervis had been members at the church. Since she and Pervis had already eaten breakfast, she covered a breakfast plate with saran wrap for Joy and sat it on top of the stove to keep it warm.

"There, that's that," Eva said proudly looking at her accomplishments.

The shrill buzzing noise of July flies was nature's way of warning that the day's forecast would be a definite reality. A fan identical to the one upstairs but smaller cooled the downstairs was mounted in the dining room window set at high speed. Arthritis in Eva's knees disallowed her of the benefit of enjoying air conditioning.

"Joy! Come on down to the front porch now! Bring your comb and brush and the Dixie Peach too. I want to give those locks of you're a special touch today," Eva yelled upstairs.

"Oh boy, she remembered!" In no time, Joy was downstairs and on the glider with the requested items in hand and waiting for her grandmother to come from the kitchen.

"Good gracious, child. That was quick. I covered your breakfast plate and sat it on the stove but, I wanted to comb that head first." Eva chuckled. "Come on then and let's get started. Sit down on this pillow between my knees and let's see what becomes of this thick mop of long tangled mess."

Eva plopped down in her rocker and began using those skilful fingers. With each part the comb made, Joy could feel the cool of the air on her scalp as her grandmother created a corn rowed hairstyle. For the first time in a year, Joy's hair was getting the motherly attention it needed. Petula's knowledge of hair care was null-and-void. As Eva finished a cornrow section and repositioned Joy's head to continue, Joy became lost in vivid image of precious moments when her Mom used to show her how to put on lipstick, and daintily blot off the excess with a tissue. She also remembered a time when she had tried on her Mom's favorite pair of beautiful silver and red rhinestone dangling earrings. Many other memories streamed through the recesses of her mind like the flowing current of a rippling mountain spring.

"Granny, did you comb Aunt Barbara and Mom's hair like this too?"

"I sure did. When I braided their hair, I wouldn't have to comb it each day. In fact, I'm combing your hair in the style your mother use to wear when she was your age but, you'll have to stop squirming so much."

"Sorry, Granny, I'm tender headed."

"You mean to tell me that with all this hair on your head, you're tender headed?"

"Yes, Granny."

"Poor little you, I'll try my best not to pull too hard, okay?"

"Okay. Was Mom's hair long like mine when she was my age?"

"Yes indeed, and it was just as thick."

"Turn your head, sugar. Just a few more braids and I'll be finished."

"You know what, Granny? Once…I made Mom really mad."

"What'd you do?"

"Turn you head this way, sugar because in a few more minutes I'll be finished. What were you going to say?"

"I was going to say that I made Mom really angry with me…but just one time."

"What did you do?"

"Well…Mom was getting ready to go out to supper at an award ceremony on the base and the captain wanted his people to bring their wives."

"Uh-huh, and what else happened?"

"I took a pair of her favourite earrings from her jewellery box and tried them on. Then I did the stupidest thing."

"What was that stupid thing, Joy," Eva asked as she was working on the last braid.

"I stuck one of her earrings in a wall socket in her bedroom and the sparks flew everywhere. Mom had to throw the master switch to bring the lights back on. I knew for sure I was in for a good whipping because of the black smug all around the wall socket but, Mom was only angry because she said I could have electrocuted myself. She didn't even tell Dad I was the reason the wall was smudged up."

"There are lots of things children get way with from time to time. Because she was the kind of loving mother I know she was…she took the blame for the wall damage…right?"

"Right Granny," Joy marvelled at what her grandmother said because she had lots more incidents of the goings on in New Jersey to tell her too.

"There you are, Joy. All finished. Child, you look as pretty as a picture. Take a look at yourself in the hall mirror."

As she stood up, her rear end was a bit sore from sitting in one position but she didn't care. She darted down the hall and stood in front of the mirror. A hanging mass of braids hung down the middle of her back like a gorgeous curtain. Three long braids hung against the side of her face to her waistline and Eva decorated the end of each braid with different color wooden beads she'd found in her sewing basket.

"Oh, Granny, it's gorgeous! It's the first time I've had a hairdo like this. Look at all the rows of braids! My head feels like its breathing.

GRANNY'S PLACE

Thank you, thank you, thank you, Granny," Joy said as she hugged her grandmother.

"You're most welcome, baby," Eva smiled tenderly. "Let's get hopping, Miss Beauty Queen. Harvey will be here to pick us up before we know it. You eat some breakfast while I bathe and get myself together for church."

Joy washed down her last mouth full of cheese and eggs with a gulp of ice-cold milk. She was hungry and enjoyed her food. She smiled to herself. She was so very happy.

The bathtub was filled, soap suds bubbled, water splashed, perfume was spayed, outfits were examined in the downstairs full-length mirror and Harvey was right on time. Before leaving the house, Eva made certain the bow behind Joy's dress was evenly spread then she looked in the mirror again to make sure her own hat was positioned just right too.

Honk! Honk! Honk!

"Come on, sugar. The taxi is here!"

"You sure are looking lovely this morning, Joy and you look absolutely ravishing too, Miss Eva," Harvey complimented.

"Oh hush up, Harvey. I'm going to say a special prayer for you," Eva joked.

Harvey drove up into the church parking lot into the one of the three spots reserved for taxis. The W.B.F.C. had initiated the parking spaces as a special reward to Harvey for his taxi business and his faithfulness in picking up so many fares free of charge on Sundays.

Joy, Eva, and Harvey waited in the church foyer to be ushered into the sanctuary after Reverend Leyton finished praying and before he began his sermon he'd preached for the fifteenth time. After a round of Amen's, the left and right aisle doors were finally opened. Led by Deaconess Jones who was dressed in her starchy white uniform matched with white shoes and gloves, Eva and Joy strutted down the red-carpeted aisle towards the front of the church to be seated with the rest of the Deaconesses. Heads turned in their direction and Eva acknowledged all looks with a soft smile and a nod of her head. However, the majority of the whispers stirring about were of the sweet looking preteen following close behind. Joy's three layer petticoats bounced under the hem of skirt of her dress, which was made of green chequered, pink, and mint green taffeta. The waist, accented with a wide deep green satin sash was expertly tied. Eva and Joy proceeded to sit down on the front pews below the altar. Four red-carpeted steps led to the podium and then the choir stand. Joy spotted her grandfather among the Senior Choir members who were seated in the choir stand. He winked and Joy responded with a beaming smile. Joy sat next to Eva and Eva sat next to Mrs. Bremond who responded with a traditional saintly church façade. Looking out over the congregation, Joy spotted Jamaal sitting next to his Mom and gave him a discrete wave with her lace-covered hand. Jamaal eyes bucked as they feasted upon the lovely sight.

"Boy!" Jamaal said to himself. "Is that really Joy?" He could feel a blush coming and was a little embarrassed by the new sensation he felt rise from the pit of his stomach.

The choir sang, the ushers ushered, everybody fanned, the offering was offered, the sermon was preached, and the benediction was given. For reasons only know by him, Reverend Leyton insisted on preaching about hell fire and damnation on this hot day of all days. Instead of saving souls, the soda machine was emptied. Beautifully attired and completely wilted but fanciful dressed, members and visitors poured out of the double doors of the church like a heard of sheep squeezing through narrow barnyard gate. The sanctuary was totally vacated in twenty minutes flat. It was time to go home to Sunday suppers and front porches or stand in groups on the front lawn of the church and pass along the latest news.

"Man, I thought I'd melt. I've never known the temperature to get so intense and the church was hotter than usual," Harvey said as he drove the Tazells and Joy home.

"It was miserably uncomfortable under my choir robe too. I though Reverend Leyton would never stop preaching," Pervis said while losing his tie.

"Wasn't it hilarious when Reverend Leyton said, 'I guess I'll close now' and in a back pew somebody said 'good'… Eva added. "I giggled so much that my ribs hurt."

"Yep, I heard that too, Miss Eva", Harvey answered. "But I lost it when Reverend Leyton retaliated by starting an excerpt of his sermon all over again. If Mrs. Bremond's cousin hadn't fainted because of the heat, we'd be listening to 'How Ugly Satan Is' all over again."

"I'm hungry!" Joy said. The three adults howled with laughter at Joy's summary of the whole Sunday situation.

The taxi pulled up to the front porch on South Fourth Street. Harvey took off his suit jacket and loosened his tie to get comfortable before he sat down on the glider. His white dress shirt was damp with perspiration but he still maintained a tailored appearance. Several younger church sisters always made a concerted effort to try to attract his attention whenever he was seated during Sunday service and Harvey always made a concerted effort to avoid eye contact. He was one of the men who was in the position of being an eligible bachelor with a sizable bank account and a paid off mortgage. Those two facts made him a desirable target for Suffolk's lonely heart club. Eva was partly responsible for his dilemma, as she had spread the word that he would be a wonderful prospect for someone but Harvey managed to stay shy of her efforts...so far.

"Be right down, Harvey," Eva yelled as she slipped into an airy cotton duster. Just as she made her way down to the bottom of the stairs, the telephone rang.

"Hello? Well, my gracious! It's so nice to hear from you, Barbara. How's Henry doing? That's good to hear. Glenda will be coming down for a visit? Sure! That'd be wonderful and you know your Dad will be on pins and needles until she gets here. Now stop talking nonsense, Barbara. Send down my other grandbaby. You know we don't mind looking after her at all while you and Henry are away. You and Henry work so hard, and yawl deserve a vacation. She'll be on the nine o'clock morning train tomorrow? No problem. In fact, Harvey is here right now so I'll let him know so he can meet the train. All right, Barbara and don't worry about a thing, honey. You and Henry have a wonderful time. All right, baby. I'll make sure to tell Pervis too and goodbye for now, darling."

Harvey and Purvis were on the front porch engaged in one of their man-to-man conversations about the cost of new automobiles and building materials. Seated at the end of the glider next to the living room windows, Joy had changed into her pink blouse and short-set Eva bought uptown at J.C. Penny's. As far as she was concerned, the glider was her exclusive territory on the front porch but she didn't mind Harvey's presence at all. She liked and respected him. "I wonder what it would have been like if he was my Dad instead of the one I have." she pondered without knowing Harvey had so often thought the same thing.

"That was Barbara and Henry on the phone, Pervis," Eva interrupted without regard for the conversation in process.

"Really, how are she and Henry doing?"

"The two of them are going to the Bahamas on a cruise ship."

"That boy really knows how to move around in the world. He takes good care of Barbara too. Yep! That's my boy," Pervis said.

Eva continued. "Barbara said because they're going to be gone for so long, they're sending Glenda down on the train to stay with us for the whole summer. Won't that be great to have the grand girls together for the summer, Pervis? Oh, Harvey! I told Barbara that you'd pick up Glenda at the train station. She doesn't trust any other driver. Is it okay?"

"Now Eva, Harvey might have had another appointment or something before you…or even a hot date," Pervis teased.

"Hush up, Pervis. You're embarrassing Harvey."

"That's okay, Pervis. I'll be more than happy to pick up Glenda Wednesday morning," Harvey replied with a sheepish grin on his face. The men liked to tease one another. "What time will her train get in, Miss Eva?"

"She should be on the nine o'clock train which will put her in Suffolk by one."

"That shouldn't be a problem. Calls for taxi service are always slow on Wednesdays anyway."

"It'll be nice to have company for Joy," Pervis remarked. He loved it when there was a house full of family. It reminded him of when his girls were small and the house stayed full with their friends or maybe it was the fact he was from a home situation were many folks in one house was something common. No matter…he was just glad Glenda was coming.

"Isn't that good news, Joy?" Harvey said, readily detecting a slight frown on Joy's face.

"Now my summer is going to be ruined by that spoiled brat of a cousin of mine," Joy said under her breath but…Harvey heard it all.

THE LAST PIECE OF CHICKEN

It was a Tazell family tradition. All kinfolk gathered together at 139 South Fourth Street during the Christmas holidays. Glenda was the Christmas surprise for Eva and Pervis when Joy was seven and Glenda was six years old. Not only had she been adopted but, she was lacking a large degree of melanin. In fact, she was so light skinned that she was mistakenly classified as Caucasian in her upstate Oneonta private school.

It was during that Christmas that Glenda showed off her Christmas gifts. She bragged about how she'd gotten everything she had wanted from her list. She was spoiled rotten. Even though Joy hadn't seen her in a while, she was older now but, still spoiled rotten. Most of all, Joy resented having to share her grandparents with the uppity pain in the neck.

Henry headed his own law firm in New York City and Oneonta and Barbara was teaching English at Oneonta University. Henry had a competitive nature in every sense of the word. Anything he aspired to do…he did with success. His firm hadn't lost a case. It was noted for those efforts by a display of numerous awards on the wood-paneled walls of both his offices. He wanted to be something beyond the briefcase totting, blue-collar worker who was contented to share office space with identical cookie cutter images seen in Black corporate America. Barbara had the strength of character that always meshed well with his personality.

Henry was a trim build. Every day, he was donned with tailored apparel that complimented his deep brown complexion. His thick, silky black hair was the result of genes past to him through Sioux Indian blood and his skin was as smooth as silk too. Standing six foot four inches tall, he was indeed Barbara's soul mate…just as Arvis had predicted that wintry night so long ago.

Barbara and Henry advanced their careers as they planned but, for Barbara, one thing was missing, she wanted to be a mother. She knew of her inability to have children because of the car accident but, when Henry noted her depression about the issue, the two talked it over and agreed to adopt. He assured his wife that his love for her had nothing to do with her inability to bare children. After many more nights of discussion, they set in motion the plans to adopt a child.

Glenda had turned eighteen months old when Henry and Barbara finally completed over a year of a mountainous mess of applications, background checks, and financial investigations. Barbara appreciated the levelheaded stalwart proficiency of her husband during those trying times. Without his gentile comforting and words of encouragement, Barbara knew she wouldn't have been able to withstand the pressures of constant interviews and unexpected appointments. It had always baffled Barbara as to how the social offices, with its maze of regulations, made it so difficult to assist responsible couples to qualify to adopt when so many children needed to be part of loving families.

After what seemed like an eternity, Glenda Marie became a permanent part of the Johnson household. Barbara was elated and immediately began to involve her daughter in every activity she felt was the best and would enhance her child's physical and mental capabilities. The only drawback was that Glenda had grown into the plus sizes at a young age. Barbara hoped gymnastics and ballet lessons would address the problem. She'd already given four private gymnastic instructors nervous breakdowns not to mention three episodes of fleeing piano teachers. Glenda had no doubt made Beethoven roll over in his grave at her final piano recital.

By summer visiting South Fourth Street, Glenda's weight had increased by three pounds and her size sixteen dresses at age ten alarmed her mother. Barbara threw up her hands and cried on Eva's shoulder about her concern for her daughter.

Eva knew the purpose for this summer's visit was more than an ordinary, casual visit for Glenda. She wasn't worried because she also knew there was an emotional core in Glenda that needed addressing. Still pouting over Monday's arrival, Joy helped Eva set the dining room table.

"Why can't Uncle Henry let Glenda stay with his relatives in New York?" Joy asked.

"Now, honey. I can already sense the reason you're asking me that question. I know Glenda can be a bit testy and may spoil your summer days but she's still your cousin and you have to remember that. I suppose in the process of her parents showing their love, they spoiled her. You can't blame Glenda for their love for her. Try to help me out and show a little patience with her. Okay?"

"All right, Granny. I'll try real hard to do that just for you."

"No, sweetheart but I want you to do it because you really want to."

As they began to place platters of yummy food on the table, the Leytons pulled up in their 1939 chrome laden Ford. Its black shiny exterior sat on wide-rimmed white walled tires. The massive thing got a waxing and polishing from Ben's Garage each Saturday…rain or shine, hot, cold, good weather, or bad weather.

"Come right in, Reverend Leyton," Pervis greeted. "And how are you, Mrs. Leyton?"

"Good afternoon, Pastor…Mrs. Leyton," Harvey added standing to his feet as they entered the porch. All started the walked into the dining room.

"The table looks just fine, Joy," Eva complimented as she placed a platter of batter fried chicken next to the steaming country ham.

"We finished everything just in time, Granny because I hear the Leytons talking on the front porch."

"I do too so, let's go greet our guests, Joy." Eva and Joy were halfway to the porch but, met the in the dining room instead.

"Oh, how wonderful of you to stop by. Joy and I just finished setting the table a few minutes ago. Why don't you freshen up a bit and then we'll all be seated at the table," Eva said.

"You sure we're not putting you out, Sister Tazell?"

"Of course not, Reverend Leyton, you know you and Mrs. Leyton are welcome at any time."

Harvey and Pervis', snickering like little children, sat down at the table while the Leytons freshened for the feast. They knew fun was soon on the way.

Reverend Leyton had been pastor of Tabernacle Christian Church for over thirty-five years. He'd seen the church building grow from a single-room wooden framed structure to the enormous brick sided edifice it was. Because of the dedication of the members of his congregation who were carpenters, brick masons and electricians., it came to be…free of charge!

Helena and Helen were their married twin daughters who lived in the new suburban part of town. As teenagers, the twins weren't exactly at the top of the popularity list as far as their peers were concerned. That was mainly the case because something was missing in their gene cells at birth making them the ugliest twins this side of Timbuktu. When the family announced the wedding plans during a Sunday service, invitation or no invitation, the entire town attended the double wedding. Everyone was burning with curiosity as to who the husbands would be. All were shocked to see these handsome fellows walk down the aisle as if they were blind to the attachment on their arms. Helena gave birth to twin girls and Helen gave birth to twin boys. Fortunately, the babies had the genetic makeup of their fathers.

"Praise the Lord, Sister Tazell!" Reverend Leyton bellowed, as he eyed the supper table. It was laden with platters of cabbage, macaroni and cheese, collard greens, a large ham surrounded by pineapples and cherries, batter fried chicken, butter beans, string beans, fried corn, homemade rolls, three pitchers of lemonade, a long rectangular pan of cornbread, a similar pan of peach cobbler, stewed tomatoes and Pervis' pitcher of ice tea.

"Reverend Leyton, you sit here," Eva said.

"Mrs. Leyton, you sit here next to the Reverend. Pervis, you take your seat at the other head of the table. Joy and Harvey; yawl sit beside each other across from Mrs. Leyton."

The oak chairs seemed to creak and moan as the Reverend and his better half lowered their ample posteriors.

Once all were seated Eva asked, "Reverend Leyton, would you say grace?"

"Why certainly," Reverend Leyton replied as he finished tucking his cloth napkin in his shirt collar and stood up. "Let us bow our heads and close our eyes. Lord, we're all thankful for the bountiful blessing we are about to receive, and may it nourish our bodies for Jesus' sake. Bless the hands that prepared it and laboured so hard and long. May we always find fellowship with these folk and others…in Jesus' mighty, mighty Name we pray…Amen."

"Amen," everybody else calmly echoed.

Conversation topics began and consisted of how hot it was in church, how Joy is the perfect likeness to Arvis, how the Senior Choir needed more practice, how many jars of canned peaches Eva donated to the church pantry, and pass the cornbread, please.

Reverend Leyton was going on and on about how he got his inspiration for his sermons in between a mouthful of greens and candied yams. While the eating commotion was going back and forth across the table, Pervis' caught Eva's eye and Eva's eye caught Harvey's eye as all three watched to see which one of the holy couple would reach for the last piece of batter-fried chicken. Mrs. Leyton won! Pervis stuffed his mouth with corn bread to hold back the yelp of laughter that was welling up from the pit of his stomach. Harvey muffled a chuckle by pretending to wipe his mouth with his napkin. After shoveling down the last mouthful of his second helping of peach cobbler, the Reverend reared back, patted his stomach and struggled to his feet. If his chair had the capacity of audible expression, it would sigh with relief.

"Well Sister Tazell…your cooking was certainly as motivational as always. Sister Leyton and I have to leave you now for its time for us to let you spend the rest of your Sunday with family."

"How about taking home a paper p of peach cobbler with you, Sister Leyton?" Eva asked knowing already what the answer would be.

"Oh! God bless you, Sister Tazell."

"Yes-sir-re, God bless you indeed, Sister. That's a mighty fine way to say goodbye," Reverend Leyton added.

"I'll say my goodbye too, Miss Eva," Harvey said.

"Oh no, Harvey, must you leave too?"

"I've got to get an early start in the morning…remember, Miss Eva?"

"Oh, yes! Well all right then."

After everybody left, Pervis sat down in his rocker on the front porch and began to browse through the pages of Sunday's Suffolk News Herald. Still preoccupied with thoughts of Glenda's arrival, Joy mindlessly helped Eva clear the dinner table and start the kitchen clean up routine. She didn't have the nerve to raise a conversation about her cousin again but somehow she felt that this cousin would be an infringement on her summer stay in Suffolk…and Jamaal. She felt angry for feeling so selfish but just couldn't help it. She'd never had the experience of living with someone else almost her own age even though she'd heard her Mom speak of wanting her to have a baby brother... before Jasper's obnoxious behavior came into full bloom. "Oh well," Joy thought to herself as she opened the cabinet to put away supper plates. Maybe Glenda's coming to stay for the summer won't turn out to be such a bad deal after all."

"Whew! We've finally finished and I'm pooped," Eva said.

"Make sure you pack away a portion of that yummy peach cobbler for my lunch tomorrow, honey," Pervis hollered down the hall.

"Just never you mind, Pervis," Eva hollered back. "After all these years, you know you don't have to remind me how to look after your lunch box." Pervis let it go at that.

Taking their seats on the porch, Joy and Eva joined Pervis in quiet relaxation as the tranquillity of the imminent evening approached. Each mulled over the events of the day once again. The disappearance of the last piece of chicken at the dinner table became the main topic of discussion.

"I thought I'd bust a gut over the Leytons at the dinner table."

"Now Pervis, behave. We have young ears on the porch now," Eva said.

"Eva, you know I don't mean any disrespect for the Leytons but the way I see it is if you're going to preach about hell fire and damnation then why not preach about gluttony as a way to get to that hot place too?"

"Well...even though he's our pastor, there something in what you say."

"Reverend Leyton should have retired years ago," Pervis continue. "He should have let someone else take over the pulpit. You know, Eva, we need new blood in the pulpit. There's been a steady increase of young people in the congregation. Young folks today have sharp minds and are quick thinkers and there's more out there to distract them from a life of faith. They need to know that real spiritual leadership is not afraid to be accepting it."

Eva listened intensively and knew that her husband was speaking the truth...and knew Joy was anxiously waiting for her reaction to Pervis' statement. In the past, Eva and Pervis had never let their children see a division of any kind between them. If there was a difference of opinion expressed, the discussion was always out of the earshot of the siblings in the family.

"Pervis, you're entitled to your opinions and all and it's true when you said we're getting more and more young folks on the church roll. Actually, you know who I wish was in the ministry?"

"Who, honey?"

"Harvey Ellis because he's the kindest, sweetest and most decent fellow I know…besides you, of course."

"That's wonderful of you to say, Eva. I haven't told you before but Harvey and I have talked about that very fact but right now, he's happy with his current responsibility as a youth pastor. Because of his efforts, those young people have really grasped the different church programs designated just for them. Why, the young people actually come to church because of him and if anybody knows how to pass the Word along, it's the young people."

The Tazells and their granddaughter sat quietly, rocked, and listened to the serenade of chirping, croaking, and splash of bullfrogs jumping into the stream down the hill. Stars began to blanket the evening sky and the fragrance of honeysuckle vines floated thick in the air as if Mother Nature had sprayed herself with perfume. The rhythmic rocking of Eva and Pervis' metal chairs on the linoleum kept in perfect time. Pervis had a special name for the end of the day. He called it the family's "No Anger…No Wrath Time". If there was anything that happened during the day or if there were any thoughts or memories that harboured tension, there would be a mental dumping before bedtime. No excess baggage of grudges or bickering carried over into the next day. It was from that belief that the "end of the day" ritual practices were held in most homes on the front porch in the summer and in the livingroom during the winter.

"Well…tomorrow will be another long day for me. The other fellows and I have some parts to do a special shipping order to go get out at the plant. I'll probably have to put in some overtime tomorrow night, Eva."

"I understand, Pervis. I hope you and your crew get everything done. I'll be sure to pack extras for your lunch."

"Okay, Eva. Hey, Joy!" Pervis yelled. "Wake up, baby! We're going upstairs now and call it a night."

"Time for me to stretch out these legs of mine but I must admit they held up pretty good for me today," Eva said.

"I've got news for you, old girl. They've always been in pretty good shape to me."

"Now Pervis don't get so fresh," Eva giggled, as Pervis grabbed her from behind and tickled her. Eva let loose an ear-piercing squeal as she struggled to get away from her husband's clutches. She still responded to his seductiveness the same way she'd done when he had stolen his first kiss years ago. Tonight, she let him steal another. They'd been robbing each other that way for years. Joy followed close behind them and loved to watch her grandparents frolic and play like teenagers.

Each said goodnight followed by a rhapsody of snoring. Joy gazed into the night out of her window and flip-flopped restlessly as the thought of Glenda's arrival drew closer. Finally, sleep came back to her. She blew a kiss at her Mom's small photo and dropped of to sleep.

GLENDA MARIE JOHNSON

BEEP! BEEP! BEEP!

Excited and giggling, Glenda swung open the rear door of the taxi before Harvey came to a full stop at the front gate. Carrying her portable pink and yellow record player, she mounted up the front porch steps like a plump waddling duck. Her mass of black, shoulder length silky curls bounced and wiggled with each step she made. Harvey follows her to the porch carrying a large powder blue, leather suitcase and a matching overnight bag each monogrammed with the letters "GMJ".

"Salutations everybody," Glenda shouted with an out of town northern accent and overdone aristocratic pretension.

"Oh brother," Joy moaned. "This is worse than I thought. She looks like the Gerber Baby all grown up!"

"Glenda hopped into Eva's arms and gave her grandmother a bourgeois peck on the cheek as if rewarding Eva for some kind of servant's job well done.

"And who is this, Granny?" Glenda asked pointing to Joy.

"Why, Glenda! Don't you recognize your cousin Joy?"

"My, my, my, look at you, cousin. You've grown so much that I would never have known who you were…especially with that absolutely charming and adorable hairdo," Glenda said. "That style is rare upstate."

"That rips it! Joy muttered to herself as Glenda and Eva made their way upstairs. "…and just when I was going to give that knucklehead a chance." Harvey was laughing so hard to himself as he drove away that he could barely see the road but one thing was for sure, a major change was coming for Glenda whether see knew it or not.

"Let's go inside and get you settled in your room. It's right across the hall from Joy's," Eva said, as she hobbled up the steps dragging Glenda's overstuffed suitcase with her. Annoyed, Joy hopped up the stairs past Glenda to Eva, snatched the suitcase out of Eva's hand, stomped to Glenda's bedroom and threw the suitcase on the bed.

"Ignoring Joy's actions for the moment, Eva asked, "What in heaven's name have you got packed in that thing, Glenda?"

"I brought just a few summer items, Granny. Well…of course, there are some of my favorite books in there too."

"Whoever heard of packing books?" Joy mumbled.

"I like to keep up with the latest literary achievements for teens and beside that, Granny…I'm this year's Spelling Bee first place winner for the third time. Reading is most important to me. That's how I learn new words and phrases."

"I'll bet you're carrying a giant bottle of diet pills too," Joy said below her breath as she watched her cousin waddle up the stairs.

Glenda expressed pure elation over the spaciousness of her bedroom. Joy plopped the heavy suitcase down in the middle of the bed. She was perfectly satisfied to have her Mom's old bedroom.

"Whew! That is that! I'll leave you two so you can get reacquainted," Eva said, grabbing the corner of her apron and fanning her sweating brow. "I have some mending to do so I'll see you both when you're ready to come down."

"Gosh! It's good to get a change of scenery," Glenda chimed while she looked out of her bedroom window. "I think I'm going to enjoy this country life for the next few months."

"Yep, I guess you'll have to get use to ordinary country folks like us," Joy replied while sitting in a soft upholstered armchair next to Glenda's bed.

Still flapping her jaws non-stop, Glenda meticulously hung up twenty-four summer outfits. The rest of her suitcase inventory included three pairs of sneakers, two pairs of patent leather dress shoes, a pair of Buster Brown loafers, silk ballet slippers and of course…books.

"Can you really dance in those things?" Joy asked, pointing to the ballet slippers.

"Certainly I can, Joy. Haven't you taken ballet lessons too?" Glenda asked, with a look of genuine shock at Joy's question.

"Well…I didn't want to say it before but I would have completed my advanced lessons but the instructor I had moved to Europe last year," Joy replied sarcastically.

"Really," Glenda asked, not realizing she was the butt end of a joke. She just exploded into another torrid of 'I've done this versus

I've done that'. Without making a sound and while Glenda's back was turned, Joy quietly withdrew from the presence of the Prima Donna's room and tipped downstairs to the front porch. Still jabbering, Glenda twirled around to show Joy a bottle of perfume she'd bought as a present with her own allowance…but Joy wasn't there.

"I wish I knew how to make people like me," Glenda said, flopping down on the edge of her bed with disappointment. A tear rolled down her cheek. Groomed for all the social graces there was one thing she longed to have…a real friend. Not even her parents knew of the cruelty she'd experienced at being the target of heartless pranks for being the chubbiest girl in her class. Having finished her unpacking, she started downstairs but before she did, she made sure to ware her 'glad-face' to hide her façade of loneliness.

"…all done?" Eva asked.

"All done, Granny," Glenda replied politely pretending not to notice Joy.

"May I sit next to you on the glider, Joy?"

"Help yourself," Joy said, flippantly not caring if Glenda did or didn't.

"I was sorry to hear about your Mom's death," Glenda said as sympathetically as she knew how. "I had the flu and a terrible stomach virus so Mom felt it was best for me to stay at home."

"So…that's why you didn't show up, eh?"

"Yes, Joy," Glenda replied, happy to have initiated some kind of conversation with her cousin.

"Well…that's okay. I suppose if you're sick that you're sick", Joy said tersely.

Sitting in Pervis' rocker, Eva pretended to search for a spool of thread in her basket. She'd been listening to the conversation at hand and keenly observing Joy's chilliness towards Glenda even after Joy had promised to try to understand her cousin's conflicts. Eva knew Glenda was high-minded but that was no excuse for Joy's rudeness. She'd never shown favoritism where her daughter's were involved and was not about to begin with her granddaughters. She decided it was time to put an end to Joy's attitude immediately.

"You know something, girls? Sitting here watching you two brings back memories of the time I was a youngster your age."

GRANNY'S PLACE

"You mean you can remember that far back, Granny?" Glenda asked.

Joy rolled her eyes around in disgust. "Boy, that fancy education sure didn't do you much good, Glenda."

"Sorry," Glenda mumbled.

"Sure I can remember that far back, Glenda. Would ya'll like to hear a true story about something that happened back then?"

"Oh yes, Granny," Joy remarked, remembering Eva's story about "Aunt Jemima".

"All right then and listen close. I was about twelve years old then and it was terribly hard for Black folks in those days but my family had many years of experience under the belt of knowing how to make the best of hard times. Anyway, it was late autumn and the leaves on the trees had finished changing from springtime green to endless shades of yellow, orange, and red. I tell you, there's nothing prettier than watching Mother Nature change her seasonal outfits."

"I know what you mean, Granny. We've lots of trees in our backyard too," Glenda said.

"So! New Jersey's trees change colors too," Joy snapped. Eva shook her head in dismay over Joy's unsavory behavior but continued her story.

"As I remember, there was this rich white family by the name of DeLoach who owned acres and acres of land. When their son and daughter grew up, they moved away, began lives of their own, and didn't visit their folks too often either. Old man DeLoach was a kind spirited old gent. Because he and his wife could no longer care for their land, and really didn't need to, Mr. DeLoach decided to rent out the land by acres rather than let it sit and grow wild. He spread the word around that his land was for rent and had a line of black and white folks the next week. The contract each had to sign or make a mark was simple enough. All need be done was to harvest the two acres of land for seven years and fill the DeLoach barns with twenty per cent of the produce at harvest time. At the end of the seven years, if the renter wanted to purchase the land, it was his for a low, low price. I'm here to tell you that with a deal like that, folks clamored to the DeLoach doorstep like ants around a sugar cube and my Mama and Papa got in on the deal too. As it happened, a family by the name of Williams had

GRANNY'S PLACE

acres right next to ours. Their two teenage boys, who were two years apart, looked like twins. James, the older brother was a friendly and generous soul but his brother Rufus was always complaining or brooding about something. After each harvest, Mr. Williams allowed each boy to glean the acres."

"What do you mean 'glean', Granny?" Glenda asked.

"It means to collect whatever leftover crops left along the edges of the field after a harvest," Joy said, obviously irritated by Glenda's interruption. Eva continued.

"Mr. Williams told his boys they could keep the errand profits from any ideas they came up with in selling their gleanings. He wanted them to be as creative as possible. James had the idea to take his vegetables, arrange them carefully on a cart, and haul them into town to sell. Rain or shine, no matter what kind of weather it was, James merrily went to the market. On the other hand, Rufus hung around the house and jealously eyed his brother's efforts. James has sold every bit of his vegetables and asked his father to keep his earnings in a safe place. Whenever Mr. Williams asked Rufus about his earnings, Rufus just whined and made lots of excused. I mean to tell you that the boy sulked and brooded and got meaner with each passing day."

"Finally…the winter weather set in over the land. Everything was frozen and covered with snow. Columns of smoke rose from cabin chimneys as hard working families enjoyed the fruits of their labor. Christmas came and because of his hard work, James was able to buy a humble gift for his parents and Rufus.

By this time, malice had replaced anger and Rufus hated his brother. The sky was clear and bright on Christmas Eve day. Ice cycles hung from the windowsills and the wintry air kept them intact. Deer scratched around for bits of grain in the frozen fields."

"At his Mama's request, James went to the well to draw up a pail of water. Rufus was outside already gathering wood for the fireplace. His spirit was as sour as a lemon. When he saw James leaning over the edge of the deep well, his face twisted with the wickedness he'd been brewing in his heart. Like a stalking bobcat, he crept up behind James and pushed his brother into the deep dark well. He waited beside the well until her heard the last of his brother's gurgling pleas for help as

James disappeared under the water. Then it was over. Rufus went back into the house with a smile on his face."

"As some time went by, Mrs. Williams noticed James was taking longer than usual to draw up a single pail of water and asked Rufus had he seen James while outside. Rufus lied and said that he been on the backside of the house and hadn't noticed his brother. At that, Mrs. Williams began to wring her hands with worry. Mr. Williams put on his coat to go outside and search for his boy. Rufus, pretending to be concerned too, joined his parents. They searched for hours calling out for James but got no answer. They imagined that a bear got him and dragged him off or a wolf attacked him but there were no bloodstains or animal tracks found in the snow. They walked to all the neighboring houses in the bitter cold weather. My Papa offered to join them in their search and they were grateful for his help. I wanted to go too but my Mama was afraid I'd catch a death of cold so I stayed put at home. The search went on for hours until it was too dark to search anymore. When night had completely blanketed the woods and fields, all went home promising to rejoin the worried parents for the search in the morning."

"Christmas came but it was a sad day for the Williams family. After everybody searched again for many hours, all assumed the worst. Neighbors comforted the Williams family and returned to their own homes. Rufus was still pretending to be worried about the disappearance of his brother but deep down inside…he was glad."

"A whole year passed. Rufus was feeling smug because at last he was getting all the attention from his parents he felt he deserved. He'd kept his wretched secret of James' demise locked away in his evil heart. Still another year passed but fate had not forgotten Rufus' heinous deed because something peculiar happened on the exact same day of the year the original wrong was committed."

"What happened, Granny," Glenda asked.

"He was content his vile action hadn't yet been found out. Rufus went to the well in a happy-go-lucky whistling mood but an unspeakable thing happened."

"What happed to him, Granny," Joy asked, with her face partly covered with the pillow.

"As Rufus leaned over to pull up the pail filled with water, his eyes bulged out of his head at the sight looking back at him."

"What did he see, Granny," Glenda whined. Joy covered her face with a pillow and Pervis almost hee-hawed outloud. His wife was doing an excellent job in getting her point across.

"There on the shimmering surface of the well water was the image of a face."

"A face," Glenda asked, now sitting on the edge the glider and shaking like a leaf. "Whose face?" she managed to ask again.

"It was the face of James. His poor spirit could rest no longer. He was weeping pitifully and pleading for Rufus to pull him out of the dark cold wet grave. Rufus was so terrified that his knees buckled and he fell to the ground beside the well in a heap. He began to yowl like a wounded puppy. After several minutes, he got up enough nerve to peer back into the well water. He whimpered and begged his brother to forgive him for the awful sin he'd done.

"Did James forgive what he'd done, Granny," Glenda asked.

"He did forgive him but there was one condition. The condition was that Rufus must confess what he'd done to his parents before the New Year began. If he didn't, a curse would fall on him. When Rufus heard the condition, he wailed even more."

"Gee Granny, I'd hate to be in Rufus' shoes right now," Joy said, a bit distressed. "What was the curse?" Eva smiled and continued with her tale.

"It was this. If Rufus didn't confess before the New Year began, he'd become completely mute, grow desperately lonely, be shunned by other people for no reason and…he'd lose his sanity. When Rufus had been outside too long, Mr. Williams came out remembering what had happened to James. He found Rufus on his knees beside the well. He gently put his arm around his son's shoulder and asked what was troubling him. It was the perfect time for Rufus to tell all that had happened by the well but he didn't have the courage to tell the truth. He never realized how much his parents loved him. Perplexed and thinking that Rufus was still grieving over the loss of James, he led his trembling son back into the house."

"Time went on little by little and minute by minute. As the New Year grew closer, because of his fear and stubbornness to confess what he'd done, Rufus slowly began to lose his soundness of mind and talking and formed words with more difficulty. He couldn't even do the simplest chore."

"I think I would have told the truth," Joy said, smugly. Eva smiled again. Joy put her face behind the pillow again.

"What happened next, Granny," Glenda asked more bravely.

"By now, Rufus couldn't say a word and most of the time he'd walk around the fields with a blank stare in his eyes. From then on, he was no help to himself or his parents and the family lost everything and had to move before the next planting season."

"What did the neighbors think about the way Rufus was acting?" Glenda asked.

"I don't remember what other folks thought but I'll let you in on a little secret."

"What Granny?" Joy asked.

"My Papa always suspected that Rufus had something to do with James' disappearance. He also knew Rufus was jealous of James and showed it often. Papa was a great believer in a person getting his real 'comeuppance', so Rufus loosing his mind and all was no great surprise to Papa. From then on, nobody saw Rufus much. Word got around that he built a shack at the edge of the woods and only came out of the shack to glean a few scraps of food to eat. Soon, all was forgotten about that day. But…one wintry morning…my Papa found Rufus' body draped over the edge of the same well where James met his demise. One of Rufus' arms was pointing down at something inside the well. Terror was eternally frozen on his face and twisted it so horribly that it even shook up Papa, who wasn't a scary kind of fellow. Papa found a piece of burlap and covered Rufus' stiff body the best he could and laid it down near the well. He was gone about fifteen minutes or so to get the undertaker when Papa heard a loud splash and ran back towards the well as fast as he could. Rufus' body was gone and never found again. It was hard for Papa to explain because Rufus' body froze so stiff that there was no way possible it could have fallen into the well on its own. After careful examination of the area, Papa said he found scratch marks on the edge of the well wall. As time passed on, the story of Rufus Williams became a folktale told to youngsters in front of warm fireplaces during the Christmas season to warn them of what could happen if they were hard-headed or hard-hearted. The strangest part of the tale was that around harvest time, one or two farmers would tell of a shadowy figure roaming aimlessly along the edge of the field with a pail and howling something like, *'I'm sorry, James! I'm sorry!'* Now grandchildren of mine, can you tell me what you think is the moral to this story?"

Looking at each other, both shook their heads like puppets on a string.

"No? Well the moral of the story is that no matter what you do or say, no matter how long it takes, deeds and words are like seeds. You can be sure of one thing…those seeds will grow in your heart and you can't escape the harvest that you'll reap one day."

Glenda looked at Joy and Joy look back at Glenda.

"Would you like to see my drawings in my picture diary, Glenda?"

"Sure I would Joy, and would you like me to show you some dance steps I learned in my ballet class?"

"That would be great, Glenda," Joy said, putting her arm around Glenda's shoulder. Satisfied she'd gotten her point across; Eva sat back and rhythmically rocked in her chair.

AND NOW THERE WERE THREE

Meals were always a special part in the kitchen on South Fourth Street and there wasn't a day when breakfast, lunch, a snack, and supper didn't get served with clockwork precision. Eva's kitchen was her kingdom and the entire Tazell family clan never interfered with any judgements from that room. Each generation of family youth who had the privilege of residing or visiting, remembered the culinary delights that tantalized and satisfied their palettes each day. This afternoon's snack was sandwiches abundantly stacked with slices of cheese, home cooked ham, lettuce, tomatoes, and mayonnaise topped with a tall ice-cold glass of Kool-aid.

"Joy, Glenda…its time for your snack," Eva yelled from the kitchen. The cousins responded by racing downstairs to the kitchen. Both said grace in unison and gobbled down the snack Eva had waiting for them.

Sounds carried well in the house because there was a twelve-by-twelve inch grate in the corner of each room that allowed heat from the large portable stove in the diningroom to rise and warm the upstairs.

"May we go out for a walk after we've finished our snack, Granny?" Glenda asked.

"Yes baby, but try not to stay out in the sun too long if you can help it and…don't talk with food in your mouth. You might choke," Eva answered.

"Yes ma'am," Glenda responded meekly. Eva was so glad to see Glenda beginning to relax and act her age.

"When you're finished eating, put your dishes in the sink because I'm going back on the porch to finish my mending," Eva instructed while walking down the hall.

"I'll say one thing, Joy," Glenda said while wiping off the table. "I for one will never forget that story Granny told us on the front porch yesterday."

GRANNY'S PLACE

"That story was something else, Glenda. I don't want anything to do with 'bad seeds'," Joy said as she thought about her Dad. Glenda thought about the mean things the girls in her ballet class said to her. Each wondered what seeds would grow under those circumstances.

"We've finished eating and cleaned everything up, Granny. Can we go now?" Glenda yelled down the hall to the front porch.

"Yes, but make certain y'all get home on time for supper and remember not to go too far!"

"We won't, Granny," the cousins yelled back in unison. With that said they ran out the yard gate and disappeared up South Fourth Street. Midway, Joy led Glenda off to the side of the road and took a shortcut through an empty lot of land and down a narrow grassy path. They passed by the rickety back porches of some of the houses with clotheslines laden with sheets, towels and pillow cases. From the look of the linen, it'd been hanging on the clothesline for a day or so.

"Golly, Joy," Glenda said. "Where are we going?"

"...to visit with Jamaal."

"Who's Jamaal?" Glenda asked as she heaved trying to keep up with Joy.

"He's a real good friend of mine and Granny and Granddaddy are real good friends of his parents. We plan summer activities together each time I come down. I want you to meet him, okay?"

"That's fine with me, Joy but please don't walk so fast. I've got to get use to all this adventure stuff...especially the heat," Glenda said puffing. She gave her brow a wipe with the hem of her sleeveless blouse.

"All right Glenda. I tell you what. Just ahead is my favorite spot and you'll like it too."

Joy continued a bit ahead of Glenda as images of her oasis in the forest formed in her mind. She smiled to herself as she wondered if Mother Nature had made many new things grow. They arrived at the spot just in time to get out of the relentless heat of the sun. A burst of air gently whipped tree limbs. As far as the eye could see, an expansive meadow dressed in tall blades of grass and wild flowers swished in every direction that the wind dictated.

"Come on, Glenda! We're here!" Joy shouted, grabbing her tortured cousin by the hand.

Glenda wasn't use to the new sensation of grass gripping the calves of her legs or perspiration dampening her clothes. Running with Joy at this pace made her feel as if she were going to pass out but she mustered up all the energy she could so as not to disappoint Joy…or herself because there was no way she was going to jeopardize creating a long-lasting friendship with her cousin.

"Yikes," Glenda yelped.

"What's the matter?" Joy asked, still trotting with Glenda's hand in hers.

"That thing over there flew in my face and bumped me on the nose!"

"Oh silly, that was a horsefly, Glenda," Joy laughed.

Just as she promised, Joy led Glenda to a stream of translucent water flowing gently through a rocky bottomed ravine. The massive branches of a weeping willow tree cast a welcoming shadow over the stream. Glenda dropped to her knees and splashed a handful of clear water on her face and neck and scooped up one handful of water after another to drink until her thirst was quenched. Joy climbed up on a nearby boulder and stretched out on her back. She lifted her mass of braids to allow the breeze to cool her neck. Glenda joined her.

"Glenda, I'm sorry about the way I treated you when you first came. I know Granny cleared up most of everything when she told us that story. I swear, I'll never offend you again."

"That's okay, Joy because I'm sorry too."

"You are? What do you have to be sorry for, Glenda?"

"I was showing off a bit with all my stuff because…well…I didn't know how to react to you."

"That's not exactly the same thing but I get what you mean. Is all forgiven?"

"Sure it is, Joy. Let's start new today…right now," Glenda said, reaching for Joy's hand to shake it to seal their covenant. "Let's take off our shoes and slash around in the stream."

"But…we'll get all wet," Glenda said.

"Are you kidding? That sounds like a good idea with all this heat. Besides, we'll dry off long before we have to leave for home." They had a grand time of kicking and splashing water everywhere. Their voices echoed through the woods and across the entire meadow. Today…Joy and Glenda were a part of the sounds of Mother Nature and other's of God's creatures.

"Betcha I can get you wet all over first," Joy said slapping up water in the stream with her feet.

"Betcha you won't Miss New Jersey," Glenda hollered back.

Both made a sudden belly-flop in the middle of the stream at the same time. Glenda howled with laughter as Joy swam around in the water like some weird fish with its butt up in the air. The girls enjoyed themselves until their toes began to wrinkle. Waterlogged and out of breath, the cousins climbed out of the stream and relaxed on top of the sun-drenched boulder to dry. They peered between the branches of the weeping willow tree and stared into the cloud filled sky. Challenging her own imaginary skills, Joy played a guessing game with Glenda to see who could recognize something from the cloud formations.

"I see and elephant," Joy said, pointing to the sky.

"Yes, I see it now and I see a frog," Glenda said. The topic then changed to current fashions, what the new school year might be like, what they wanted to be when they grew up, graduating from college, and of course…boys. They'd become so involved in their skyward creativity that they hadn't noticed their clothes were completely dry.

"All this reminds me of one of those paintings you see on the wall in a store furniture display. You know what I mean, Glenda. I'm talking about the ones that hang on the wall above the couch in the livingroom."

"You sure have a terrific imagination, Joy. Are you going to study art in college? From the looks of your picture diary, you have a natural talent. I've never seen a diary like that before."

"I suppose I will, Glenda but what do you want to be when you get older?"

"I don't know exactly but it will to do with law. Daddy is so organized and admired and I love to find out about things, you know…dig down real deep."

"You love your parents a lot, don't you Glenda," Joy said.

"I have to confess I do, Joy. They're two great people."

"Jamaal said he wants to be a veterinarian and wait until you see all the little animal hospital he and his Dad built."

"Hadn't we better get going so we'll have time to spend there before we have to start home?"

"You're right so let's get going," Joy said.

Dried by the sun, they continued their walk along the grassy pathway that curved around the edge of the meadow. In the distance was the Wilson home. In the center of the twenty-five acre homestead was a voluptuous ranch style house. Black wrought iron railings supported an L-shaped porch with wrought iron railings and blue and white stripped awnings with matching shutters that shaded the entire porch. White cape-cod curtains accented a large bay window lending a soft contrast to the outside white aluminium siding of the house. The grass and shrubbery surrounding the house were immaculately trimmed. A freshly painted white-picked fence defined the borders of the spacious lawn. Dave built the house as a wedding present for Debra.

Dave and Debra Wilson were hardworking folks who prided themselves in managing their own crops. Both came from families who made their living toiling the earth. A summer drought Suffolk suffered five years ago set the atmosphere of fear stricken neighbors who sold their homesteads to quick talking land developers but the Wilsons did not give in to the modern carpetbagger's wiles. Now the only thing most of his neighbors had let was a bogus contract and years of regrets. David taught Jamaal that if all else fails; hold on to your land as long as you can.

David was an expert carpenter too and tried to pass on this talent to his son. He designed and built most of his family's home but today was spent mending fences around his property. Debra was an excellent homemaker and knew how to stretch and save a dollar. If one penny went somewhere, she'd have a receipt. For some unexplainable reason, Debra refused to trade in one item in her kitchen and that was her wood burning, cast iron stove handed down to her from her great-grandmother. The stove was an antique and was her pride and joy. It was handed down through many in her family and made a wedding gift from her parents. David tried in vain to convince his wife to let him buy an electric modern stove but Debra wouldn't hear of it. She had talked about the cast iron stove with Eva who congratulated Debra with three cheers and a hoorah for sticking to her guns. Today, Debra was at the Emmett's' home helping with the endless washing of clothes and soiled diapers.

Joy and Glenda walked around to the back of the house where they found Jamaal cutting wood for the stove. It was one of his every-two-weeks chores. Rain or shine, stacking wood on the back porch was an all-the-time chore. He'd have finished hours ago but he stopped several times to fool around with Samson, the family's eight-year-old bloodhound.

"Hi Jamaal," Joy said, shading her eyes from the sun.

"Hey Joy," Jamaal said, driving his axe into a chunk of wood and remembering how lovely she looked at church Sunday.

"I thought I'd stop by and introduce you to my cousin, Glenda Johnson who's visiting all the way from Oneonta, New York. That's way upstate New York," Joy said. "She'll be spending her summer vacation here too. I hope you don't mind Jamaal, but I brought Glenda over to see your animal hospital. Do you have a minute to take her on a tour?"

"I sure do," Jamaal said, bursting with pride and glad for a reason to get out of the scorching heat of the sun. Samson, panting heavily because of the heat, remained sprawled under the shade of the back porch underneath the steps. He had the instinct not to get in the way of the hot ball in the sky. In the meantime, Jamaal led the girls to the backside of his Dad's tool shed sitting to the edge of the huge backyard fence.

"I like your sign, Jamaal," Did you make it?" Joy asked.

"Yep, I did it by using a piece of hot iron to burn the letters into the wood."

"Jamaal's Animal Clinic," Glenda read. "I must admit, that's very impressive."

"Thanks Glenda. I did all the lettering myself." Jamaal said. "Of course, I used Dad's tools and he lent me a hand from time to time but the whole building project took only a week. I worked long hard hours each day but it was worth the effort."

Constructed with scraps of lumber and old chicken wire, a well-designed animal hospital resulted. It could house ten animals in separate compartments no bigger than a sheep that needed medical treatment…that wasn't too serious for the future veterinarian to handle. A mesh floor allowed for easy spray cleaning with a hose and sturdy twelve-inch stilt legs supported the structure. The wooden roof slanted downward at a forty-five degree angle so rain could easily drain off the top.

"The whole thing is a wonderful idea," Glenda cooed. "It's great that you care so much about animals the way you do. Why I was in the 4-H Club in New York and…"

"Er…Jamaal…have you had any patients lately?" Joy interrupted, giving Glenda a few 'who-care-about-the-4-H-club' looks.

"I gave medical treatment to a wounded baby fox's leg about two weeks ago," Jamaal said, proudly.

"Wow," Glenda gushed. "I'll bet it was cute and cuddly." Glenda briefly reverted to her old self. Joy suspected her cousin wasn't use to being around boys. It bothered her a bit to know Glenda was trying to work her feminine wiles on Jamaal.

"What other animals have you admitted to your hospital, Jamaal?" Joy asked.

"H-m-m-m let me see. Well…I've registered three rabbits, a raccoon, two squirrels, three chipmunks, five kittens and even two mice," Jamaal said.

"What was your most difficult case so far?" Glenda asked.

"That's easy to answer because it was no doubt my own hound, Samson. He broke his leg and that's what gave me the idea to start the hospital. It was a serious case. Dad, Mr. Jenkins, Mr. Adams, and I were on a hunting trip," Jamaal said as they all walked back to the shade of the back porch and sat on the steps. "We'd gotten up before the sun came up in the morning. We found a great spot to fish and set up a campfire to cook what we'd caught. I remember Dad telling everybody to hurry up and finish eating so we could start hunting for deer because Samson was sniffing the air something fierce. Finally, we started through the woods and before we knew it, we were on the trail of the biggest buck you ever did see."

"Excuse me for cutting into your story, Jamaal but what's a 'buck'?"

"A full grown male deer," Joy said, irritated.

"Anyway…Dad had his rifle aimed between the eyes of a huge buck when a bobcat jumped out of nowhere. Samson started howling, and took off like lightning and cornered the bobcat up a tree on a hill but he stepped on a patch of loose rocks and down the hill he rolled.

GRANNY'S PLACE

I caught up with Samson first and the came Dad. The problem was obvious to us both because Sampson's bone was sticking out of his leg. When we got home, Mom made an ointment out of crushed herbs and axle grease. She set the bone straight and wrapped up his leg in a splint and after some months of healing, you can't tell that he had an accident at all. My first patient healed up just fine. That ladies…was my first case."

"Good old Samson," Joy said, as she patted the dog's head.

"But listen, you guys," Jamaal said. Mom will cook-my-goose if I don't get this wood cut before she gets home. It was nice of you two to stop by," Jamaal said, as he shook Joy's hand as an excuse to touch her. Joy trembled with delight and Glenda…well…she was just Glenda.

The sound of the axe shopping on the pieces of wood made Joy look back over her shoulder. Jamaal had grown taller this summer and his bare chest revealed well-developed muscles that moved in perfect harmony creating a symphony of music inside her that she'd never before. Besides being creative, he'd been on the honor roll since kindergarten. More than ever, this summer Joy was glad they were best friends.

"Hey, wait a minute," Jamaal hollered. "I forgot to ask you something, Joy," he said as he interrupted their walk back down the path.

"What is it, Jamaal?" Joy asked.

"Did you get permission from Miss Eva to go on that wagon ride with TJ?"

"Yes and granddaddy thinks it's a good idea to hang out with TJ for an afternoon," Joy replied.

"Really Joy? Why did he say that? I didn't think he would."

"Because granddaddy said most people don't care about TJ because he looks and acts so different and hanging around with TJ would be like talking with a living history book and we'll sure learn things that we can't find in a book."

"Who's TJ?" Glenda asked feeling left out of the conversation.

"Glenda," Joy began draping her arm around Glenda's shoulder. "Do you know the expression 'a picture is worth a thousand words'?"

"Yes I go, Joy."

"Then wait until you see TJ before you as any question and I guarantee your mind will be satisfied."

"Nevermind that Joy, just follow me because I have something to show you guys. Wait until you see this and the give your opinion," Jamaal said, leading the way. "Samson and I found it yesterday. I was messing around when Samson and I came up to this mess of steep hills covered with loads of moss and Devil's Shoestrings. The place was almost hidden at the top of that hill over there," Jamaal pointed. "As Samson and I got closer and moved away some vines and stuff, we saw the entry to a cave. See it?"

"Yes, I can see it and it looks spooky to me," Glenda whined.

"Golly Jamaal, it looks like it's been there since the beginning of time," Joy said, staring at the massive mound.

"Actually, I found this cave because Samson kept barking and barking and looking up at something and that's what got my curiosity. I literally had to drag Samson away from the place."

"Sound mysterious but exciting," Joy said.

"Excuse me if I missed something but usually dogs bark like that to warn you about something," Glenda said, having gotten her nerves back in order.

"She does have a point, Jamaal," Joy said.

"I now but when I tried to set a date to go with TJ all he'd say was 'You'll know when the time is right'."

"Both of you give me a headache with this 'TJ obsession' of yours," Glenda said. "I wish you'd make up your minds and do whatever it is you're going to do."

"All right, Jamaal. Count me and Glenda in on your cave adventure," Joy said.

"Great ladies and how will tomorrow morning about nine o'clock do you? TJ will be at our place earlier tomorrow morning to deliver some lumber for Dad and I can tell TJ the news then."

"Sounds good for us and we'll see you tomorrow morning," Joy waved, as she and Glenda started down the path back home.

"Okay! See you then," Jamaal shouted back.

"Do you and Jamaal find places to explore each summer?" Glenda asked.

"Uh-huh, but we take turns each summer. Last summer I found a place to explore and this summer it was his turn."

"Well…he most definitely found a place," Glenda mounded. "When did you first meet Jamaal, Joy?"

"Granny and Granddaddy have known the Wilsons for years but Jamaal and I only became friends four years ago. We met in Vacation Bible School."

"…in Vacation Bible School?" Glenda interrupted. "Haven't you met any other girls around town to do stuff with?"

"Not really because most of the girls around here are off to summer camps or visiting relatives out of town. I'm visiting from out of town too….remember?"

"You're lucky, Joy."

"Why do you say that, Glenda?"

"Because my Mom and Dad use to ship me off to summer camps too but this time I'm glad they shipped off to Suffolk."

"I'm glad too, Glenda."

THE HOUSE

The table was set and the blessing said as roast beef, homemade buttery mashed potatoes, homemade gravy, string beans, creamed corn and cornbread criss-crossed in four directions as each reached for another helping of something. Nobody seemed to notice the sultry heat of the kitchen. The only relief was a counter top oscillating fan that blew the heat from one corner of the kitchen to another.

"Three cheers for Granny," Glenda added. "The gourmet stuff Mom likes to cook doesn't begin to match the taste of this food." Pervis almost choked on a mouthful of ice tea from that statement because he'd tasted Barbara's cooking too. Eva wiped her mouth with her napkin…a long time.

When Pervis was able to take another swallow of ice tea he asked, "What do you girls have planned for tomorrow?"

"We're going on a wagon ride with TJ," Joy said.

"I sure will be glad to see this mystery man you keep talking about, Joy," Glenda said.

"That's great girls. Of course you've cleared everything with Granny first," Pervis said.

"It's fine with me, Pervis."

With the help of Glenda and Joy, Eva put her kitchen in order and then the ladies made a speedy exit to the front porch to join Pervis. Eva plopped down in her rocker with a 'Thank you, Jesus' while Pervis continued to pat his stomach until he belched. Joy and Glenda playfully shove each other to see who would sit down on the glider first. Then four contented family members began to engage in sharing the events of the day. Pervis expounded on the goings on at the shipyard, Eva went on about the W.B.F.C. while Glenda and Joy jabbered about their walk to see Jamaal and his animal clinic.

"Granny…by the way," Joy said. "Not only will we be riding with TJ tomorrow but Glenda, Jamaal and I have planned a nature hike for tomorrow. Can we go with him…pleas-s-s-e-e?"

GRANNY'S PLACE

"Say yes Granny, because it will be my first adventure outing for the summer," Glenda added.

"Sounds like a good idea to me, don't you think so Pervis?"

"Sure Eva, and hiking through nature keeps the mind clear and the heart strong."

"You know something, Pervis? You and I have that annual church committee meeting tomorrow night and we both know how that can drag on so with the girls on a nature hike too, they won't have to sit around on a hard church pew and be bored to death with grown folks business."

"You're right, Eva. "What time to you plan to leave, Joy?"

"Jamaal said he'd be by at eight o'clock in the morning," Glenda interrupted.

"That's just in time," Eva said. "The church meeting starts at nine o'clock and you'll have plenty of sunshine because the weather man announced the temperature was going to each one hundred-three degrees but the July Flies have already told us that."

"If Mom knew I was about to do something that would risk getting a skinned knee she'd drop down in a dead faint," Glenda giggled with mischievous delight while enjoying the cool breeze created each time the glider swung back and forth. Eva pondered the real meaning behind her granddaughter's statement and knew her daughter's over protectiveness came from her car accident years ago.

"You know something else?" Glenda continued. "I loved to hear Granddaddy say grace before each meal because it's a practice we don't always do at home. We only go to church when we feel like it because Mom says that religion is a manmade thing and whatever a person feels or thinks about a higher power should be his or her own business. Dad never challenges her or says how he feels but he never says anything to avoid an argument that he knows will start."

Eva's rocking chair came to an abrupt halt. "Pervis, did you hear what I think this child said?"

"Oh mercy," Pervis said under his breath. "Glenda really mashed Eva's corn this time."

"Eva honey, don't get your dander up because nowadays everybody feels they have a right to their own opinions," Pervis added.

"Opinions you say? What about the Lord's opinions? His opinion doesn't change at all for anybody and never will."

To quell the icy tension, Joy said, "Granddaddy, tell one of your stories"…as if she and Glenda hadn't had enough story telling already.

"Sounds like a good idea, Joy. Mmmmm…let me see now…"

The setting was perfect for the storytelling idea. When the last remnants of sunlight spread over the horizon and the evening sky rolled in, the front porch became a stage featuring imaginary players who turned into shadows with familiar voices. Joy and Glenda scooted closer together in preparation for the story. Glenda's last words still echoed in her mind but Eva's rocker was back in motion again.

"How about I tell you of this house…139 South Fourth Street?" Pervis asked.

"You mean about this very house?" Joy asked.

"Yes, about this very house," Pervis replied.

"Lights, camera, action," Glenda exclaimed.

"We'll start in September in the year 1933," Pervis began.

"Boy, that was sure a long time ago," Glenda said, tucking her legs under Indian style.

"Shush, Glenda," Joy hissed.

"As Eva already told you, we had saved enough money to leave the hustle-and-bustle of the New York City life. Remember Millie Bowers?"

"Yes Granddaddy," Joy answered. Glenda was confused.

"Who's Millie Bowers?" Glenda asked.

"Hush girl. I'll tell you later," Joy said.

"Just before your grandmother and I moved, Millie received word that her Uncle Roland died. Since she was the last living member of her entire family, she inherited everything including this very house."

"You mean the house where we're living now?" Joy asked.

"Yep, the very same one and here's how it all happened. One day, she stopped by our apartment to gab for a while and the house came up in the conversation. Since she hadn't seen or heard from her Uncle Roland for years, she was surprised to learn he'd left her his property. Millie knew we wanted to move south, so she offered it to us. She didn't know it, but the price she quoted for the sale was half of what we'd saved. Eva and I knew we'd run across a blessing and we jumped at the offer. Millie said she didn't know much about her uncle except that he was very secretive and rarely had visitors to stop by but he was and expert housekeeper and kept the property up and in good condition. I told her I wanted to make sure and she was okay with that so before Eva and I made our move, a friend of mine who was a truck driver too, had to make a run to Suffolk. He'd agreed to make a quick stop for me and check out the place. With the delightful report be brought back, Eva and I started packing."

"Where's Millie Brown living now?" Glenda asked.

"The last letter we got from her was about the middle of last year," Eva answered. "In her letter, she let us know she'd gotten married…for the third time." Pervis was glad that his wife was relaxed again.

"We didn't have much furniture to speak of," Pervis continued. "The only items we had were our bedroom furniture and the girls' cribs and a dresser. Millie told us that we were welcomed to any furniture left in the house. To our pleasure and surprise, the place was fully furnished but we changed all the bedroom furniture anyway. The thought of sleeping on someone else's bed gave me goose-bumps!"

"Good old Millie," Eva said, reflecting on the good and bad times they had at the Lewis house.

"Everything was settled and I started my first day at work at the Navy yard in Norfolk. Eva did her homemaking thing and met our new neighbors. One day, after I came home from work and supper was over, Eva and I sat on a bench in the side-yard. We watched Arvis and Barbara toddle around in the spacious and grassy back yard. Since the yard was already well fenced in, we let the girls play to themselves and went inside the house to finish a painting the girls' room. Since it wasn't dry yet, we piled into our bedroom. It was crowded but we were happy."

"One night in particular, we were absolutely exhausted and decided to turn in early and then…just about midnight…Eva frantically shook me awake. I asked her what was wrong and all she could say was 'listen'." …and then I heard it too."

"What did you hear, Granddaddy?" Glenda asked.

"Yeah Granddaddy, tell us," Joy urged. Joy sat motionless and Glenda let out a tiny squeal in anticipation of what Pervis would say next.

"Eva was right and we both heard a moaning sound like someone was in pain. I jumped out of bed and reached for my flashlight. I whispered to Eva to stay with Arvis and Barbara and she squeezed my hand and told me to be careful. I tiptoed downstairs to investigate. Just as I reached the landing at the bottom of the stairs, I felt an eerie chill go right through me and then I heard the front door slam shut with a fierce bang. It was so loud until I looked to see if the thing was still in its hinges. As soon as it quieted down a bit, I unlocked the front door and shined the flashlight beam outside on the porch to check the lock on the screen door. Everything was undisturbed but when I locked the front door back and turned to go back upstairs, I heard a loud crashing sound coming from the diningroom. It sounded as if all Eva's best dishes smashed to smithereens. Eva heard it too and was standing at the top of the stairs calling my name to make sure I was okay. I told her I was fine and to go back into the bedroom with the girls."

"I shined the light into the diningroom expecting to see a mess of broken dishes on the floor because the only furniture was a buffet with an antique hutch on top. That's where Eva displayed all the china Nancy Green had given her. But…to my surprise…not a dish was broken. My heart was pounding so hard that I though it would jump out of my chest. The strange commotion finally stopped and I went back upstairs. Oddly, Arvis and Barbara slept through the whole ordeal and Eva and I were glad they did."

Pervis paused for a while to light his pipe and chuckled at the sight of his granddaughters. Joy and Glenda squeezed up so tight beside each other that not even air could pass between them.

"Are you two sure you want Pervis to finish the rest of the story?" Eva asked. "What you're about to hear next might keep you awake for the next few nights."

Joy hugged her knees against her chest and thought for a moment, Glenda did the same, and then together…they nodded "yes". Eva chuckled and said, "Younglings today sure are a different breed."

"All right then here we go," Pervis began. "A week passed since that awful night and Eva and I still felt uneasy and couldn't get rid of the feeling it wasn't over yet. It was as though we could sense a presence in the house like invisible eyes watching us. We even talked about finding another house but we'd used up most all of our savings and that gave us no choice but to stick it out. We kept the girls insight of one of us at all times and were determined that no intruder was going to make us give up on years of hard saving only to see our dream driven away by some invisible bully."

"A few days later, the shipyard closed early. The temperature in the manufacturing plant rose above ninety-eight degrees. I was almost home when Mr. Genie, our across-the-street neighbour greeted me."

"Oh, is that the empty house over there with the weeds and wild bushes around the house?" Joy mustered up the nerve to ask.

"Yes baby, but the house didn't look like it does now."

"Although we'd only greeted each other in passing, Luke Genie seemed anxious to introduce himself to me. One evening he invited me to join him on his porch for a glass of lemonade."

"What did he look like, Granddaddy?" Glenda asked.

"Mr. Genie was a short, dark-skin man with raven black hair that was naturally slick and shiny. He retired from the Planter's Peanut factory when he was seventy years old. Mrs. Genie died two years before he retired. After ten or fifteen minutes of polite conversation, he asked me a question that completely caught me off guard. He knew that Eva and I would be plagued by strange noises and groans when we moved in our house. I told him the whole story and when I'd finished, he just sat in his chair without saying a word. A deep frown creased his brow. Ever so seriously, he asked me if I believed in ghosts. I almost dropped my glass."

Joy and Glenda were as still as store mannequins and Eva was reliving those terrible nights. Blanketed with the darkness of night, they sat quietly on the front porch. The only light came from the rays of a full moon and a dull flickering street lamp that played host to a mass of swirling and fluttering moths and a few other winged night flyers.

"Luke leaned forward in his chair," Pervis continued. "He stared straight into my eyes without blinking and said, 'You must build all around your house. You must add onto all sides with new lumber but before you nail one piece of lumber or pour one bucket of cement, you must bless all the building materials with a special simple prayer. You must say, *Because he loves me, says the Lord, I will rescue him; I will protect him, for he acknowledges my name.*"

"Psalm 91:14", Eva said softly.

"So-o-o-o that's why the upstairs and downstairs rooms open into a porch instead out outside," Joy shrieked.

"That's why the back of the refrigerator sticks out into a side porch instead of attached to the kitchen wall," Glenda said nervously.

"Both of you are exactly right," Pervis smiled, puffing his pipe.

"Granddaddy, when did you start smoking a pipe?" Glenda managed enough nerve to ask.

"When I started telling this story," Pervis answered. Everybody embraced the moment with howls of laughter.

When the front porch was quiet again, Glenda and Joy vowed to sleep together in tonight.

"Go on with the story, Granddaddy. What happened next?" Joy said.

"Luke also told me to be sure to spread a layer of three inch deep, new top soil under the entire house before sealing it up. This very porch we're sitting on now is a new addition too and the porch is a solid block of cement."

"How did you and Granny keep from getting pestered by the ghostly thing while construction was going on?" Joy asked.

"That's an excellent question, Joy. In fact, that's the very question I asked Luke."

"Pervis, it's getting late and we have a full day tomorrow," Eva interrupted.

"Oh no, Granny, please let Granddaddy finish telling us the story," Joy said, moaning with disappointment.

"You'll just have to wait to hear the rest of the story another time. Now you two skedaddle upstairs and get ready for bed," Eva said sternly.

With only a nightlight burning, the cousins huddled together under Glenda's bedspread. They whispered and giggled until finally falling to sleep.

Pervis was snoring and Eva was reading Psalm 91. *"How can evil overtake or plague come near? For He orders His angels to protect you wherever you go."* After closing her Bible, Glenda's words about spiritual matters came back to her mind. She was determined that both her grandchildren attended church every Sunday. Plumping up her pillow, she looked at her snoring husband, reached over to his nightstand and removed his pipe.

"Amen, Lord and goodnight."

THE HIKERS

Jamaal had a big sty on his left eye. His Mom mixed up an old country remedy and rubbed it into the infection. Glenda was whimpering about a headache and Joy had a runny nose. It was as if the boogie-man put a curse on all of them. Today's planned hiking excursion was. When Eva told TJ of the problems, he said he didn't mind and set off for parts unknown. He already suspected there would be some problems so he and Josie meandered back into the woods.

THE SHOPPING SPREE

COCK-A-DOODLE-DO!

Old Colonel was three hours late again. Eva saw Pervis off to work and sat at the kitchen table sipping her second cup of coffee while reading the morning paper.

"H-m-m-m, chicken legs are twenty-five cents per pound today. When the girls wake up, we'll all go uptown and do a bit of shopping… if they're feeling all right this morning. This will give me a chance to buy new clothes for Joy," she said. Her thoughts drifted back to the day Joy first arrived in Suffolk. Eva secretly inspected the sparse wardrobe Joy unpacked and told Pervis of her discovery. Both agreed that shopping for some new clothing was in order for their grandchild.

"Jasper should be ashamed of himself. He should never have allowed Joy's wardrobe to come to such a state but he wasn't what you considered 'a normal state' himself," Pervis said, as he left for work that morning.

Glenda always had the best and had all the advantages that came with attending a prestigious private school. She was a member of several youth groups, traveled extensively, received private ballet lessons, modern dance, and private singing lessons. She was given anything her little heart desired.

Deprived of the extras because of Jasper, Joy still excelled at what she did. Eva couldn't put her finger on it but there was something special about her oldest grandchild that was to be admired. Joy had the strength of character of an older more experienced person and she accomplished whatever she had a mind to achieve. Eva was determined to do all she could to encourage that trait and erase bad memories. This morning…it would be a shopping spree.

Eva turned the newspaper to the community page. *The Starshine Brownie Troop #24 camping trip will be…etc…etc.* The article brought back the memory of the time she and Pervis visited Arvis during one of her frequent hospital stays. When they arrived, Arvis was upset and

GRANNY'S PLACE

highly concerned for Joy's health and well-being. She told her parents about her next-door neighbour, Tamara Hooskadile. Tamara was to keep a keen eye out for Joy. As an example of her worriment, she told Eva and Pervis of a past incident.

One day after school, Joy went home to the officers' apartment section of the apartment complex for her monthly Brownie meeting. It was the home of Cindy Miller, a fellow Brownie Trooper. Cindy's mother was the troop leader.

Joy was a new member but had progressed in earning her badges one after the other. Arvis even gave extra piano lessons to acquire the money needed to buy her a uniform. Joy walked with Cindy to her house. They were early for the Brownie meeting so Cindy used the extra time to show Joy her collection of foreign dolls. Joy especially liked the African doll adorned with authentic Kente cloth outfit. After a while, the troop meeting officially started as all troop members had arrived. They said the Brownie pledge together, badges were awarded, information about new badges was given, and all troopers applauded when the cookie fundraiser amount was announced. The next order of business was a cooking lesson. Mrs. Miller made certain they washed their hands. With aprons on, she gave instructions for making the chocolate chip cookies.

Treats like chocolate chip cookies were a rarity at the Bailey home. Each time Arvis shopped for groceries, she'd have to slip in a little surprise for Joy's school lunch because Jasper was strictly a meat-and-potatoes man. A bowl of oatmeal or unsweetened cornflakes made everybody's taste buds go on strike except his.

They played more games and the date for next month's meeting was set. Each trooper chose three cookies to take home. By the end of half an hour, all Brownie's left…except for Joy. Even though she had a bridge party to attend, Mrs. Miller didn't blame Joy for Jasper's lateness.

"The walk homes isn't to far and I'll be all right," Mrs. Miller.

"Are you sure you'll be fine?" Mrs. Miller asked.

"Don't worry about me, Mrs. Miller. This Brownie Trooper has everything under control," Joy said, saluting. Mrs. Miller laughed and sent Joy on her way.

Joy was embarrassed to be a potential problem because she wanted to be the best Brownie ever especially since she was the only black in the troop. No prejudice came from Mrs. Miller or the other troopers but Joy took pride in everything she wanted to achieve.

Jasper got home early to pick up Joy from the Brownie meeting but because of drinking four unmixed drinks of Tanguray, he forgot why he was home early. With a slur in his speech, he called Mrs. Cottcreeve in an attempt to locate the whereabouts of his daughter. Frustrated by her answer, he ended the conversation abruptly by slamming down the phone. With a few choice words, he fixed another glass with Tanguray and flopped down on the livingroom couch. Finally, he heard Joy's key unlocking the front door. Like a kid, he hid behind the front door as Joy stepped inside. Like a ferocious beast awaiting an unsuspecting prey, he snatched the startled child by the neck and threw her to the floor tearing her new Brownie uniform to pieces. Animalistic savagery twisted his face as he took off his military belt and beat Joy with the brass buckle all over her thighs and back.

With each strike of the belt, he tried to unleash some kind of personal frustration he'd had for a long time. Because she lived right next-door and heard Joy screaming, Mrs. Hooskadile pounded on the livingroom wall and warned Jasper stop hitting his daughter. He ignored her the first time so she banged on the apartment door again telling Jasper to stop beating the child or she would call the police. Jasper stopped. He didn't want the police involved. The former heavyweight-boxing champion from Russia kept banging on the door until he stopped his devilment.

Still sobbing, Joy broke free of his grasp, ran upstairs to her room, locked the door, and sprawled across her bed. Covered with burning and bleeding welts and clutching three crushed chocolate chip cookies in her hand, she continued to shed tears until she fell asleep.

Eva's eyes filled with tears. She hadn't forgotten one detail of the incident told to her and Pervis that day. She folded the newspaper and pushed it aside, walked over to the kitchen sink with her coffee cup in hand, raised her head to the ceiling and reaffirmed the promise she and Pervis made. *"Hell will swallow up that man before he lays another hand on our grandchild!"*

GRANNY'S PLACE

With their hair completely in disarray, Glenda and Joy stumbled into the kitchen. "Good morning, Granny," Joy said yawning. Eva responded with a backbreaking hug for each of her granddaughters. They didn't know how to deal with the sudden show of affection and Eva saw the puzzlement on their faces and said, "I hope Granddaddy's tale didn't frighten you rascals too much."

"Oh-no," both girls said in unison, thinking they solved the reason for the smothering hug. "We liked every spooky minute of it. When Granddaddy finishes the story tonight, I know what sort of picture I'm going to draw in my picture diary," Joy said.

"After this summer, I won't have a problem thinking of what to write for my back-to-school essay," Glenda said. The cousins continued to chitchat while helping Eva set the table. Eva prepared one of her usual breakfast menus of homemade buttermilk flapjacks, warmed slices of smoked ham, orange juice and a large bottle of Aunt Jemima dark syrup. All bowed their heads while Glenda blessed the table. Eva smiled warmly.

"Girls how about we do a bit of shopping uptown today?" Eva asked. "I read Sears-'n-Roebuck is having a fifty percent sale all over the store and I don't want to miss that."

"Great, because I love to shop," Glenda chirped. "Mom and I use to drive all the way to Manhattan, New York to shop. We'd check into a fancy hotel on Friday, do our shopping and whatever else came to mind and drive back home Sunday afternoon."

Joy kept her eyes on her plate and stuffed her mouth with the last bit if flapjacks. She pretended not to listen to Glenda's shopping fun because shopping was something she never had a chance to experience with her Mom.

"You two go on upstairs now and hurry and get ready because I've called Harvey already and he said he'd be here in fifteen minutes."

"Okay Granny," the girls chimed, as they scrambled upstairs start dressing.

"Twenty-eight, twenty-nine...thirty," Glenda recited, as she brushed her hair. "No time to count to one hundred today," she said, putting her brush down on her vanity table. Holding a small package behind her back, she stepped across the hall into Joy's bedroom.

"What are you staring at, Glenda? You give me the creeps when you do that," Joy said.

"I didn't mean anything but…this is for you," she said, awkwardly handing Joy the present.

"What's this?"

"Open it and see."

"Gosh Glenda, a bottle of perfume and the bottle is shaped like the Sleeping Beauty slipper," Joy grinned. "This is my first bottle of honest-to-goodness perfume. Thank you so very much."

"It's my way of saying, let's be friends forever and never forget one another. It also says I wish you were my sister…instead of my cousin."

"Those are the most thoughtful words I've ever heard, Glenda. A cousin wouldn't think like you do…but a sister would."

"Y'all come on downstairs because Harvey is here now," Eva yelled upstairs, interrupting the cousins' moment. Two pair of feet lumbered down the stairs and onto the front porch.

"Hi, Mr. Willis," Joy greeted.

"Good morning, ladies. Somebody sure smells good…or is it the honeysuckle vine I smell?" The girls blushed at Harvey's remark as they climbed on the back seat of his taxi.

"I've decided the girls and I are going to do the town today, Harvey," Eva announced, as she slid onto the front seat.

"You sure picked a scorching hot day to shop, Miss Eva. I don't think we've ever had weather as hot as this for a long time," Harvey said, as he drove up the street. "I spoke with Dave a little while ago and he's worried because his well water is mighty low and other farmers are feeling the effects of all this heat too…and no rain is in the forecast."

"That's a shame, Harvey. We really need some water in the ground because our well water is low too and my hens haven't laid a single egg in four days," Eva said. "Some days of hard rain would sure do everybody good."

"Actually I shouldn't complain because this heat is a blessing in disguise. Folks who usually walk or ride the bus call me instead and that's excellent for business."

Joy waved at her favorite statue on top of the Planter's Peanut factory. The immense statue of Mr. Peanut seemed to show no concern for the heat as he stood royally and shinned on top of the plant. Harvey parked in front of the Sears-'n-Roebuck store.

"Meet up back here in about an hour, Harvey," Eva said.

"All right, Miss Eva. Remember, as far as Lucille is concerned, the day is yours."

"Hurry up, girls. We're only at our first stop to shop."

A refreshing blast of cool air enveloped their bodies as they stepped into the foyer of the store. Glenda and Joy followed Eva up the escalator to the third floor. Joy's eyes widened as big as silver dollar when she caught sight of rack after rack of all kinds of girls' paraphernalia.

"May I help you, please?" A thin-lipped store clerk with a southern drawl asked.

"Yes you can," Eva answered. "My granddaughters are shopping for dresses and whatever you have to compliment their choices."

"Right this way, ladies." She directed another clerk to assist Glenda while she assisted Eva and Joy.

"I don't know which rack to look on first," Joy said.

"Take your time, darling."

The clerk walked Joy through rack after rack of dresses, tops, shorts, jumpers, and you name it and handed outfit after outfit as Joy tried them on in the dressing room. She was having the time of her life. Jasper never sanctioned shopping for her own clothes so this was something new for her. Glenda took a moment to pull Eva to the side.

"Granny, I brought my own shopping money so you don't have to spent anything for me. Would you mind if I spent my money to buy something for Joy? I thought I'd ask you first because there's no way I want to hurt Joy's feelings," Glenda said, showing Eva a one hundred dollar bill.

Eva looked lovingly into Glenda's big black eyes. "Are you sure you want to do that, sweetheart?"

"Yes Granny. I'm sure."

Joy was in and out of the dressing room and modeling every outfit in the mirror…and grinning all the time. She near ran the sales clerk crazy. To relieve the clerk, Eva helped with Joy's selections and chose panties, socks, belts, slips and all kinds of accessories to match. Glenda calmly selected two pair of denim short sets. She liked the gold buckles bibs on the denim tops. She also bought a fancy light blue, short-sleeve t-shirt and a pink t-shirt just like the blue one and a few other items. With the sound of the final chin-a-ling of the cash register, each of the trio carried three large shopping bags out of the store. As they crossed Main Street and climbed into Harvey's waiting taxi, they reminded him of Mother Goose and her goslings close behind. He helped with the bounty and made sure the car doors were secure. Joy thanked her grandmother umpteen times.

"Looks like you three emptied all the shelves in the store," Harvey teased.

"Never you mind about us, you big silly," Eva joked back. "You'll do the same thing with your new 'somebody special' if I have anything to do with it."

"Yes...er...where do we go next?" Harvey sheepishly asked, not wanting to encourage more conversation on the subject.

"The Poultry House is the next stop, Harvey. They have a sale on chicken already cut up and I want to get a few cases."

"Your wish is my command," Harvey said with mock obedience.

"Boy, you're a mess," Eva said, wiping her sweating brow with her handkerchief.

"Granny, can Glenda and I ride to Dairy Queen while you're in the chicken store...if Mr. Ellis won't mind."

"All right, honey. Harvey won't mind the extra stop. A double dip of ice cream sounds like a good idea. It's getting hotter and hotter out here. Harvey, the last stop will be the icehouse. I've got something in mind for the weekend."

"Okay, Miss Eva." With that said, Eva walked around the corner to the Poultry House.

Harvey found a parking space under the shade of an oak tree by Dairy Queen. The three had a good time eating their ice cream cones and chatting about nothing. Harvey kept a check on the time.

"We'll need to get back to the poultry store soon, girls."

"Okay," Joy said. Glenda ate the last bite of her cone. They got back to the Poultry House just as Eva came out with a stock boy pushing a cartload of four cases of chicken.

"The next stop is the ice house, Harvey and then home it is," Eva said, proud of her poultry purchase.

GRANNY'S PLACE

"Thanks for everything, Harvey and especially for giving us this day. I know what a busy man you are and adjusting your schedule to help us shop is appreciated so very much." "You're welcome anytime, Miss Eva. I enjoyed every minute too and the girls and I had a grand time eating our ice cream cones together and Glenda certainly can carry on a conversation," Harvey smiled.

Harvey had lost count of the number of times he'd taken Eva uptown to do her shopping and he'd taken Arvis shopping in the past too. He regretted never making a real effort to get to know her...permanently. When they got back to the house, he carried the heavy cases of chicken to the kitchen for Eva while Joy and Glenda ran upstairs with the bags of shopping goodies to Joy's bedroom.

"Have a good day, Miss Eva and tell Pervis 'hello' for me."

"I sure will, Harvey. See you again soon. Bye now!"

Eva knew how excited the girls were and left them to themselves, and busied herself with getting the chicken cleaning started.

Joy emptied her shopping bags and spread her new clothes on her bed. She stared at the menagerie with amazement and gratitude.

"Is that all you bought for yourself, Glenda?"

"I got what I wanted," Glenda said, holding out her arm. The bracelets and a few accessories are enough for me. Oh yes, I almost forgot. I did buy something for myself. I bought a pair of denim bib shorts and I bought a pair for you too, Joy."

"Why did you buy a pair for me, Glenda?"

"I knew you won't mind if I bought them but I got them so we could dress alike and mainly because it gave me a chance to buy something for my 'big sister'." Not only that, overalls are a relief from those fluffy outfits Mom buys for me and besides that, I needed something to wear for our hike tomorrow."

"I don't know what to say, Glenda. I've never had jeans like this before," Joy said, with trembling lips. The cousins hugged tightly for a long time. When they finished, both had the same thought about Jamaal and the hike.

"I wonder if Jamaal's pink-eye problem is over," Joy said.

"I hope it is, Joy. He's supposed to take us on that cave adventure or something like that. We've got to remind Granny to pack a good lunch for us."

"Knowing Granny, she'll make sure we have plenty to eat and drink," Joy said, sarcastically. "And…there's another little thing you forgot about."

"What, Joy?"

"You know you have one of those 'girl things' for Jamaal."

"What? You must be nuts. You're the one who has his nose wide open. Anybody can see that when he's around you." They continued to giggle and tease each other. They gabbed endlessly about the shopping trip as they finished hanging up the new items.

"I feel an afternoon nap coming on. We've had a full day and I want to hear Granddaddy tell the rest of that story tonight," Glenda said.

"You're right, Glenda," Joy yawned. "Granny is busy in the kitchen anyway."

She went upstairs and changed her clothes and ate a snack before she began cleaning the chicken. Joy and Glenda continued to sleep. Summertime meant you slept when you want and you get up when you wanted to get up.

THE SAGA CONTINUES

The outside temperature had cooled down to a comfortable ninety-three degrees why Joy and Glenda woke up. They washed up a bit and beautified themselves in the mirror.

"Let's go down to the kitchen and see if Granny needs any help. That's the least we can do to show how nice it was to take us uptown yesterday," Joy said.

"Great idea and I'll race you downstairs. The last one down is a rotten egg," Glenda squealed, getting ahead of Joy…for the first time.

All four cases of chicken soaked in the back porch sink filled to the brim with baking soda and water. Eva put aside a large bowl full of pieces for tomorrow's breakfast.

"Is there baking soda in the water, Granny?" Joy asked.

"Of course there is, baby. I always soak chicken in baking soda before I start cleaning each piece. The soda takes off all the yellowing off the chicken skin and leaves just plump, clean chicken pieces. Usually I let the pieces soak overnight but it's too hot today."

"Can we help with that, Granny?" Glenda asked.

"You sure can, Glenda. You can begin by handing me those freezer bags over there," Eva said, pointing to the top of the back porch freezer. "Joy, while Glenda helps me do this, I need you to set the table for supper and then help us finish up here. Then the both of you can go up to the end of the street and wait for Granddaddy's work van."

"Whoopee!" Both girls remarked.

"By the way…don't worry about your lunches for tomorrow's hike. I've already packed them and have them ready in the refrigerator before you sleepyheads got up."

They helped Eva pack away bags of chicken in the back porch freezer and retreated to the swing seat under the magnolia branches.

"I hope Granddaddy finishes the story about Mr. Genie, ghosts and things that go bump in the night," Glenda said.

"I hope so too, Glenda. In fact, I wish this summer lasted forever. I hate thinking of going back to New Jersey," Joy said. Glenda didn't realize the real reason Joy made the remark.

"I hear Granddaddy's whistle," Glenda shouted, as they ran out of the yard and up the street.

"Hi Granddaddy," they chimed together.

"Well hello there, Sweetmeat and Peaches. How are you feeling today?"

"We're doing fine, Granddaddy but why did you say 'Sweetmeat and Peaches'," Glenda asked.

"You mean I never told you about that?"

"Nope, but what does that mean," Joy asked anxiously.

"I use to call your Mama 'Peaches' and Glenda's Mama 'Sweetmeat'. Since you two remind me of your Mamas, you'll be 'Peaches II and Sweetmeat II', is that okay?"

"Sure Granddaddy. We don't mind at all," Glenda said.

"What did you two do for the day," Pervis asked.

"We helped Granny put away oodles of packs of chicken in the freezer," Joy said.

"Be honest, Glenda. We looked at all our new clothes again," Joy said.

"I'll bet you left the store shelves empty," Pervis joked.

"Those are exactly the same words Mr. Ellis used yesterday," Joy remarked.

"Last one through the gate is a rotten egg," Glenda hollered as they approached the yard gate.

"Glenda, what's with you and rotten eggs?" Joy laughed. Pervis howled with laughter at the playfulness of his granddaughters. When he stepped into the back porch, he put his metal lunch box on of one of the freezers, walked to the kitchen sink, and kissed Eva on the back of her neck. Joy and Glenda loved to see their grandparents smooch. They all sat down to have super. Eva surpassed her cooking knowledge again with her platters of superb, finger-licking foods. Full of delicious leftovers, Joy and Glenda helped Eva with the kitchen clean-up. Pervis exited to the next event of the evening…the front porch.

"One, two, three and push," Joy said, showing Glenda her technique of setting the glider into a rocking motion. The scent of honeysuckle blossoms perfumed the evening air. The humidity of the day chased away a wisp of cool breeze.

"Granddaddy would you tell us the rest of your story about Mr. Genie and all," Joy begged.

"They've been waiting for this moment all day, Pervis," Eva said.

"Well then girls…hold your hats but I'll only begin if one of you can tell me where I stopped in my story," Pervis teasingly responded.

"I remember, I remember," Glenda shouted, waving her hand in the air as if going to answer a question in her classroom. "You stopped at the part when you asked Mr. Genie how to keep the ghosts away while you finished building around the house."

"Sounds like you're cornered, Pervis," Eva laughed.

"You win, Glenda."

"Luke Genie," Pervis continued, "did indeed tell me how to keep the apparitions away while I worked on the house. He told me to place two three gallon metal buckets filled with pieces of old cut up tires sprinkled with sulphur. Then he told me to set the buckets on fire and put one under the east side of the house and one under the west side. I had to do that each night to keep the ghost away. Eva and I agreed we'd rather deal with the smell of burning rubber and sulphur rather things that go bump in the night."

"We knew about Millie's uncle, Theodore Bowers but we didn't know much about his wife. We knew her name was 'Elaine'. Everybody knew they kept to themselves and their socialization with neighbors was null and void. At the very beginning of Fourth Street, when folks sat on their porches in the early evening, they'd hear the Bowers fussing about most anything. The only time nearby neighbors caught a glimpse of Elaine was seeing her hang out laundry or piddle around the yard. On the other hand, Theodore was known around to be a cussing stingy fellow. He also had a strange habit of hiding his money in ditches around the house because he never trusted bank security. If you started him on the topic of banks, you'd never get a word in edgewise. He'd go on and on to describe every bad thing he could think of about banks and most times he'd say the same things over and over."

"What was his job at the peanut factory?" Joy asked.

"For twenty years, Theodore worked in the conveyer belt unit and according to others, never missed one day of work in all that time.

GRANNY'S PLACE

He was a despicable man but as an employee, you couldn't get a better worker."

"What was another one of his bad habits, Granddaddy?" Glenda asked.

"For one thing Glenda, he was so miserly that he wouldn't use his vacation days unless he was made to do so by his boss. Thirdly, he ate a baloney sandwich and an apple for lunch for years. But…one day…during the lunch break, he was sitting with other workers whose character was known to be shaky. He interrupted others eating lunch with boisterous laughter and bragging about his house being safer than a bank."

"Mr. Genie overheard part of the conversation and in the locker room after work, he took it upon himself to warn Theodore about the danger of telling those particular men about his money that was buried somewhere in the yard."

"How in the world could his wife stand him," Joy asked. Glenda looked at her cousin with curiosity.

"Lots of folks had that question in mind too Joy. Neighbors knew Elaine couldn't take another minute of Theodore's bulling and harsh words. One day, while Theodore was working, she packed her little bit of belongs and moved to her spinster sister's house across the county. When Theodore came home from work and read the note his wife left, his attitude was good riddance to bad rubbish. After a few days, Mr. Genie noticed that it seemed as though nobody was home at Theodore's place but didn't want to exchange anymore words with the man after the locker room incident."

"Boy, it sounds like he was an awfully cruel man," Glenda said. "You have no idea Glenda," Joy thought.

"He was indeed a cruel man Glenda, but everything cruel he'd done, he was about to experience in a different way."

"What do you mean, Granddaddy?" Joy asked.

"Joy, life has a way of paying you back for everything you've done and Theodore had lots to pay back."

"How did life pay back Theodore, Granddaddy?" Joy asked.

"About a month after Elaine left, for the first time, Theodore didn't show up for work two days in a row. Three more days past and still there was no Theodore. Others thought he finally used some of

GRANNY'S PLACE

his vacation time. Remember those fellows he was talking with in the lunch room?"

"Sure, we remember," the cousins said in unison.

"Supposedly concerned about his absence from work, the two queer acting friends told Theodore's concerned boss they would stop the house and check on the man. Early that same evening, the sneaky friends knocked at Theodore's front door but there was no answer. They decided to enter the house anyway and were shocked at what they found."

"What did they find, Granddaddy," Glenda asked nervously.

"They found Theodore sitting in front of his television...dead as a doornail!"

"Sounds like his number was up," Eva said.

"It sure was Eva. Word got back to Elaine fast."

"Poor Elaine," Glenda said.

"'Poor thing' my foot, Glenda because Elaine couldn't wait to get the man in the ground, cash his insurance check and take off for parts unknown never be heard from again."

"As usual, rumors flew around town and one of the rumors was Elaine got out of town so fast because she was involved in Theodore's strange death. As the authorities investigated, they found some kind of plant taped to the underside of the Theodore's chair."

"Boy, that does sound strange but did Elaine really have anything to do with her husband's strange death?" Glenda asked.

"I don't really know, Glenda. I think Elaine was suspected because she was from Haiti and had some bizarre customs. That fact was enough fuel to get the tongues around here wagging."

"Where did Elaine bury Theodore? Is he buried out at Jericho Cemetery," Joy asked.

"Yes but the grave was left unmarked and the cemetery caretaker hired wasn't the best bookkeeper at all. No one bothered to find out where Theodore was buried and cemetery office burned down the next year. The caretaker died six months later."

"Golly Granddaddy, that's creepy," Glenda said, as she inched closer to Joy on the glider. "What happened to their home?"

"It stood empty for three years until the day Millie told us about it. If Theodore hadn't been such a worry-wart about the upkeep of the house, Millie wouldn't have been able to sell the place to us."

"It's hard to believe Millie had an uncle and aunt like them," Joy said.

"You can say that again, Joy because Millie was such a lovely person."

As they continued to chat about Pervis' tale, night made its entrance and the familiar night sounds began. Something was flip-flopping and splashing around in the stream at the bottom of the hill. The street lamps were lit but they didn't provide the light needed to illuminate things around it. As a result, everything and everybody was shrouded by a shadow.

"Great-day-in-the-morning," Eva groaned as she rubbed her knees. "There has got to be some rain falling someplace nearby. My knees are aching and giving me a fit."

"A thunderstorm is coming? You get a real kick out of knowing if your knees predict something," Pervis teased.

"Man, leave me alone," Eva chuckled. "I'm going to fix a hot cup of chocolate for each of us to warm us up because it's getting chilly out here."

"That sounds delicious, Granny," Joy said.

"While I fix the chocolate, you and Glenda go upstairs and get that calico quilt off top of the linen trunk in the hall."

"It's so dark up their now," Glenda whined. "How will we see?"

"Granddaddy place a light switch at the bottom of the stairs right over there," Eva pointed. Joy, get Granddaddy's cardigan out of our bedroom and make sure to bring down a sweater for you and Glenda."

While the girls were upstairs, Eva set up TV tables on the porch. To satisfy everybody's nighttime munchies, she carried out a platter filled with pork chops and homemade rolls. Joy and Glenda lumbered downstairs with the goods, and settled on the glider and wrapped the quilt around their shoulders. Eva wrapped up in her shawl that she kept hanging by the telephone stall in the downstairs hall.

"Are y'all ready for me to finish the 'Theodore and Elaine' mystery?" Pervis asked. His question was answered by a resounding "yes".

GRANNY'S PLACE

"Here we go. After the dust settled regarding Theodore's death and Elaine's disappearance, a rumor started up about the money he was supposed to have buried somewhere on the property. The next thing Mr. Genie told me made the hairs on the back of my neck stand up."

"What did he say, Granddaddy? What did he say?" Joy anxiously asked while Glenda held her end of the quilt with her teeth.

"On a hot balmy night around midnight, Mr. Genie was suddenly awakened by the noise of a commotion coming from Theodore's house. He jumped out of bed to investigate. He tiptoed onto his front porch to get a closer look. He watched as two men dressed in dark clothing waving their arms in the air like they were trying to fan away a swarm of bees. They tumbled over each other yelped and screamed all the way up Fourth Street. The light of a full moon revealed it was Theodore's two so-called friends who'd been secretly searching around for Theodore's money. They ran so fast until their tattered coat tails waved behind them like flags blowing in a hurricane. Remember before he died, Theodore bragged to them about buried money on his property and it got the best of those greedy boys. Mr. Genie was about to go back into the house but something caught his attention again."

Their hot chocolate cups drained, Glenda pulled the quilt over her head and Joy sat motionless with a pork chop bone sticking out of her mouth. Eva giggled at the sight of her grandchildren.

"Mr. Genie thought the two men set Theodore's house on fire because he saw smoke streaming from under the house. Mr. Genie rubbed his eyes again to make sure he saw what he thought he saw. He told me he saw something that made his blood run cold. Beads of sweat were on his brow and his mouth was as dry as cotton. The smoke did something he had never seen before."

"What did it do, Granddaddy?" Glenda whined.

"The smoke rose towards the sky until it formed a big cloud… and stopped in mid-air. Like a living nightmare, the cloud took the shape of Theodore Bowers. The smoky apparition shrieked in a ghostly, death defying way. *'Nobody comes between my money and me! Whoever tries will die'.* Then with lightening speed, the smoky spirit swirled into nothingness and shot back under the house."

Pervis paused telling the story and took his last sit of hot chocolate. Without saying a word, Joy and Glenda sat quietly and absorbed

GRANNY'S PLACE

the strangeness of their Granddaddy's tale. Simultaneously, they turned their heads towards the house across the street...Mr. Genie's now old, vacant and dilapidated house. The house created a loathsome shadow against the night sky. Pervis chuckled to himself because his granddaughter's silhouettes resembled two bumps on a camel's back with two sets of eyes to boot."

"One thing more," Pervis continued, "I believe everything old man Genie told me and it motivated me to get the construction work done on around the house all the sooner. The work took six months to finish but after that...Eva and I were never bothered by ghostly intruders again."

"Why was Mr. Genie so sure that telling you to construct something new around the entire house would work, Granddaddy?" Glenda managed to ask.

"Because when Luke Genie was an eleven year old boy, his father had to do the same thing to their home too."

Eva phoned Debra to say the hike wouldn't be until tomorrow because one of Pervis' stories lasted longer than expected. That was all right with Debra because one of Jamaal's hospital patients needed his attention and he had to go in town with Dave to get some needed medicine.

The evening was ended. Pervis was snoring and Eva finished reading her Bible. That night, Joy and Glenda slept between their grandparents.

THE FIRST ADVENTURE

Eleven o'clock Wednesday morning, Old Colonel was flapping his mangled wings and crowing the best he could. Pecking the ground, the hens ignored the master of their domain.

Eva busied herself in the kitchen and took out the lunches she'd made for her grandchildren and Jamaal yesterday. She couldn't understand it but she had a strong urge to pack plenty of food for the new hikers. Twelve homemade BLT sandwiches, two meatloaf sandwiches, two dozen oatmeal cookies, a quart size plastic container of carrot sticks, two dozen legs of plump batter fried chicken, a quart jar of her homemade watermelon pickles, two dozen rolls, and two bags of twenty pieces of Horehound. Thickly sliced meatloaf sandwiches for Jamaal were waiting too because she knew they were his favorite.

Arm-in-arm and wearing their overall sets, Joy and Glenda stood staring at themselves in the door mirror in Glenda's room. The only difference in the outfits was Joy's t-shirt was yellow and Glenda's was light blue.

"Even though we don't resemble one another, we really look like sister's in these outfits don't we Joy?" Glenda said.

"We sure do, Glenda." The two hopped downstairs to the kitchen like proud peacocks.

"My, my, my, don't y'all look as sweet as can be," Eva said.

"Thank you, Granny," Glenda said. "Joy and I wanted to look alike for our outing."

"Well y'all certainly did a good job with that but I want you to do something else for me now."

"What Granny?" Joy asked.

"Look in the hall closet and get two of your school book bags. I want to use them for your hiker treats," Eva replied.

"Sure thing, Granny," Joy said.

Joy opened the hall closet door under the stairs. She pulled the light-bulb string hanging in the center of the closet ceiling to turn on the light, grabbed her book bags off the back shelf, turned off the light and ran back to the kitchen. As she did, Jamaal knocked on the kitchen screen door.

"Come on in, son," Eva said.

"Good morning, Miss Eva," Jamaal replied. "I came over so Joy, Glenda and me can get started because we've got to beat the afternoon sun." He noticed how cute the girls looked…especially Joy.

"We're almost done helping Granny pack our lunches, Jamaal," Glenda said.

"Here Glenda, stuff this plastic tablecloth in the book bag too," Eva said.

"Joy, do you have a flashlight and first aid kit? Mom packed one in my backpack in case we need it along with her homemade first aid stuff," Jamaal said.

"That was smart of your Mom," Eva said. "Her healing secrets were around long before all the concoctions they sell in the drugstores."

"Gosh Miss Eva, I almost forgot to tell you. Mom said she wouldn't be able to make the church business meeting because of a terrible backache."

"That's okay, Jamaal because I'm not feeling too well myself."

"All right, Miss Eva but we better be on our way now," Jamaal said.

"Y'all have a good time and make certain you're careful along the way and try to get home before it gets dark. Pervis and I will be home from the church meeting at five o'clock."

"Miss Eva, don't you fret one bit. Dad made sure I have everything planned out and even made notations in a pocket notebook for emergencies," Jamaal said, sticking his chest out.

Eva watched them go past the side of Mr. Genie's vacant and dilapidated house and down a hill filled with weeds that was Mr. Genie's prized garden. But…when they went past the front porch, they didn't notice Pervis sitting in his rocker going over the notes for the church meeting. He watched as the trio disappeared down the grassy trail. Eva finally joined her husband on the porch. The air was already humid and muggy. Pervis notice his wife was limping.

"Has your knee been bothering you this morning?" Pervis asked. "I've never seen you limp like that before."

"To tell you the truth Pervis, I woke up this morning feeling poorly. My knee has swollen for the first time in years and the aching is something fierce."

"That settle's it. No church meeting for you today. Sitting on those hard benches will worsen your condition too."

"But Pervis I…"

"No arguments from you because I won't change my mind on this," Pervis said, sternly as he escorted Eva to the livingroom couch. He didn't have to coax Eva very much because she secretly wanted to stay home anyway. Her mind was on Jamaal and her grandchildren and she had even prayed a silent prayer as they left for their hike. She couldn't dismiss the thought of some kind of impending danger. The ache in her knee alarmed her because the last time she felt pain like this was that wintry night when Barbara and Arvis had that terrible accident.

"I have to leave for the meeting now but is there anything I can do for you before I leave?" Pervis asked.

"Turn on the television for me, Pervis because the noise will keep me company and I'll most likely fall to sleep too. I'll be just fine and don't worry so much," Eva replied. As Pervis kissed his wife goodbye, Harvey and pulled up and blew the horn in his taxi and the longtime friends were off to the church. David was in the car too.

"Eva's eyes became heavy with sleep but she managed to say a prayer outloud. "Please Lord, there's something amiss but You know what it is and I leave the whole thing in Your capable hands. Watch over my grandchildren and Jamaal and keep them safe." Soon after praying, she drifted into a deep sleep. In the distance, the sound of a melody played on a harmonica floated through the livingroom windows.

"TJ brought Dad a load of seeds early this morning, Jamaal said. "Since Mom wasn't going to the church meeting because of her backache, she asked TJ if he would mind doing a little fence mending since he was all ready over our way. Sick or not sick, Mom can't stand it when she sees there's something to be done."

"That sounds a bit like Granny, Jamaal," Joy said. "By the way, Jamaal, I thought we were supposed to go along with TJ on his wagon for this hike?"

"We were but TJ suddenly pulled out. I guess he had something else more important to do. I guess that's why he and Dad gave me direction and all. It's okay though because he said we'd do the same another time."

"There you do again with this TJ fellow," Glenda said. "Who is this guy anyway and please don't give me that guff about 'a picture is worth a thousand words' just because I've never seen him before."

"I promise to tell you everything I know about TJ when we get to the cavern," Jamaal said, keeping up a steady pace.

"…a 'cavern', Glenda said.

"…you remember Glenda," Jamaal said. "I told you about a cave when you and Joy came by my house the other day…remember now?"

"Oh you mean that spooky place you had picked out," Glenda replied.

"That's the place but at the last minute yesterday, TJ told me about a cavern which is bigger than the cave I discovered. Dad told me the location and it sounded like a safe place too."

The three continued to walk through the density of towing pine trees, oak trees and wild growth of all kinds until they came to the edge of an immense meadow. The meadow was split straight down the middle by a rustic path formed by the constant pounding feet of travelers. The path hadn't been used by sojourners in many years and Mother Nature had reclaimed the zigzagging territory with the growth of flowery weeds. It had been years since a vehicle dared traverse the potholed dirt road.

Sounds of clicking bugs and insects warned each other of a human invasion. As the happy hikers continued their afternoon quest, they entered a world innocuous of city surroundings that threatened nature's boundaries. To Jamaal's delight, a jackrabbit darted across the clay road with lightening speed and scurried into a clump of shrubbery on the opposite side of the path.

"What was that?" Glenda hollered, almost jumping out of her skin.

"It was probably one of my former patients," Jamaal joked.

"Your wits astound me, Jamaal," an aggravated Glenda replied.

"Nevermind about Jamaal's teasing, Glenda," Joy said. "There's nothing around here that'll harm you."

Their path began to narrow and empty into another grassland field. The hikers stood in awe as they gazed at nature's untouched masterpiece. The breathtaking view couldn't be described with words. All kinds of wild flowers swayed back and forth at the command of a warm summer breeze. Butterflies of different designs created a fluttering kaleidoscope of magnificent hues. Strung between delicate limbs of a growing oak tree, a spider's web adorned with the dewdrops of the morning, glistened like diamonds. A warm of knats seemed to hang in midair and performed a ritualistic dance. Squawking crows flew high overhead and disappeared into a cloudless horizon.

"It's like a perfect work of art," Joy marveled.

"I hope nothing changes here in a million years," Glenda sighed. With Jamaal leading, the three crossed the field in single file.

"We'd better pick up the pace because it's getting hotter by the minute. I want to reach the edge of the wood over there before the sun hits the middle of the sky," Jamaal said, pointing to the edge of the meadow.

"Have you ever been to the cavern before, Jamaal?" Glenda asked.

"…nope," Jamaal said.

"Then how do you know we're going in the right direction? It seems as though we've been walking for miles. I thought TJ told you how to get there," Glenda moaned.

"In case you've forgotten Glenda, I brought a compass with me. Didn't you know folks from Suffolk have a nose for directions?" Jamaal joked.

"…that's real rich, Jamaal,"Glenda said.

"I have a map TJ sketched for me. According to this map, we'll find a stream of natural spring water at the edge of the woods. Besides that, I think TJ wanted us to see those meadows and all the beauty of nature. We'd have missed those sights if we'd taken the route I had planned for us."

They reached the edge of the forest and the towing pine and oak trees sheltered the weary hikers from the heat of the day.

"Good old TJ. He really knows directions," Jamaal said. He dropped his backpack to the ground, took off his shoes and socks, rolled up his pants legs and jumped into the stream of water that cascaded over rocks and boulders. Joy and Glenda followed suit. The three splashed around romping a playing delightfully. They drank water from their canteens, filled them again and lay back on the boulders next to the stream under the shade of a huge pine tree.

"Does this remind you of something?" Glenda said.

"It sure does," Joy replied.

Jamaal spread his map at the base of the oak tree that shaded Joy and Glenda. "Here's where we are now," Jamaal said. "We'll be at the cavern before you know it."

"Okay Jamaal but lets grab a bite to eat before we push on," Glenda suggested.

"I'm for that, Glenda," Joy said, rubbing her growling stomach.

After the girls ate and Jamaal wolfed down a meatloaf sandwich, they sprawled out on a cushion of pine needles at the base of the oak tree. Stretched out on his back, Jamaal folded his fingers behind his head and stared up through the branches. Joy leaned on one elbow and chewed a twig while Glenda rubbed alcohol on her aching legs. Two squirrels scampered up and down a branch of the oak tree as if playing a game of tag while a pinecone lost its battle with gravity.

"Well…we've spent enough time enjoying nature so we better get going," Jamaal said, breaking the solitude of the moment. "Better refill the canteens too because according to my map, the cavern is half a mile through these woods. "Boy-oh-boy, this knapsack sure is heavy. My Mom must have packed everything but the kitchen sink."

Joy and Glenda didn't notice the small patch of foreboding clouds forming on the horizon but Jamaal did and it made him uneasy. As he and the girls trekked their way to the cavern, he noticed the woods had become silent and there were no animals in sight. Jamaal now knew that the two squirrels were not playing but scurrying for home. One of the things his Dad taught him when on their camping trips was to read the signs of the forest. Jamaal strongly sensed that bad weather was on its way. Without breaking his pace and letting the girls see what he was doing, he checked his compass again.

"The cavern should be just over that hill to the north of us. We should see it in a few minutes.

"Thank goodness for that," Glenda said. Out of breath too, Joy nodded in agreement.

GRANNY'S PLACE

Within five minutes they were standing at the foot of a tall, massive rocky cliff. Devils' Shoestrings had grown from somewhere on top all the way to the base and formed a natural ladder. Wild shrubbery and knotty branches of all kinds protruded from crevices and cracks in the face of the cliff. The cavern entrance was camouflaged by moss and weeds.

"How in the world are we supposed to get to the top?" Glenda said, patting the ground with her foot.

"...climb," Jamaal said.

"You've got to be kidding, Jamaal."

"This time I have to agree with Glenda completely," Joy said. That looks like a dangerous climb if you don't know what you're doing."

"I hate to break up this conversation but if you look over your shoulder you'll see why I wanted us to get to the cavern in a hurry." Joy and Glenda turned around just as lightening flashed silently in the distance.

"That thunderstorm will be here before you know it so I suggest we stop gabbing and start climbing. I've done a lot of climbing..."

"...with Dad," the girls said in unison.

Jamaal was first to start up the cliff to test each foot hold with his weight and constantly glanced over his shoulder to see if Joy and Glenda were following close behind. He used his shirtsleeve to wipe the sweat from his brow and took the last step upward and threw his leg over the cliff edge. He made it.

"Just place you foot on the exact same rocks I did," Jamaal yelled down. "Don't forget to use the vines too."

"Don't be afraid, Glenda. Granny said Devil's Shoestring vines are as strong as rope," Joy hollered, following close behind her cousin's heels.

"I did it too, everybody," Glenda squealed as she lifted herself over the cliff top. "It's your turn next, Joy."

Lying on his stomach and still breathing heavily, Jamaal reach down for Joy but felt his shoulder bone snap as he reach down to grab her wrist. His shoulder had pulled out of joint and he grimaced with pain. Joy was dangling, screaming and kicking in midair with only Jamaal's grip on her wrist between her and the rocks below.

"Quick Glenda, I need your help," Jamaal puffed. Glenda scurried to the edge of the landing and lay on her stomach next to Jamaal but began to panic when she saw her cousin hanging in the air.

"No baby stuff right now, Glenda. Reach down and try to grab Joy's other wrist. You've got to hurry. I can't hold on much longer. You can do it, Glenda. I know you can."

"Joy," Glenda yelled. "Reach for my hand! Grab my hand!"

During a moment of sanity, Joy managed to catch Glenda's hand while Jamaal held on to her other wrist.

"Try to get a foothold on something near you and push yourself up," Jamaal shouted.

Joy manuvered her foot into two knotted Devil's Shoestring vines and with the last bit of her strength, pushed herself upward as hard as she could. Glenda and Jamaal were now able to reach her elbows. With one last heave, Jamaal quickly locked his arms around Joy's waist and threw his weight backward. Laughing and crying at the same time, the three friends embraced each other as they became a tangled mess of arms and legs.

"Joy, are you okay?" Glenda sniffed.

"I am thanks to you and Jamaal," Joy replied. She looked into Jamaal eyes and he looked back into her's. Glenda smiled as the two openly expressed what they felt for each other.

"Jamaal hurt his shoulder," Glenda said, breaking the spell of the two heartthrobs.

"Oh Jamaal, is there something I can do for your shoulder?" Joy asked with girlish concern.

"There sure is," Jamaal said, as he reset his shoulder by hitting it against a rocky wall.

"...what?"

"Lose some weight," Jamaal laughed, hiding his painful expression from the girls. Joy mistakenly gave him a slap on the same shoulder.

"Ouch," Jamaal hollered. Instead of slapping me, look inside my knapsack and get that container of salve Mom made up. That stuff will heal anything," Jamaal said. Rubbing on the salve and moving his arm up and down, he sighed with relief when the pain completely disappeared.

"Jamaal, let's explore the cave now because I don't like the looks of those clouds over there. I think they're storm clouds," Joy said, pointing towards the edge of the meadow.

"Good gracious! First we almost loose you and now a thunderstorm," Glenda whimpered. "What next?"

"Chin up, Glenda and let's find out how to get inside this cavern. You and Joy help me clear the entrance and throw aside this brush and small tree limbs. Don't get rid of the dried tree limbs because we can save them for a camp fire," Jamaal said.

"What a mess," Glenda complained, dumping an armload of twigs beside the cavern entrance.

"I can't wait to see inside," Joy said.

"I can't wait either, Joy," Jamaal said. "…but I hope we're not invading the privacy of some fury family."

"You don't really mean that…do you Jamaal?" Glenda said.

"I was just joking, Glenda," Jamaal laughed.

"Nevermind that Jamaal, but now that we have the cavern entrance cleared how are we suppose to get inside? The entrance is so small," Glenda said.

"Looks like we'll have to crawl on all fours but we have to get a move on because that storm is getting closer by the minute. I go first and then you and Joy follow when I signal you to come inside."

"Why do we have to wait, Jamaal?" Joy asked.

"I want to check to make sure the place is safe."

"Well…hurry up and check it out because I don't want to get caught in the rain."

After what seemed like an eternal wait, Jamaal called Joy and Glenda to crawl through.

"Wow, Jamaal," Joy said. "The dirt floor looks like it's been swept clean."

"Not only is the floor dry, but have you noticed that we all are standing straight up? The temperature is here is cool too."

"Have you noticed something else?" Glenda said.

"…what?" Joy and Jamaal said in unison.

"Turn off your flashlight, Jamaal."

"Hey! Everything lit up! Where does the light come from, Glenda?"

"It's that white powdery substance on the cavern walls. It's called luminous algae. It's a harmless chemical element that reflects the slightest source of light. I saw the same thing in a huge cave my parents and I toured last summer."

"Does it ever stop glowing, Glenda?" Joy asked.

"It only stops glowing when it doesn't have any light to reflect."

"In that case, let's start building a fire and let it do all the reflecting it wants," Jamaal said. "I have a feeling everything's going to turn out fine for us and we're going to have a blast too."

They walked around following one illuminated path after the other leading into dark tunnels that they decided not to explore. Back in the main cavern, Joy noticed that the smoke created by their campfire rose up and exited through a hole on the ceiling that was well rounded as if formed by human hands.

"Look up there, you guys. See that hole in the ceiling? It makes a perfect chimney," Joy said.

"It looks like it was made on purpose but how could a person reach that height?" Glenda said. "Boy…this place is getting stranger by the minute. First…the hole in a tall ceiling, second…a smooth dirt floor, third…illuminated algae…and you know something else? Check out that fresh pile of hay over there. I have a strong feeling somebody has been here before."

Wind blew through the small opening at the mouth of the cave.

"You guys get everything settled and unroll the blanket in my knapsack. I'm going back outside and collect more wood for the fire," Jamaal said.

Once outside, Jamaal observed the sky. It was dark and the sun was nowhere in sight. A massive streak if lightning flashed down to the horizon like ghostly fingers. Wind blew through the small opening at the mouth of the cave. Hurriedly, he collected many armloads of firewood until he was satisfied he had enough. He crawled in and out of the cavern entrance until the wood pile was inside. He thought of his chopping wood chore at home and briefly reminisced that he wished he was at home this very moment.

"Jamaal, make sure you place the fire right under the hole in the ceiling," Glenda said.

"…already done, Glenda."

GRANNY'S PLACE

In the excitement and coziness of their new surroundings, they rehashed the trek to the cavern, Joy swinging in midair and Glenda's whining. The warmth of the dancing flames of fire was so relaxing. The walls of the cavern twinkled and glittered like thousands of tiny Christmas lights as the summer storm roared outside. Glenda pulled out a container of baby wipes from her backpack and handed them to the other hikers. The three giggled and laughed with delight. Finally, they thought of their present circumstances.

"What the matter, Jamaal," Joy asked, as he stretched out on his makeshift mattress. "Why do you have that frown on your face?"

"I was thinking of the map TJ drew for our hike."

"What about the map? It got us here didn't it?" Joy replied.

"Yes, but TJ told me we'd find lots of other caverns but in some way, he intentionally wanted us to find this particular one."

"Why did he pick this one out, Jamaal? Maybe if he'd chosen a different one, Joy might not have almost bought a ticket to the Great Beyond," Glenda retorted.

"When I asked him why he picked out this cavern he looked me straight in the face and said, 'Trust me, Massa Maal'."

The three summertime friends decided it to pay serious attention to their stomachs. Eva's sandwiches and treats were more delicious with each bite. All conversation ceased as food was munched, the flames crackled, the wind whistling outside, thunder rumbled, and lightning flashed across the sky.

"Granny says when you hear thunder and lightning like this, angels in heaven are moving things around and cleaning house," Joy said, hoping to relieve tension and calm her nerves too.

"Cleaning house? That noise sounds more like somebody's being moved out to me," Jamaal joked. "Okay Glenda, I know the look on your face means 'shut-up'. You're really going to give me a mean look when I tell you we're in for an all night stay in Hotel Cavern."

"But Granny and Granddaddy and your folks don't even know which cave we're in or if we're safe from the storm, Jamaal," Joy said.

"...but Dad knows we're in this cave. Not even TJ knows where we are. We've got plenty of food to eat and we're warm," Jamaal said. "I've been through a storm like this before when Dad and I went on a camping trip. That's when I learned all the safety tips and finding this cave in time is a good thing for us."

Joy and Glenda decided to take Jamaal's advice and carefully stored the remainder of the food. They heard loud popping. Jamaal peeped out of the cave entrance to see what was making the noise.

"What was making the popping sound, Jamaal," Glenda said, trembling again. "Are the cavern walls falling in or something?"

"It's nothing like that Glenda. Hail balls the sizes of Kansas are bouncing off the cave outside. Imagine that!"

SEARCHING

Golf ball size hail pelted the metal roof of the house waking Eva from her deep sleep. The telephone rang several times before she was able to get her hurting knee functioning and answer.

"Hello Pervis. You have to stay there because of the storm? I haven't seen anything like this for years. I hope the farms haven't been hit too hard. No, the children haven't come home yet. Does David know which cave they're in? TJ drew a map for Jamaal and the girls and knows what cave they're in? Okay, I'll wait until you call again. I love you too."

RESCUED

Flames of the campfire hungrily licked the air warding off dampness. Jamaal searched around the cave floor for any loose stones he could find to add them to the pile at the cave entrance. Thunder rolled and lightning flashed angrily. Trees that once stood majestically prostrated themselves to the command of a relentless gale. Joy and Jamaal sat quietly listening to the turmoil around them but Glenda began to panic and whimper...again. With earsplitting rumbling, another roll of thunder exploded.

"I can't stand this anymore! I'm getting out of here! I want to go home to my Mom and Dad!" Glenda cried hysterically. She ran towards the cave entrance and frantically started to pull away the rocks. Jamaal followed behind her.

"Glenda, stop! You'll be just fine but you have to stay inside out of the storm. You wouldn't last a minute in that mess out there." He led her back to the warmth of the campfire and sat her down next to Joy who put her arm around her cousin's trembling shoulders.

"I'm all right now, Joy. I don't know what got into me. I guess I'm not use to a lot of things...and thunder like this is one of them."

"That's okay, Glenda," Jamaal said. "Joy and I won't let anything happen to you. Right, Joy?"

"Right," Joy said.

"Thanks, Jamaal," Glenda sniffed. "I'm glad I had my first real adventure with you and Joy. It really makes me feel special...and it's better than spending the summer with a bunch of snobs racing canoes."

"You know something, Glenda? This is a good time to tell you everything concerning TJ," Jamaal said.

"Tell me, Jamaal. What about that strange character?" Glenda asked.

"One morning I came to Miss Eva's house because she had asked Mom if I could pick peaches. It was Joy's first time picking peaches so Miss Eva told her to help me. We were almost finished when I saw, coming into the yard, this odd-looking fellow and his mule pulling an old flatbed wagon. Joy and I could hardly believe our eyes. This fellow looked like the Uncle Ramose character from that story about Huckleberry Finn but…I noticed his eyes first," Jamaal said.

"What was odd about his eyes," Glenda asked.

"They weren't odd at all Glenda, but they were big and bright and twinkled like diamonds. My folks taught me never to assume the worst about a person and I stared at TJ only because he was such a strange looking individual. Dad also said the strangest thing about TJ."

"What did your Dad say, Jamaal?" Glenda asked.

"He said whenever he's somewhere around, you can hear him playing his harmonica."

"What's strange about that, Jamaal," Joy asked.

"Dad said that if two people were side by side, one might hear the harmonica and the other one might not. There's lots of storied flying around about the man but when he's around, whatever's wrong…turns out right and that's what's strange."

"What you've said is so true, Jamaal. I've never seen the man before but the first time he has ever seen me was by the peach tree. I remember he looked me straight in the eye and told me that I'd be a great artist someday and I'd also be a great influence in many lives. What really stunned me was his knowing that I kept a picture diary. The man had never met me before and there's no way he could have know that but he knew…somehow," Joy said.

"I never told anybody this before Joy," Jamaal said. "…but TJ came by my house a few weeks ago. I was in the backyard chopping wood for Mom's stove. TJ asked me if I wouldn't mind getting him a glass of water. I was only gone about five minutes but when I came back out, a six food high pile of wood was chopped and stacked neatly against the side of the porch. I just stood like a robot staring back and forth from the wood pile to TJ. TJ took the glass of ice water from my hand, smiled with that twinkle in his eyes, drank the water, said 'thank you' and left."

The trio sat in silence and stared into the campfire.

"…listen," Jamaal said.

"…to what?" Joy asked.

"I don't hear anything," Glenda added.

"That's the whole point!"

"Jamaal, this is not a time for riddles. What do you hear because I don't hear a thing," Glenda said, somewhat irritated.

"Maybe it's that secret recipe Granny used to make his meatloaf sandwich," Joy joked.

"For cry outloud, Jamaal," Glenda said. "Would you just tell us what it is?"

"…silence…I hear absolutely nothing. I don't hear thunder or hail stones bouncing off the cavern walls. The storm has passed," Jamaal said excitedly while pulling away the rocks from the cavern entrance. Joy and Glenda join in to help.

As they crawled through the entrance, three pairs of eyes peered at the sky. It revealed an aurora of colors and a rainbow crowned the clouds. Stars struggled to reclaim their place in the heavenly canopy but the sun stole their brilliance. Birds were tweeting and chirping. Bullfrogs croaked as Nature seemed to sing with joy. The hikers took a deep breath to fill their lungs with fresh air.

"This is absolutely wonderful," Glenda said. "Now we can be on our way home."

"Not so fast Glenda, it's not going to be as easy as you think. The thunderstorm rearranged the cliff and blew away the Devil's Shoestring vines away. We have no choice but to stay her until our folks can find us."

"But how will they know where to look, Jamaal?" Joy asked.

"Yes, what are we supposed to do 'Mr. Genius with the Map'," Glenda added.

"Take it easy, Glenda. We'll be okay."

"That's right, Jamaal," Joy said. "We're home free, Glenda. Put a smile on your face. Everything will soon be over."

The forest gleamed as sunrays reflected off the rain soaked foliage. The hikers crawled back inside the cavern to gather their belongings into their backpacks. Jamaal made certain the campfire was out with water from his canteen. They went back outside…and waited.

GOOD NEWS

Eva was kneeling on the sofa and praying when the phone rang for the umpteenth time. Waiting in line for use of the phone in the pastor's office, Pervis had finally gotten through to his wife again. He said he and other church members were stranded at the church because of road outages due to flooding.

"Have you been able to contact Harvey?"

"Not yet, Pervis but his whole company has been barraged by calls for transportation where possible."

"Dave tried to call his house and check on his wife and find out about Jamaal but the telephone service was out of order," Pervis said. "He's really concerned about both of them. Don't you fret and worry about anything because the Lord has already worked out everything and will keep the kids safe wherever they are. I've reminded Dave that he's taught Jamaal well when there is an emergency to handle. To call Debra and call us when you've reached her. That will give Dave some peace of mind."

Eva did just that. "Hello Debra? Lord your husband and Pervis will be so glad I was able to contact you. The phone lines were down over you way and your husband was worried sick and near in tears about you. You can make it here? Be careful Debra, because Pervis said some roads were flooded. You're going to ride one of your horses to get here? Girl…you are something else. I'll see you in a half an hour.

While waiting for Debra to arrive, Eva went into her domain and began pulling leftovers out of the refrigerator. She set up the dining-room table as if a king or queen was coming for a visit.

"Eva! I'm here! Where do you want me to tie my horse?" Debra yelled.

"My, my, my you're a sight for sore eyes," Eva yelled, throwing open the kitchen screen door. "Dave will to do his own special bunny hop when he sees you, girl. Jamaal will have a fit too."

STILL IN THE CAVE

"What was that?" Joy asked.

"Oh no, not again with 'what's that noise'," Glenda chided.

"Hush up Glenda, and listen. You're right, Joy. I hear it too," Jamaal said, cupping his ear with the palm of his hand.

"It sounds like music," Joy whispered.

"It is music! It's harmonica music," all three shouted.

"YIPPEE! It's TJ," Jamaal shrieked.

They stood near the edge of the cliff and looked up and down the horizon straining to find the source of the familiar sound that filled the entire rain soaked grassland spread out before them. Still searching for their tattered rescuer, the hikers looked and listened even harder. The harmonica music became louder and louder…and then…stopped. Several minutes passed but no sight of TJ.

"What do you suppose happened, Jamaal?" Glenda asked disappointed.

"I wish I knew, Glenda," a bewildered Jamaal said.

Several more moments of deafening silence passed. Images and thoughts of home began to fade in the minds of the hikers when suddenly…

"Hey thar y'all," TJ said.

Joy, Jamaal and Glenda spun around. There he was as big as day and standing behind them.

"But…but…but," was all Jamaal managed to say. Glenda and Joy stood transfixed and motionless like two doll cutouts. TJ cackled at the astonishment he'd caused.

"How in the world did you get up here, TJ?" Jamaal asked, after gathering his wits.

"Gotha yo' stuff 'n follow me," he motioned to the cavern. Once inside, TJ disappeared as he walked down a path not familiar to the hikers. The three followed reluctantly not because they didn't trust TJ but because they could barely see in the dark. TJ didn't seem to have a problem seeing anything. Pushing aside a pile of straw, he pointed to a crack in the stone wall.

"Dis is whar we's gonna go thru," TJ said. With one finger, he touched the crack in the stone wall. Creaking and scraping...the wall opened revealing another algae illuminated cavern.

"What the...," Jamaal gasped.

"Glenda, you wanted to know about TJ and now you're getting to see him first hand," Joy whispered to her bewildered cousin.

"Incredible," Glenda whispered back.

"Pissst,"

"What Glenda?" Joy said.

"Have you noticed something?"

"No. What?"

"The campfire is out and there's no light coming in anywhere."

"...and?"

"So...what light is activating the algae this time?"

TJ was the only one in the cavern. Joy gasped at Glenda's observation. It was true. Light was being reflected by something or...someone.

"TJ, who are you really?" Jamaal asked. "Things just seem to happen for the better when you come around."

TJ smiled and his eyes twinkled. "Josie told me 'bout everything," he said.

"Huh?" the hikers said together.

"Sho' 'nuff," TJ said.

"Excuse me, but it's a little hard to believe that a mule told you where we were and that we'd be caught in a thunderstorm," Glenda said. "Okay...let's have it, how did Josie tell you where to find us?"

"Well Josie and me, we was having breakfast and she said she saw pale stallions gallopin' 'cross da sky dis mornin'."

"Josie saw pale stallions...and told you...I mean talked to you?" Joy said.

"Sho' 'nuff, Miss Glenda, cause when Josie sees pale stallions ridin' 'cross the sky it means bad wetha."

"Well that one up on Doctor Dolittle," Glenda replied.

TJ motioned to the inquisitive trio to follow him once again. Moving in single file, they turned their bodies sideways to squeeze through another narrow opening. Finally, they were in another smaller cavern. Jamaal turned on his flashlight.

"TJ, this passage leads to a dead end," Jamaal said.

"Naw it don't," TJ said, pointing straight ahead.

Jamaal directed the beam of his flashlight down the corridor but all he could see was another wall of stone and another narrow opening.

"How are we supposed to get through there," Glenda whined.

"Weese got ta suck up a gut and crawl."

"Do you want to use my flashlight, TJ", Jamaal asked.

"No sir 'cause I knows whar I's going," TJ replied. His eyes sparkled wildly.

They crawled one behind the other with Jamaal in the rear. "My brand new coveralls are getting filthy not to mention the toes of my shoes getting all messed up too," Glenda said.

"For goodness sake Glenda is that all you can think about now? I'm thinking of seeing Granny and Granddaddy again," Joy retorted. "Just crawl and shut-up…please." Jamaal was glad to hear that.

The dirt tunnel began to slope downhill but after some minutes more of crawling, it opened into a smaller cavern but they were able to standup this time. Of course, an illuminated alga was all over the place.

"Jamaal is your flashlight turned on or off?" Glenda asked.

"…off."

They followed the natural sight source and soon found themselves standing outside in the middle of age-old pine trees. Josie was munching on grass and waiting patiently for her master. The hikers could barely believe their eyes. TJ was delighted to see Joy, Glenda and Jamaal absorbed with their hiking experiences. He knew this expedition would be remembered by the trio for the rest of their lives.

"Y'all betta git on bode de wagon. Weese got ta stop by da church 'n pick up a Pappy 'n a Grandpappy dats waitin' ta see deys chillins." The weary but elated hikers threw their knapsacks on the back of the wagon. They were on the way home.

"TJ, tell us about that cavern and all those passageways," Jamaal said.

"I was in a cave like dis when somebody I know was born…way 'round on the otha side of da world. Life is like that cave you found.

GRANNY'S PLACE

It's full of surprises and unexpected avenues all the time. You have to be strong to adjust."

"Hey you guys," Glenda whispered. "Could he be talking about Bethlehem?"

"What made you think of 'Bethlehem', Glenda," Joy asked.

"I don't know. The word just came out of my mouth."

"Have you noticed something else?" Jamaal asked the girls.

"What now, Jamaal," the girls answered in unison.

"With his last statement, TJ used perfect English."

The hikers sat quietly as the wagon pulled them towards home but they felt a strange new respect for their rescuer. To them, the cavern was no longer just a cavern but a memorial of a very special adventure.

"TJ can I come and sit next to you?" Joy humbly asked.

TJ nodded his approval and Joy moved from the back of the wagon and onto the wooden buckboard seat. Touched by a wave of compassion, Joy threw her arms around TJ and kissed him on the cheek.

"Thank you for everything, TJ," she whispered in his ear.

"Yo welcom', L'll Miss 'n everythin's gwanna be jes fine." TJ was speaking of…in the future.

"We always wanted to ride with you one day, TJ and we sure got our wish," Jamaal said.

"Dat's truer than you think, Massah Maal…so true."

By the time they reach the edge of the last meadow, the sun had dried up all the rain but an infinite number of wild flowers had already blossomed and reached up as if standing at attention. The grassland appeared to be covered with a magnificent carpet. Mother Nature had summoned water, her most precious resource, back to the deep recesses of earth. Josie trotted down the narrow path around the middle of the meadow the hikers traversed earlier in the morning. Josie turned the wagon around a corner once again.

"TJ…"

"Yes 'sum, Missy Joy?"

"Please excuse my manners but I forgot to introduce you to…"

"…Missy Glenda." This was no ordinary man and Joy said no more.

"There's the church," Jamaal shouted.

GRANNY'S PLACE

The devastation and havoc the storm had done to the community could be seen everywhere. By some miracle, some homes totally escaped the wrath of the storm. Many had already begun a feeble but noble clean-up attempt to flooded streets and yards, clogged sidewalk drains filled with debris. Other storm complications hampered their efforts. Broken tree branches piled in the middle of the church lawn for lack of space to put them elsewhere. Fortunately, the church had become a safe haven for many of now homeless families. Dave took a moment's break from new trash being gathered and looked up from his chore to wipe his brow. His heart near leapt into his throat at the sight of what was approaching.

"Everybody" Dave shouted. ...it's TJ and the kids!"

Josie sloshed down the flooded street without breaking her stride. TJ directed her towards the church yard. Dave ran to the wagon before it could come to a stop. Jamaal, Joy and Glenda jumped off the wagon. Pervis squeezed his Sweetmeat and Peaches and planted kisses on their foreheads and cheeks. Dave tearfully hugged his son. Others cheered TJ and surrounded his wagon and Josie. They patted his back and shook his hand in appreciation for all he'd done. TJ patted Josie on her nose and she secretly smiled back at him.

"Y'all betta hop on bode, Mr. Pervis 'cause weese gots ta let yo' wives know 'bout dis good news too," TJ said.

"Okay TJ, we'll do just that," Dave said.

A tearful but happy entourage hopped on the wagon. In fact, everyone else who needed a ride home was welcomed to come along too. Once again Josie plodded along at a steady gait oblivious of the added weight and hoopla. One by one, neighbors whose roads were still impassable were dropped off in front of their homes. Next was South Fourth Street. Ignoring the pain in her knee, Eva and Debra hurriedly opened the gate for the noble steed that tirelessly hauled the most precious burden in the world as they wept with elation at the sight coming into the yard. A second barrage of hugging and kissing commenced among the seven family members followed by tons of questions. TJ thanked Josie again and loosened her from the wagon and placed her in the shade of the magnolia tree for a rest.

Once inside all silently joined Eva in prayer. "Lord, I thank You for answering my prayer and Debra's too. I thank You for keeping our family members TJ and Josie safe and sound," Eva wept, raising her hands unashamedly towards a bright blue heavenly canopy.

"Amen,"...everybody shouted.

"TJ," Pervis began. "We can't thank you enough for what you've done this day. Please stay with us and share in our celebration of the return of our grandchildren. We'd all be honored if you could.

"Yes TJ, please do," Eva added.

"Well…I s'pose Josie and I could stay jes a bit."

"Yahoo!"….the three adventurers yelled applauded.

The diningroom table was displayed an abundance of tantalizing dishes and bowls of delights. An extra chair of honor was brought in for TJ. With heads bowed once again, Pervis blessed the table. Spoons, forks, and arms moved up and down from plate to mouth. Laughter filled the house as platters of food were emptied of their contents. Dave leaned back in his chair after downing a second ample slice of peach pie.

"Eva and Debra…that was the greatest…but Debra and I want you and Pervis to know we never have supped with finer people. It's been a real pleasure to have you for friends all these years but today we all have a new friend," Dave said, pointing to TJ. "TJ we all want you to know that you can park those feet of yours under the table at my place anytime you have a mind to stop by. Josie can graze on our place anywhere she wants."

"The same here TJ," Pervis added, holding his glass of ice tea up in a toasting gesture as the rest followed. Then the men folk, young and old withdrew to the front porch and the ladies, young and old helped tidy up the kitchen and diningroom. The kitchen was finished and the females joined the men on the front porch. The main topics were the events of the day and not one detail was left unmentioned. After hours had past, TJ stood to announce that he and Josie had to leave.

"Do you truly have to leave now TJ?" Debra asked.

"Fraid so, m'am," 'cause I don't want Josie ta feel left out."

"Before you go TJ, will you play a tune with your harmonica?" Joy asked.

TJ looked at Joy with that familiar twinkle in his eye that shielded a secret only he knew. He pulled his harmonica from his patched jacket pocket and an immediate hush fell over the porch. TJ began his solo. He began to play "He".

GRANNY'S PLACE

"HE can turn tides and calm the angry sea
HE alone decides who writes a symphony
HE lights ev'ry star that makes the darkness bright
HE keeps watch all through each long and lonely night

HE still finds the time to hear a child's first prayer
Saint or sinner calls and always finds HIM there
Though it makes HIM sad to see the way we live
HE'LL always say "I FORGIVE"

HE can touch a tree and turn the leaves to gold
HE knows every lie that you and I have told
Though it makes Him mad to see the way we live
HE'LL always say "I FORGIVE"

The music was spellbinding and it was as though an entire orchestra accompanied each note of TJ's harmonica. The soothing diapason melted away hurts, doubts and fears for all who listened. Oddly, no birds chirped and no July Flies buzzed. Only a cool breeze enveloped the family gathering. There wasn't a dry eye on the porch. After a long moment of quietness, Dave and Pervis rose from their seats and walked over to the glider where TJ was standing. The three men embraced for a long time.

"I undastans…and so does HE."

Eva had packed a bundled of food for TJ when she came from the kitchen but now was the time to give it to him. "I wish I had more to give, TJ," Eva said, wiping her eyes with the corner of her apron.

TJ smiled, waved by to all and went into the yard to hitch up Josie. Pervis and Dave remained standing on the front porch steps to holler out a final farewell to TJ. They waited…and waited.

"I'd better go to the back of the house and see what's holding up TJ," Pervis said.

"I'll go with you Pervis," Dave said.

When the two men reached the backyard, they were astounded to find absolutely no one. They returned to the front porch not dumbfounded.

"Is there something the matter, Pervis," Eva asked.

"You're not going to believe this, Eva. TJ is gone."

"What do you mean? How could he be gone? We all have been sitting right here waiting for TJ and Josie to pass by. There's no way out of the yard except through the front gate," Eva said.

Everybody then realized that they had made the acquaintance of someone unique. A breeze suddenly rose again and rustled the treetops. The fait sound of harmonica music echoed in the far distance. The summer constellation strained to make its debut against the rays of a setting sun as the Wilsons waved their goodbyes.

"Are you sure you don't want to give Harvey a call for a taxi ride home?" Pervis shouted. "It will be dark by the time you get home."

"That's all right," Dave yelled back. We'd rather walk and discuss…well…you know what I mean."

Pervis nodded in agreement.

IT'S NOT YOUR FAULT

Eva and Pervis sat in silence on the front porch listening to the familiar sounds of nocturnal creatures. The darkened night sky was now filled with zillions of shimmering celestial bodies. Neither noticed that Glenda and Joy had retreated upstairs to get rid of the dirt and grime of their cave adventure. Glenda was in the tub submerged up to her neck with scented bubble bath. Joy sat on the edge of the tub holding her new set of baby doll pajamas on her lap.

"This summer is going by too fast, Glenda."

"I know what you mean, Joy. It always happens that whenever you're having fun. The time seems to just fly by."

"Maybe I can live with you in New York when summer vacation is over."

"I'd love it, Joy. We'd be like sisters for real but what about your Dad?"

"I hate my Dad. I hope I never see him again," Joy replied, running out of the bathroom in tears and dropping her baby doll pajamas on the floor. Covered with suds and her oversized bath towel, Glenda hurried to her cousin's bedroom.

"What's going on, Joy and why do you hate your Dad so much?"

"Before I tell you anything, you've got to promise not to repeat a single word to anybody…not even Granny or Granddaddy."

"That's an awful big promise you're asking me to keep, Joy."

"Do you promise or not because that's the only way I'm going to tell you anything."

Glenda realized the seriousness of the situation and wanted Joy to trust her. Above all that, her curiosity got the best of her.

"Okay Joy, I promise."

"I'm going to run away a few days before my Dad comes to take me back to New Jersey."

"But…why? Where will you go?"

"I don't care where I go as long as I get away from him."

"What has you so frightened you can't even tell our grandparents. Don't you trust them?"

"Of course I do but you don't understand, Glenda."

"...then tell me something I can understand, Joy."

"Before I made the train trip here, Dad said if I told anybody what was going on, he'd put me away in a reform school."

"Joy, your Dad was just trying to cover his tracks and one of the ways is to threaten you. He's trying to control you that way because he knows you're fearful of the results. Granny and Granddaddy would put their lives on the line for you so you don't have the right to deny them...anything," Glenda said. "Whatever it is, they'd have the law after him and you can count on that. Think about it. He's brainwashed you into not saying anything to the two people who you love."

Joy pondered her cousin's words and looked at her admiringly. Even though Glenda was terrified in the cave, she was not afraid to speak her mind.

"Let's finish bathing Glenda, and then I'll tell you everything," Joy said.

An hour had passed. The cousins rubbed themselves with bath creams and body perfume. They settled on Glenda's bed to talk.

"Go ahead, Joy. I'm ready to listen."

First of all Glenda, he beats me until I'm covered with scars so bad that I can't even change into my gym clothes for a week. Most of the beatings are for dumb little things like turning off my radio two minutes late."

You mean there's a specific time you can listen to your own radio?"

"Yep...and it's only an hour before bedtime."

"Sometimes he whips me for things that are his fault but he never admits to making a mistake." Joy was crying again. Glenda held her hand but said nothing.

"Then sometimes...sometimes...more often since Mom died..."

"Go on Joy, let it out. You have nothing to fear here so get it all out."

"...he comes into my room at night and jams his finger in my vagina. When he finishes, I'm sore for a week. He won't stop until he feels me being satisfied...you know what I mean by satisfied? He even makes me put his...his...thing in my mouth."

"Yes Joy, I know." Glenda began to tremble…but not from nervousness…but from anger. "I know I promised to keep this secret Joy, but I don't think this is a matter we should try to hide or settle by ourselves."

"You mean we have to tell Granny and Granddaddy? You mean you're going to break your promise?"

"Now hear me out, Joy. My Dad told me that anyone who performs sexual acts with his children is a criminal of the worst kind and needs to be put in jail. If I haven't said it before I'll say it again…you haven't done anything wrong but the wrong has been done to you. You're the victim. Please don't keep this to ourselves and let Jasper get away with it. This kind of act needs to be exposed."

"I know what Dad did was wrong Glenda, but do you think our grandparents will believe me?"

"Are you kidding? I believed you yet we haven't known each other with closeness like this until just this summer. They love you so very much. You want to know something else?

"What Glenda?"

"I think they already suspect to hear this kind of thing but you have to be the one to bring it to them…not them to you."

"I was so afraid, Glenda because the same thing happened to a friend of mine back in New Jersey. When she told her story, her Mom didn't believe her. It effected how she acted with other kids and almost flunk in school. She ran away from home but the police caught her and brought her back home. To end it all, she killed herself by eating rat poisoning. I have nightmares about her sometimes." Joy's was crying again.

"Listen Joy, Granny and Granddaddy must know. I'm going to give you one week to make up your mind and if you don't they are going to hear it from me."

Joy could hardly believe the mature wisdom and fairness of Glenda's words. The deal she presented left no room for excuses. She was right about Granny and Granddaddy and it would be a relief to tell them the whole mess.

"You're right, Glenda. I'm going to come clean and unload this mess."

"Good, now dry your eyes and let's go downstairs before Granny and Granddaddy think we've drowned in the tub."

Glenda went down first to give Joy a bit more time to get herself together.

"Where's Joy, Glenda," Eva asked.

"She'll be down in a...oh here she is."

"My goodness, you two smell like a garden of lilacs," Pervis commented.

Joy sat on the glider close to her cousin. "I'm going to tell them everything Sunday," Joy whispered in Glenda's ear. She wanted to tell them Sunday not because she was hesitant to do so but because she need time to organize her thoughts and make absolutely certain not to leave out the smallest detail. Glenda was right. Jasper needed to be exposed.

"YAHOOOOOOO," Glenda yelped.

The startled grandparents looked at the girls and then at each other. Joy and Glenda giggled so hard until they could hardly catch their breath.

"That must have been joke," Eva said to Pervis. The cousins laughed even harder.

THE JOHNSONS

Glenda had always been a thinker. She was an honor student but always contemplated the idea of becoming a lawyer like her father.

Oneonta, New York resembled a Norman Rockwell painting but it was the environment she knew. Her neighborhood consisted of community of professionals cloistered in an historical section of town where the elite lived. The homes were of one Victorian style or the other. The only observable differences were the personalized renovations of property by individual families. The front of each residence was adorned with a long driveway edged with elaborate lighting, the latest landscaping trends, and manicured, spacious and meticulously kept yards. Glenda loved her undisturbed, picture perfect world and all it embraced.

When it came to her well-being, Glenda's parents left no stone unturned. They gave her every advantage towards developing into a well rounded person. Presents on her numerous birthday parties were expensive and Christmas gifts were off the charts. But like her cousin, she was lonesome and the awful facts Joy's situation had confided enabled Glenda to focus outside her untarnished surroundings in Oneonta. This particular summer she understood there are tangible heartaches in this world in spite of fortunate circumstances not experienced in her life.

In the comfort of his library, Glenda shared Saturdays with her Dad. She sat near his side and watched him read through piles of office papers and bundles of legal jargon and had a tremendous sense of security at just being in the same room with him. She and her Mom made a special trip to New York to buy her Dad his antique desk a week before Christmas. Her favorite memory was curling up in one of her Dad's leather wing backed chairs in front of a glowing fireplace while reading a book from her Nancy Drew collection. There were the Saturdays she and her Mom joined her Dad in his office to discuss family business or community matters. Especially in the winter after the meetings, the three would flop down in front of the warmth of the huge fireplace on oversized pillows from India and eat handfuls of popcorn and just enjoyed being together.

"Glenda," her Dad expounded on one of those Saturdays, "...the circumstances that we are fortunate to have are not a part of everyone's life. But I especially want you to never forget is that you have a choice to determine for destiny. With that choice, we can't always escape circumstances but we can handle the outcome of the circumstances. If you're faced with an obstacle, examine all the ways to go over under or around it. You are a treasured part of the destiny of your Mom and me. That was the Saturday Glenda learned she was adopted. She was adopted but loved more than Joy was loved by Jasper...her natural father.

The inhabitants of South Fourth Street became embedded in dreams and images of the last two days but...all dreamed of TJ.

FINALLY REVEALED

There wasn't the usual Sunday morning hubbub of preparation as was normally the case because it was the first time in twenty-five years, church service was canceled. Prayer groups were organized by the W.B.F.C. and the Tazell home held their services in the diningroom. Much was acknowledged and thankfulness was expressed by all present and the church meeting ended.

Joy sat next to Glenda on the glider. Her eyes were swollen from crying. She'd emptied her heart of every detail of the hurts, fears, and Jasper's actions at 572 Pinebrook Road in New Jersey. She told of the cruelty dealt to her and her Mom.

Eva was seething. Pervis was infuriated. Joy was relieved. Glenda was glad.

JASPER'S FINAL CONFLICT

The highlight of the month for Jamaal, Glenda and Joy was the July 4th State Fair. Jamaal won a five foot teddy bear by toppling three sets of miniature bowling pins with a baseball. He gave his winnings to Joy.

Since the cavern adventure, the tree companions rode on TJ's wagon whenever he showed up for a chore or to give a helping hand. They had become the envy of neighborhood youth. The curiosity about TJ grew each time they'd get a glimpse of Suffolk's new hero… and legend.

It was Tuesday and the day was hot and balmy. The hikers and TJ were returning from one of their many hay rides when Joy saw it first. Parked in front of the yard gate was the green Mercury. TJ noticed Joy's reaction at the sight of the vehicle.

"Don't panic Joy," Glenda said reassuringly.

The girls climbed off the wagon then TJ turned the wagon around a few yards from Jasper's car. Jamaal remained seated next to TJ but both looked back over their shoulders observing intensely. Joy and Glenda walked towards the front porch stairs.

"Hold my hand Glenda," Joy said. She was trembling something awful but was confident that her grandparents could handle the situation.

"Remember…you haven't done anything wrong…and you're not alone in this," Glenda assured. They opened the porch screen door and could hear angered voices from the kitchen. They waited on the glider. "Listen carefully, Joy. There's something else I have to tell you and now is the time."

"What Glenda?"

"The day after you told our grandparents about the trouble with Jasper, I talked with my parents and explained the whole story to them. Guess what happened?"

"What Glenda?"

"After I told my parents about you, they said Granny and Granddaddy had already contacted them about the matter and then I overheard part of their conversation."

"What did they say?"

"I heard Granny tell Mom to calm down. She was obviously upset. I also heard Granny ask my Dad to look into this mess legally. I know for sure Dad is going to have his whole office working on this immediately."

"Gosh Glenda, it looks like I've really started something."

"All you've started was exposing the truth about some ugly facts. Had she lived, would your Mom have done differently?"

"I guess you're right, Glenda. I hope something can be done before school starts because I don't want to go back to New Jersey. Do you think Granny and Granddaddy have told Jasper everything I said about the sexual thing?"

"I don't think so Joy because some of those facts are a trump card and our grandparents don't want to let Jasper know what will come next. That's what the telephone call to Mom and Dad was all about. Knowing my Dad the way I do, he wants to keep certain bits of information secret so he has time to prepare a big legal surprise for Jasper."

The glider was motionless as the girls strained to hear the conversation in the kitchen. Then…Joy recognized familiar footsteps stomping down the hall and her heart raced. Eva and Pervis followed close behind.

"Well…there's my little darling," Jasper said with pretended surprise. "…and who's your pretty little friend?"

"That's Aunt Barbara and Uncle Henry's daughter…Glenda," Eva said, obviously irritated.

"Really because I thought Barbara couldn't have any kids since that accident she had when she was bar hopping with Arvis," Jasper said with his tactless arrogance.

"I already know about my adoption and am proud to have the parents I do. For you're information and to keep the facts straight, the next time you make reference that Aunt Arvis and my Mom were 'bar hopping', know that intelligent people don't socialize like that…like you do," Glenda said.

Glenda's answer was like a punch in the mouth. Jasper's face twisted with anger. He didn't like the idea of a twelve year old putting him in his place and making him look like a fool but he had better sense than to meddle with anything that belonged to Barbara. He still had the scar on his neck to prove it.

"You're Daddy has something to tell you, Joy," Pervis said. "It sees he didn't want to let us know until he saw you first."

"Yea well…you see…er…I'm afraid I going to have to cut your vacation short. You see…you're going to have a new Mom. Isn't that great? She doesn't live far from here so I decided to drive down and tell you about it. She and I haven't set the date yet. You've never met her before but she's good people."

The tension on the front porch was explosive after Jasper made his awkward announcement. Eva rose from her rocker like a cobra preparing to strike. Pervis was standing too.

"So this is the something you had to tell our granddaughter and couldn't tell me and Eva in the kitchen. You're a mean vicious man," Pervis said.

Eva's eyes narrowed and her lips drew tight. She ordered her grandchildren off the porch. The cousins obeyed without hesitation. They had never seemed their grandmother so angry before. Joy and Glenda made a beeline outside and sat on the bench under the magnolia tree but could still hear the verbal thrashing Jasper was getting from Eva and Pervis. At last, they saw Jasper jerk open the car door and shake his fist at Eva and Pervis.

"You better have her little butt ready to go when I come back in August or the both of you will regret it," Jasper snarled. He drove off so fast that his car tires spun and pebbles flew in all directions and hit the porch door. The nightmare had gone…for a while.

Pervis and Eva walked back to the kitchen and sat silently at the table for a long time. Joy lay on her back on the picnic bench while Glenda was on her hand and knees on the lawn searching for four-leaf cloves. Joy stared up through the lush green leaves of the magnolia tree. Her thoughts drifted back to one special night in New Jersey. She remembered her Mom being uneasy one evening and was pondering many things. Joy hoped one of them was to divorce Jasper. She'd been crying and there was a distance look in her eye. Arvis wanted to take a

GRANNY'S PLACE

walk and get away from the cramped apartment and Joy went with her too. Jasper was somewhere at a card party with some of his buddies.

This wonderful person wasn't just a mother but she was Joy's best friends too. Joy knew Jasper was always the source of her Mom's misery and often wondered how such a loving being could put up with so much confusion.

The two walked through the apartment complex silently and hand in hand. Joy perceived her Mom was waiting for something that she knew was going to happen. They continued to walk along the curving sidewalks lined with desolate looking apartment buildings. The night sky was vast and laden with stars glimmering like rhinestones. Joy looked up at the sky and imagined what it would be like to be able to jump from star to star never stopping and never getting tired. Suddenly her Mom stopped walking. She pointed breathlessly towards the sky as if discovering a treasure. Arvis pointed to the Big Dipper and then panned her finger across the night sky until she pointed to the Little Dipper. Joy squeezed her mother's hand tightly and hung onto every word of the explanation about the starry lesson. It was one of those rare moments she was able to share with her Mom without Jasper breathing verbal poisoning down their necks.

"Joy! Glenda!" Eva called, motion to her granddaughters to come into the kitchen. The cousins immediately responded, washed their hands and took a seat at the kitchen table. Eva sighed deeply but didn't say anything until she finished pouring a glass of cranberry juice for the girls, herself and ice tea for Pervis. Then she began to speak.

"First of all Joy, Pervis and I never mentioned anything to Jasper about his wicked deeds towards you. You're granddaddy and I want to save that ammunition for a later date but one thing we want you to know for sure is come hell-or-high-water, you'll never, ever have to neither live with Jasper and his demonic women nor attend that ridiculous wedding he mentioned on the porch. All Pervis and I want you to be concerned about is enjoying the rest of your summer and look forward to attending East Suffolk High School in September."

"…and," Pervis added. "We want you to completely trust us and know everything will work out okay. Do you have any questions to ask me or your grandmother?"

"Yes Granddaddy," Joy replied. "Granny, will you…"

"Will I what, honey?" Eva said.

"...braid my hair again for the first day of school."

"Oh my little Sweetmeat," Eva replied, as she hugged the only living remembrance of Arvis.

"I tell you what," Pervis said. "Why don't the two of you take a stroll to Mr. Percy's Ice Cream Polar? Just watch out for the traffic." He reached into his jacket pocket and handed each of his granddaughters a five dollar bill.

Eva stood on the front porch watching the girls skip up South Fourth Street until they disappeared from sight. Once again the remembrance of that wintry New Year's night exploded in the recesses of her mind.

MR. PERCY'S PLACE

Mr. Percy's Ice Cream Polar was the last original shop on the block. It had not changed much in the twenty years it had been there. Mr. Percy adamantly fought City Council when the plan was to upgrade stores and other businesses to attract new customers. The quaint old time shop was located in an ideal spot at the corner of Suffolk's busiest intersection. The town council wanted to buy his property but Mr. Percy fought them tooth and nail. He had the ideal spot and even more people and tourists patronized his shop after all the publicity with the council. He was a shrewd businessman and could not be budged.

Mr. Percy was a dark-skinned, round-faced man who had just enough silky hair to eliminate him from the completely bald category. His white, starched, spotless apron and a cigar stub clinched between his shining white teeth were his trademarks. Standing five feet and eight inches tall, he had a strong booming voice that cheerfully greeted customer. A framed dollar bill representing Mr. Percy's first sale hung on the wall behind an old fashioned cash register. The gold, ivory and wooden cash register sat under wall-length shelves lined with antique soda glasses. Eight sets of burgundy leather, high-backed bench seats with a chrome pedestal table in between and chrome and red top table lined the wall. A small chrome rack held napkins, straws and a laminated menu of meals, drinks and ice cream sat on each table. On the wall above the tables hung autographed glossy, black and white photos The Nicholas Brothers, Dorothy Dandridge, The Drifters, The Platters, Bill "Bojangles" Robinson, and many other noted stars and singers. The floor was an immaculately clean black and white linoleum tiled floor. Chrome and red and yellow was the color of the jukebox lent the final touch to the décor of the polar. The nostalgic, air conditioned setting, with its half-the-wall picture windows was a blessed relief from the blazing sun. Joy and Glenda were the first customers of the day. They slurped their strawberry sundaes and chatted about nothing.

"How're Mr. Pervis and Miss Eva doing these days?" Mr. Percy asked.

"Just fine, Joy replied. "These sundaes are delicious, Mr. Percy."

"Thank you, baby and how about I fix y'all a double dip of strawberry ice cream with lots of chocolate syrup and a cherry on top for your second sundae on the house?"

"Oh Mr. Percy, That would be great! Oh excuse me, but I haven't introduced you to my cousin, Glenda Marie Johnson. She's visiting Granny and Granddaddy for summer vacation too."

"Nice to make your acquaintance, Miss Glenda," Mr. Percy said.

"I'm pleased to meet you too, Mr. Percy. You have a wonderful place here."

"Well thank you, Miss Glenda. I'm going to fix those sundaes for y'all so I'll see you in a bit, okay?"

"All right," the girls said in unison.

"I'll take care of the first order, Mr. Percy."

"Jamaal," Joy said almost shouting. "What a terrific surprise."

"Hi Jamaal, won't you join us?" Glenda said.

"Don't mind if I do, Glenda."

"Thanks for paying for our orders, Jamaal," Joy said, grinning from ear to ear.

Jamaal sat next to Joy…and Glenda snickered.

THE PLAN UNFOLDS

Pervis decided to ride with Harvey and deliver sharpened saw to a few of his costumers. He also took the opportunity to tell Harvey about the situation with Joy and the run-in he and Eva had with Jasper. Harvey was incensed. It took a lot to anger him but when he listened to the hateful and demonic things done; he imagined his hands around Jasper's throat. The two rode in silence until Pervis had finished his deliveries.

"Let's stop for a bite to eat. I don't think Eva feels like being in the kitchen tonight anyway," Pervis suggested.

"That sounds fine to me, Harvey."

A week had pasted since that diabolical visit from Jasper and Eva needed to keep herself busy to keep from thinking about it. She decided to busy herself by hanging a load of freshly laundered curtains. She also wanted to occupy herself until Pervis got home. Just as she finished hanging a third set of curtains, the telephone rang. Rushing into the house, Eva threw the clothes basket on top of the back porch freezer and rushed to answer the phone.

"Hello…Henry? Thank goodness you found the time to answer. I was just thinking about you. Now you know Glenda's just fine and she's even lost fifteen pounds too. You and Barbara won't recognize her when you see her again. She and Joy are at Mr. Percy's right now. They've gotten as close as two peas in a pod. What's that? You did? They've been filed already? That ought to set Jasper back a few notches. Yes Henry, under no circumstances will Pervis and I let Joy out of our sight after today. Yes, I'll speak to Barbara now. Hi, honey! Yes and she's having a wonderful time too. Yes, she knows about Joy's situation and let me assure you that you have nothing to worry about because she's a little steam roller just like you. Sure baby, I'll tell her I talked with you and Henry and I love you too. Bye now!"

GRANNY'S PLACE

Feeling refreshed in her spirit, Eva carried the laundry basket back to the clothes line and finished hanging the curtains. "So far so good," she said to herself. Jasper is finally going to get of his comeuppins."

She thought of the contents of Arvis' last letter written to her and Pervis during Arvis' last stay in the hospital. Yes…it was time to take action to address what Arvis had written and she also stated in the letter that Joy was the only one able to start what Henry had put into action with the courts. Arvis knew she could count on Joy's inherent strength. Arvis knew well of Jasper's warped dealings and corrupt behavior. Because she was aware of her own physical demise, she knew Joy would have to complete the process of setting things straight.

Pervis and Eva never approved of Jasper's involvement with their daughter from the beginning. He was sneaky and cunning and won Arvis with manipulative charm and empty promises. When told of Arvis' impending marriage to him, they strongly suspected their daughter would have a life of misery. They couldn't understand how a knowledgeable girl could agree to marry a low-life like Jasper.

One Sunday, Dr. Diggs was a dinner guest of Eva and Pervis. He respected the confidentiality of his patients but this one time he knew he couldn't keep the test results private and told the results of Arvis recent examination. Pervis was fit to be tied not because of the circumstances but because…it was Jasper Bailey who had done the deed. Jasper's lustful demands and can't wait attitude led to a hasty wedding in a clerks' office. The marriage ceremony was more like a reading of last rights instead of nuptials being exchanged. Arvis insisted on the marriage to uphold the family honor.

Eva went into hysterics and Barbara was appalled because Arvis had only a semester left before graduation from college but couldn't attend classes because it would be obvious to all that she was in the motherly way. Barbara tried desperately to convince her sister that marriage didn't have to be the only solution to her dilemma. Eva and Pervis even agreed to raise the child while Arvis completed her studies. As usual, Jasper used his poisonous venom on Arvis' mind and gloated over the fact that he'd tainted someone from the other side of the tracks. But now Jasper was going to answer for all the misery he'd caused his wife and child.

UPTOWN

The Broadway Theater was just a few blocks from Mr. Percy's Ice Cream Polar.

"Let's see what movie is scheduled to play," Joy said while looking up and down the street for traffic.

"I think a horror flick is playing now," Jamaal said.

"Ugh...what a waste of time," Glenda said.

"I like horror films," Joy said as they crossed the street. "I remember watching my first horror film. It was a day when Mom wasn't feeling to good and asked me if I'd mind spending the day with her...like she had to ask. Anyway, she sewed and I watched the Million Dollar Movie. They were featuring the movie 'King Kong' starring Faye Ray. Boy, was that a movie."

"Yep, I saw that one too," Jamaal said, walking in the middle of his friends.

"What's a 'King Kong'?" Glenda asked. All walking ceased and Glenda became the center of attention. Without warning, Joy and Jamaal starting laughing so hard they had to hold their ribs. They looked like two drunks on a Saturday night.

"Glenda...you're a real piece of work," Jamaal finally managed to say.

"All right smarty-pants. So I don't know about 'King Kong' but have you seen the movie 'Autumn Leaves' starring Joan Crawford?"

"Yep, every fall," Jamaal said joked.

"I've never heard of the movie either, Glenda," Joy said. That's not fair. You probably made up the title and everything."

"I did not. I would never profane Joan Crawford like that," Glenda protested. "The next time you see your Dad Jamaal, ask him is there a movie called 'Autumn Leaves'."

"Aw, never mind all that. Let's just see what's playing at the theater and change the conversation," Jamaal said.

The trio resumed talking about this and that and was finally in front of the movie marquee showing the film of the day. The movie to be shown was called 'Pinky'.

"That looks interesting. It takes a lot of nerve to make a movie like that nowadays."

"Why do you say that, Glenda," Joy asked. "I saw the movie."

"It must cause a lot of problems for a person to be of one race and look like another race. What was it about?"

"It was about this girl who was black but she was so light-skinned she could pass for white. Her nickname was 'Pinky'. She wanted to study to be a nurse so she used her skin color to get into a good nursing school up north. Her black grandmother, played by Ethel Waters, washed clothes for whites to have the money needed to send to Pinky. Pinky and a white doctor fell in love and he had no idea of her real race. She finished nursing school and came home. Her first private duty nursing assignment was to a rich, sickly old white woman played by Ethel Barrymore. Secretly, the sickly woman willed all she owned to Pinky and refused to leave anything to a hateful relative who accused Pinky of killing the old woman. Pinky went through much attending to this woman. When the woman died, she was put on trial. To make a long story short, Pinky won the case, turned the mansion the old woman willed to her into a school to train black girls to be nurses. The doctor that fell for her left the scene when he found out her real race. The entire movie was a tear-jerker but almost all the white theaters refused to play the film. I'm glad I saw it because I'll never forget it as long as I live," Joy said.

Joy and Jamaal looked at each other again. This time they were just smiled. Glenda didn't realize that she was a perfect example of 'Pinky'. The companions decided it was time to go home.

"It's too hot to walk all the way back home so let's catch a bus. We may have to ride around town as the driver makes his stops but at least we'll be out of this heat," Jamaal said.

They walked back to the corner of Main Street and caught a bus just as it came to the stop. The driver wound through neighborhoods and side roads. Glenda was real excited because the ride gave her a chance to see the city. The bus parked in front of the Planter's Peanut Factory for fifteen minutes to give all who worked the morning shift a way to get home. Strategically placed fans cooled the bus since the driver turned off the motor.

The wait over, the bus filled to capacity and began its route again. It was a relaxing ride but Jamaal and the girls got off on South Third Street with some other passengers and walked the rest of the way home. It'd gotten so hot until the blacktop on the streets began to melt in spots.

"As they were about to open the gate of the South Fourth Street yard, Jamaal asked, "You guys in for another adventure tomorrow?"

"What'd you have in mind, Jamaal," Joy said.

"I thought a day of exploring old graves in Jericho Cemetery would be nice."

"That sounds great Jamaal because I always wanted to go back to that place. It's awesome," Joy said.

"Maybe I missed something but what would we do in a cemetery?" Glenda asked.

"Well for one thing Miss Brains," Joy began. "…there's a section of the cemetery where the tombstones date back before the Civil War. I think I'll be real educational for us," Joy said.

"Now the fact that it can be an education outing makes all the difference. I like historical discoveries, Joy," Glenda said.

"I'll have the chance to do some charcoal rubbings for my poster collection and hang them on my bedroom wall."

"You can think of the goofiest things Joy," Jamaal said.

"Okay Mr. Know-it-all. What were you intending to do at the cemetery?"

"Bones," Jamaal said stretching his arms Frankenstein style.

"E-e-e-u-u-u," Joy and Glenda shrieked. "That's sick!"

"Let's get there by nine o'clock to beat the morning heat," Jamaal said. I'll be here by eight o'clock sharp so be ready," Jamaal yelled as he turned off South Fourth Street midway to take his short cut home.

"Joy have you ever wondered when Jamaal will figure out that we're not 'guys'?

"Glenda you crack me up. Let's see what Granny's doing."

"Granny," Joy yelled as she and Glenda entered the front porch. "We're back! Ugh! What's that smell?"

"Hush Joy. Granny is on the livingroom sofa taking a nap."

"The smell must be from this stuff," Joy said, looking at the glass jar. It looks like she rubbed it on her knee before she went to sleep. Rain must be near again if it's had this effect on her knee."

The telephone rang and Joy rushed to answer it. Glenda covered Eva's shoulders with the thin shawl that had fallen off.

"Hello Granddaddy," Joy answered. Yes, Granny is asleep in the livingroom. Okay, I'll give her the message as soon as she wakes up."

"Who was that on the phone, Joy?" Glenda asked.

"It was Granddaddy and he wants me to let Granny know he and Harvey are finished their errands and will be home shortly."

"Let's sit on the porch until Granny wakes up, Joy."

"Okay." Glenda sprawled out on the glider while Joy sat in her grandmother's 'throne'.

"Glenda, do your parents ever argue about anything?"

"That's an odd question to ask but I have no problem giving you an answer. Sure my parents argue about lots of things. I call it a strong disagreement."

"When they do, does it upset or confuse you?"

"Sometimes it does but usually their arguments end with an evening on the town or at one of their favorite restaurants. My reward is getting permission to stay up and watch TV for as long as I want. Why do you ask?"

"I was thinking about an argument between Mom and Dad one night. I think I was about seven years old. Mom wasn't feeling well and Dad had come home late that night. She was angry with him because he'd broken his promise to her about staying out so late. Mom came into my bedroom to wake me up but I was sleep. I finally woke up anyway and we talked for a bit. She got herself together and went back downstairs and that's when I heard two women's voices.

I recognized Mom and Dad's voices but the third one...I didn't. I tipped to the top of the stairs so I could hear more clearly. Mom was shouting and telling the other woman to get out of her house. Dad was laughing and reminding Mom who paid the rent and she had no right to tell him what to do. After the woman left, Mom asked Dad why he treated her so bad. Dad said coldly and arrogantly that she was a 'catch' from across the tracks and referred to me as a job well done. Next I heard a loud slap and I didn't see it but I knew he'd hit Mom. He was always slapping her around. He even hit her with a leather belt across her back the day after she'd come home from the hospital. Mom was cleaning fish at the kitchen sink when he hit her. With my own eyes, I saw her slide down the front of the sink to the floor in such pain. My pain was not being able to help her."

"I hate to say this Joy but your Dad is not only mean but he's psychotic," Glenda replied.

"I'm going to tell Granny about this one because I'm not one going to hold back one thing from her and Granddaddy."

"If Dad every did something like that to Mom, he wouldn't have hands left to carry his briefcase," Glenda said, trying to lighten the conversation for Joy.

"Every time Dad did something mean to Mom, she have to go to the hospital. The whole mess was interfering with her health."

"Your Dad was a real trip, Joy."

"Yeah and I wish he'd take a permanent trip to another planet. The one good thing that came out of that bad time was catching the train for Suffolk and finishing the school year here. I was so-o-o-o happy."

Glenda and Joy didn't know it but Eva heard every word of their conversation through the open livingroom porch windows. "Now it all makes sense," Eva said to herself. "That's why Arvis wanted to come home so bad. It wasn't because Jasper had field duty and manuvering exercises with the army base."

During her stay at home, she was able to get her self esteem together and address her weakening health. Even though he'd retired, Dr. Diggs was available at any time to complete physical examination free of charge. The best medicine for Mom was the support she got from Aunt Barbara. Her health improved and her million-dollar smile became an everyday thing. She went back to school, finished completing courses for her degree, enjoyed any extra time she had with her daughter and successfully obtained a position as a music teacher.

Jasper's ego was deflated all over Suffolk by his wife's new independence and professional position especially since he cheated his way out of high school. Arvis enjoyed the anticipation of being in the classroom but tragedy struck once again. The summer before beginning her new teaching assignment, medical complications began to plague her

GRANNY'S PLACE

life. Intensive physical examinations at Walter Reed Hospital, led by Dr. Diggs, indicated that her kidneys were failing to function properly. In two weeks, they ceased to function completely. Dr. Diggs, Eva and Pervis, and a host of friends of the family were devastated by the news. Arvis knew she had only weeks to get her affairs in order. She wrote her parents a letter and one to Joy. They were to be opened after her death. Eva's thoughts were interrupted by Pervis' arrival home.

"Hi, Granddaddy," the girls said, jumping up and down.

"Hello there Sweetmeat and Peaches, how's everything going?"

"Fine Granddaddy but keep your voice down because Granny is asleep on the couch," Glenda said.

"No I'm not y'all," Eva said sitting up on the couch. "Come here you two and let me give you a hug for watching over the house while I slept."

Returning to the porch with Joy, Glenda said, "That was strange."

"What's so strange about a hug from Granny?" Joy said.

"Do you suppose she heard what we were saying?"

"Gosh Glenda, I hope not. She and Granddaddy have a lot to deal with already."

For privacy, Eva went into the kitchen with Pervis. "Henry and Barbara called while you were out, Pervis."

"What'd Henry have to say?" Pervis asked.

"Henry told me that all the necessary papers we needed for court were filed and that everything will work out in Joy's behalf just fine."

"That's real good news, Eva."

"But...there's something else you should know. I overheard Joy and Glenda talking on the porch. They thought I was sleep. Eva told him all that she'd heard that the grands talked about. Pervis listen to his wife's words and tried not to let his anger show.

"Eva do you know what this means?"

"No, what does it mean?"

"It means that Jasper is a murderer."

"Pervis, what do you mean?"

"The fiend systematically and deliberately killed our daughter."

"My Lord, Pervis." Eva wiped her eyes with the corner of her apron.

THE LETTER

The girls finished taking their bubble baths and when they had finished, raced down to the kitchen to help Eva set up TV trays on the front porch. The evening air was thick and heavy. Eva's knee was still aching so cooking at the oven was out and cold turkey sandwiches laden with tomatoes, lettuce, onions and mayonnaise, a big bowl of potato chips, watermelon rind pickles, fruit cocktail and a tall glass of ice tea was diner for the evening. Even though dinner had switched locations, grace was said as usual.

"By the by Glenda, I spoke with your parents early this morning while you were asleep. They send all their love. He said your writing him the letter explaining the goings on here was a very brave thing to do," Eva said.

"I just wanted to make sure Joy got the best of everything from this, Granny," Glenda answered.

"Joy, I have a letter addressed to you too."

"You do, Granny?"

"Yes and its written to you by your Mama."

Joy gently took the letter from Eva's hand. "It's time for you to read it and I want you to take your time to reading it in the privacy of your bedroom tonight. It was sealed by her and stayed sealed until it was time to give it to you."

Joy said nothing but returned to the glider as if she were walking in her sleep. Glenda chattered on about their graveyard adventure with Jamaal.

"I declare, Jamaal can come up with the strangest ideas," Pervis said.

"I'm surprised you three haven't had enough prowling around after the cave hike," Eva said. "No more about cave exploring. What time will y'all be starting out on your Jericho Cemetery trip, Glenda?"

"Jamaal said he'd be here to meet us at eight o'clock in the morning."

"Well", Eva began. "...you two will no doubt have a full day tomorrow and since you'll need to get up early in the morning hurry and finish eating. You know the saying...'early to bed, early to rise'..."

"Okay Granny," Glenda said. Joy hadn't touched the food but was just sitting on the glider staring at the letter in her hands. Glenda ate her dinner and after making sure no crumbs we spilled on the porch floor she got up and kissed her grandparents goodnight. Joy mindlessly followed without eating a bit of food. Eva and Pervis understood.

Eva and Pervis sat quietly on the porch listening to the sings of night but there was a particular kind of quietness as if nature had succumbed to a deep sleep. Far in the distance, harmonica music drifted across the tree tops as if to deliver a reassuring message. Eva smiled and Pervis nodded his head and patted his foot in time with the tranquilizing melody. Something was going to change.

Joy tiptoed into Glenda's bedroom. She wanted to share her letter with Glenda.

"But Joy," Glenda said, "Granny wanted you to read this letter privately."

"I know she did, Glenda but I think Mom would be delighted if you read what she'd written." Slowly closing the door, they huddled together in Glenda's bed, unfolded the letter and Joy began to read outloud.

My Dearest Daughter,

I'm so sorry I can't be with you now. I don't understand why I had to leave you at this time...the most important time of your life. But...if we knew all the right answers to everything, life would be dull and uneventful.

I want you to be brave. I want you to remember only the wonderful moments we shared. Remember the day you stayed home from school and I spent time sewing a dress for you while you watched the Million Dollar Movie? How about the time I dressed you up and let you spend your entire day with Mrs. McQueen, the only black woman who worked at an advertising agency. She lived neighbor across the street from us...remember? I'll bet you didn't know she was the first Black woman to be promoted to vice-president of a major advertising company. Do you still have that one hundred and fifty piece color pencil set she gave you to bring home? You didn't know it then but Mrs. McQueen told me that you were a very tal-

ented artist and that you should pursue your gift. Of course, I already knew of your talent…smile.

With the support of your grandparents, Uncle Henry and Aunt Barbara, you'll grow into a refined, educated young lady so listen to them because they want only the best for you. You must study hard and learn as much as you can but most importantly learn to listen well to two of the wisest people I've ever known…Eva and Pervis Tazell…my parents.

Darling (Sweetmeat as your grandfather calls you); you've seen and heard your father do many cruel and hurtful things. You have suffered much because of his selfish recklessness. You have every right to feel a certain way about him the way I know you do. Sweetmeat, his hatred and frustrations are his and his alone. Let him carry his burdens of guilt alone. Don't harbor any of his hate or you'll live a life as miserable as his.

Now I'm going to ask you to do something that will seem awfully hard. Joy, you MUST forgive your Dad. Forgive give him not only for his sake but for your sake too. Understand me fully, I don't mean you should tolerate any of his acts of wickedness at all! When you forgive someone of the hurts they have caused you, you will experience a freedom deep within your soul. Your Dad doesn't realize it now but he has to give an account for all he's done…and he will. Granddaddy always says, 'God is not mocked, you will reap what you sow'. I have no doubt that my mother told you the story of Rufus Williams and his brother. She told Barbara and me the same story too…smiles again!

I wrote this letter to you because I desperately want you to sow good seeds all your life so nothing but good will come back to you.

Be strong, hold your head high and walk with integrity and without fear. God's strength and love will enable you to rise above any obstacle or challenge.

Finally, I want you to know that you have always been and will always be the precious gift that has brightened my life every day. I only wish I could be with you when you grow up. Know that I'll always love you. Until we meet again…all my love.

Mommy

Joy sat very still and didn't move one muscle. She held her Mother's letter to her heart. She felt changed inside. Everything around her seemed illuminated and time seemed to stand still as she rehearsed the words in the letter over and over in her mind. *"You must forgive!"* The words continued to ring in her head. Joy realized now that her Mom had the strength of character not touched by human hands or broken by the circumstances that surrounded her life. Glenda was awestruck and knew she lost a very special aunt. No words were exchanged between the cousins and none were necessary. Silently, Joy hugged Glenda, went into her bedroom and tucked the letter under her pillow. She blew a kiss towards the photo of her Mom, turned her lamp and slipped into a deep peaceful sleep.

THE FISHING TRIP

A comforting gentle breeze whistled through the screened porch and chased away the heavy mugginess of the night. A full moon was shining and its brightness lit up the side yard. The driveway stones that made a path next to the house sparkled like baubles. Silhouetted trees resembled giant feather dusters as they swayed back and forth in the night air. Lightening bugs kept their posts around the azalea blossoms that hugged the front steps.

"Eva, what do you think about TJ?"

"He seems harmless enough to me, Pervis."

"No, I mean what immediately comes to your mind when you think of him?"

Eva pondered over the question for a moment before answering. "Pervis, I actually think TJ is just a kind old man who can be trusted but…"

"…but what, Eva?"

"Well…there's a feeling that I get deep down in my bones that he's not an ordinary kind of fellow."

"I'd say that was putting it mildly. I can't get out of my mind what Frank, Charlie and I found out about the man."

"Charlie knows TJ too? You never told me that, Pervis."

"Well there's something I've got to tell you now. I didn't before because Luke Genie made me promise not to worry my family but since he's dead now, I don't think he'll mind."

"What on earth did Luke make you promise, Pervis?"

"Remember when Frank, Charlie and I took a fishing trip to try out Frank's new boat last year? Charlie is Frank's half brother."

"Yes Pervis, I remember."

"You know that Charlie always tries to outdo Frank in everything. He's a nice guy but has a drawback of wanting to be number one. Anyway he drove down from Rhode Island just to show off his new red

Ford truck just because he'd heard Frank had bought a boat. If he heard that Frank bought something new, Charlie did the same."

"You're right, Pervis. I remember him well now that you said that. I remember him as being rather obnoxious too."

"That's right, Eva. To get started, Charlie hitched Frank's boat to the back of his truck and we were off on a Friday morning. As we drove to the Dismal Swamp Lake Charlie decided to ignore Frank's directions and took a short cut he said remembered from years ago. The short cut turned out to be a pothole filled dirt road. Charlie laughingly claimed the road condition was no match for his new truck and continued driving with Frank and me bumping up and down like jumping jacks. The woods got so thick that Charlie couldn't see so he turned on his headlights. Frank fussed with Charlie trying to convince him to turn around but Charlie refused saying his truck could take the beating and we were going in the right direction. The only thing he agreed with was to slow down. Frank looked behind us to see if the boat was still attached to the truck. Suddenly, we caught sight of an odd looking light that was huge and silhouetted the surrounding trees. Charlie inched the truck about fifty yards closer and turned off the headlights but left the truck motor running. We quietly got out of the truck to get a better look. We crept closer and closer in tall wild grass."

"Wait a minute, Pervis. Wasn't that the same road the children found when they went on that cave adventure and got caught in that awful storm and all?"

"Yep, that was the same one, Eva. Like I was saying, we inched along towards the direction of the light for a clearer view and dropped to our knees for better cover."

"I bet you three were a sight for sore eyes," Eva chuckled.

"We were scared to death too. Crawling as close as we dared, we peeped through the grass and saw the light but couldn't see what it was coming from. It looked like a full moon had fallen to earth and stopped a few feet just before it hit the ground. Then the light began to throb like it was breathing heavy or had a heartbeat. We wanted to run away but we were so frozen with terror that we couldn't move. Then the light exploded but didn't make a sound. All around us and overhead were smaller discs that floated quietly around like giant fireflies. Our eyes bulging, we watched as each light disk floated away high in the sky until they all disappeared. I have to admit, Eva it was the darndest thing I'd seen in my life. Frank was mumbling the Lord's Prayer and Charlie held his hand over his mouth to keep from letting a holler escape. A wind began to blow but increased to the strength of a gale. Charlie's derby hat flew off his head. Frank and I were still on our knees holding each other. Then as suddenly as the wind started…it stopped."

"Pervis, what you're telling me sounds like something out of Glenda fairytale book."

"Eva, I tell you it was as real as you and me sitting on this front porch."

"Pervis, you sure have my attention so what happened next?"

"We calmed down a bit but kept watching the odd sight. Only one sparkling discs remained. It started to spin faster and faster and faster. As it spun, the disc got wider and wider and at the same time it changed shape. Eva, it changed into the figure of a man!"

"Come on now, Pervis. You've got to be pulling my leg this time. You've told some tall tales before but this one takes the cake."

"Eva, this is not one of those tales and I'm not making up one word. Let me tell you what else happened and then you'll believe me."

"Go on, Pervis and let's hear the rest."

"This figure completed its formation and began walking towards us. Charlie lost it completely and repented of even burning his frying pan and anything else he'd done wrong."

"Thank goodness for repentance, Pervis."

"Now hold on to your seat because the rest of what I'm about to say confirms what I've long suspected."

"Go on Pervis, go on," Eva said excitedly.

"A spiritual tune began to play. It was played on…a harmonica."

"Are you trying to tell me that…that…,"

"Yes Eva, that powerful, wonderful, fantastic figure the three of us saw was …TJ! I've always strongly suspected something was different about the man. I suspected him every since the day he came into our yard and unloaded that lumber for me from his wagon."

Eva couldn't move a muscle. It was too much to take in but from the look on her husband's face, she knew he was extremely serious about everything he'd said.

"When did you know him before that?" Eva asked, now ignoring the ache in her knee.

"You remember, Eva. The first time we met him was that night we first met Harvey. I somehow knew the youngsters would be safe in that storm too."

"Why did you keep all this to yourself, Pervis?" Eva said. "You've never done that before."

"I didn't say anything before this because I'd promised TJ to handle everything."

"No matter Pervis, I know you're a man of your word but the main thing is that it was TJ. What happened to Charlie and Frank that night?"

"TJ stood right in front of Charlie who was still babbling like a baby and repenting. Frank and I gasped as TJ touched Charlie's shoulder. We watched intensely as Charlie began to slowly raise his bowed head and looked at TJ in his eyes. With tears running down his face, he smiled and stood to his feet. An extraordinary peace came over the man and his face looked tender and innocent. Charlie kept nodding his head as the two had a conversation about something. Then TJ moved towards Frank but didn't touch him. Curiously, TJ had a look of sadness on his face and placed his hand on his chest as if he were in pain."

"Oh Pervis," Eva almost shouted. "Frank died suddenly of a heart attack while living with that woman from across the tracks."

"Yes Eva, I know but Charlie is a missionary living in Guyana, South America. In fact we got mail from him only the other day."

"Pervis honey, what did TJ say when he came towards you?" Eva asked.

"TJ folded his arms and rocked from side to side as if pretending to cuddle a baby. His lips never moved but I heard his words in my mind. *She was heaven's gain but there is one still to remain and that I'd have to fight for her to erase the pain. Don't fret or dismay for a servant of the Lord will be present when the debt is paid.*"

Eva was mesmerized. She and Pervis stood, walked towards each other and embraced for a long moment. Tears flowed down her cheeks because both knew TJ was referring to Arvis' presence before the Lord and that Joy will have other hardships.

"Let's call it a night and sleep now, honey," Pervis said softly. He made sure all the doors were locked as he'd done so many times before. Once upstairs, the grandparents tipped into Glenda's bedroom, kissed her and then into Joy's bedroom and kissed her too.

"Once in their bed Eva asked Pervis, "What will happen to Jasper?"

"I don't know, Eva but even as mean and evil as the man is…I hope he repents one day."

"Jasper's final fate is in his own hands," Eva said.

"Yes you're right Eva, and whatever is in Jasper's heart will determine his end…or beginning. Let's get some sleep now."

"Lord, have mercies on the man," Eva whispered.

JERICHO CEMETERY

Joy slept like a log. She sat up in bed, sleepily yawned and starched herself awake. She remembered last night and reached under her pillow to make certain she hadn't dreamed. The letter was there. She skimmed through the words again as if savoring a delicious meal and tucked it safely back under her pillow.

The morning air coming through the screened large window was refreshing as if it knew exactly how she felt inside. July flies, red breasted robins and blue jays noisily chirped as if in competition with one another. The scent of fresh mowed grass and brewing coffee flooded her bedroom.

Joy heard her granddaddy's famous double whistling while he went about his tasks in front of his workshop. He'd had more orders to cut up fallen trees left after the storm.

"Nobody can whistle like Granddaddy," Joy said to herself. Then she heard another familiar sound. "Good grief! It's Jamaal!" she said, looking at her Cinderella clock. She jumped out of bed to wake Glenda but Glenda wasn't in her room.

"What's going on here?" Joy wondered.

"BOO!"

"EEK-K-K! You almost scared the socks off me, girl!"

"Good morning to you, cuz. It's nice to see you up and about."

"Why didn't you wake me when you got up, Glenda?"

"Granny told me to let you sleep and told Jamaal that Jericho Cemetery wasn't going anywhere."

"But I thought Jamaal wanted to get an early start."

"Granddaddy said there are plenty of shady trees if we need to stop and rest. Now stop asking so many questions and get dressed. Granny is keeping your french toast warm for you."

"It's a weekday today and Granddaddy didn't go to work," Joy said.

"Oh, he took off a few days. He said he needed the rest. Now will you please get dressed?"

Glenda followed Joy from bedroom to bathroom and back again chattering about the day's graveyard adventure while Joy combed her hair. Brushing it back to make a ponytail, she noticed her hair had grown with the help of Granny's cornrow styles.

"Joy, how did you get that scar on your top lip?"

"Oh that scar. I was about ten when I got it. I was playing kick ball at school during recess. The playground was all asphalt. You know the kind where games are drawn on the surface with white paint. It was my turn to kick and I kicked a homerun for my team. I lunged forward so fast I tripped over my own feet. I fell so fast, I didn't have time to extend my arms to break my fall but instead fell on my face."

"Ouch!" Glenda grimaced at the sheer thought as she visualized the accident.

"Ouch is right but that's not the half of it."

"Why do I get the feeling Jasper is in the picture somewhere?"

"Boy was he. Some of my classmates ran for my teacher, Mrs. Cottcreeve and she came running and took me to the school nurse. My face was a bloody mess and I got some blood all over Mrs. Cottcreeve's blouse. That was the first time I messed up her clothes."

"Huh? Joy, you're losing me."

"Sorry Glenda. Once we got to the nurses' office and the nurse saw me, she immediately called my Dad. The thought of seeing him hurt worse than my face. He hated to be called on his job on the post as head chef unless it was one of his floozies or drunken army buddies."

"Why did they call him? I thought Petula was supposed to be living at your home."

"She was living there for a while because Mom was in the hospital but she and Dad didn't see eye-to-eye on a lot of things so while Dad was at work on base, she left town with some fellow. Dad didn't notify my school about that tidbit of information," Joy said.

"Honestly Joy, your Dad sounds like a character out of Grimes Fairytales. What happed after your school called him on the base?"

"Forty-five minutes later, he showed up at the nurses' office. The nurse was livid about his tardiness and wasn't afraid to show it either.

GRANNY'S PLACE

My eyes were swelling shut. It was obvious I was going to need emergency treatment at a hospital. He gestured for me to follow him."

"What could the man have been thinking? You certainly didn't fall on your face on purpose," Glenda said. "Did he at least take you to the hospital?"

"Nope, he took me straight home and told me to go into the bathroom. He cursed me out the whole time because I caused him to miss time from work and said had I been a boy, I'd be able to handle such a silly thing."

"You've got to be kidding," Glenda said.

"I wish I was, Glenda because I'll never forget it as long as I live."

"Why is that, Joy?"

"Dad reached into the medicine cabinet, soaked some cotton balls with rubbing alcohol and slopped all over my face. I thought I would pass out from the pain. My eyes burned like crazy. How my skin healed without any scaring but this tiny one on top of my lip is a mystery to me."

"I just don't understand how a human being could be so cruel to another human being."

"It would make sense if one was a human being doing the cruelty was human."

"Is this one of the stories you will tell our grandparents?"

"Oh yes Glenda, it's definitely in my notes I've outlined for them."

"What did Aunt Arvis do when she came home from the hospital? She must have seen your face."

"She sure did and she was outraged. She secretly called Dad's Company Commander and told her about the whole matter."

"You said your Mom called the 'Company Commander'. You mean she was a woman too?"

"Yep, the Commander sent Dad a letter let him know he was being docked two weeks pay for leaving before time for dismissal. He never found out Mom had told the Commander everything. They became real friends after but the Commander died of cancer a year later."

"That's too bad but three cheers for Aunt Arvis," Glenda said.

While Joy was telling her tale of woe to Glenda, they hadn't heard Eva putting away an armload of towels and sheets in the hall trunk. With a heavy heart, she tipped back downstairs to the kitchen. The

GRANNY'S PLACE

stress of her grandchild's dilemma was taking its toll but with Pervis home for the next two weeks…she felt more sheltered and confident. "Lord, let this mess come to an end," she prayed silently.

"Hurry and eat your breakfast, Joy. Jamaal has been waiting patiently for a long time. Don't forget your charcoal and paper either," Eva said, handing her the drawing tools. Eva handed them the lunches she'd packed too. Remember…your curfew is before sundown."

All three waved to Eva and were finally on their way to the cemetery. Jamaal lead them through a different shortcut to Eight Street. The houses on this street were huge, monolithic and haunting relics left over from the time of hooped-skirted southern belles and wagons overburdened with bales of cotton. Most of the homes were deserted with a 'For Sale' sign on the front lawn or left in the hands of county tax collectors. With renovation, they would be excellent office buildings but because they were in the "colored section" of town, the City Council dragged its feet. Only a few proud residents still clung to an era that was lost forever. They seemed not to have heard that the South lost in the Civil War. Eighth Street was a dead end but instead of ending with Dismal Swamp, it opened right into the Jericho Cemetery gate.

"We're here." Jamaal said, pushing open the towering iron gates. "It looks like nobody's used this entrance for a while. The other street entrance is used for funerals."

Joy gazed at the morbid gate design of gargoyle images embedded between enormous spike-tipped iron bars. Images of sad-faced angels in the claws of the gargoyles looked upwards to the ecstasy of a heavenly rest seemed frozen in time. English Ivy encircled the angels binding them eternally.

The exploring trio passed through the gates and started walking down a coarse sanded path that was boarded on each side by tall weeping willow trees that were twisted and gnarled by age. The trees looked like antiquated guards who witnessed hundreds of years of pain and sorrow. The path led to grassy hills as far as the eye could see. Countless tombstones, figureheads and decorative mausoleums dotted the massive landscape. Each headstone represented the final journey of men, women and children.

"Oh gosh," Joy said. She was trembling and staring straight ahead.

"What's the matter, Joy? What did you see?" Glenda asked.

GRANNY'S PLACE

"...that big oak tree over there."

"I see it but what about the tree?" Glenda asked.

"It's that same oak tree Granddaddy told me about. It's the tree that boy was hung from long ago. He's even buried somewhere out here."

"What's she mumbling about, Glenda?"

"I don't know, Jamaal. She said something about a boy and an oak tree. Beats me."

"You okay Joy?" Jamaal asked.

"Sure Jamaal. I just had a thought that's all."

"All right then here's the plan. Let's spread out and see who can find the oldest tombstone," Jamaal said.

"Sounds great Jamaal and I'll bet I get some terrific rubbings to include in my portfolio too."

"Now you're talking Joy," You kind of had me worried there for a minute."

"Excuse me but I don't think we'll get all this territory covered today."

"That's okay Glenda. We'll just come back tomorrow." Glenda was satisfied with that and began to explore.

"Joy," Glenda called. "Don't forget about doing a rubbing for me."

"How will I know which one you want?" Joy hollered.

"You're the artist. I trust whichever one you pick," Glenda hollered back.

Jamaal went to the left. Joy went to the right. Glenda went down the middle. Each began their own systematic method of searching row upon row of mausoleums, crooked and weather beaten tombstones. Some of the headstones were engraved with a last name only... date of birth versus date of death...a poem and several other styles. Some tombstones were weather beaten and corroded with old letters that told about the gravesite. Statues of sad faced angels with chipped wings spread open and cherubs stood as if frozen in time. Doves and crosses of all shapes and sizes marked the burial places of others. Many gravesites had only flat ground level plaques to identify a grave.

Glenda was engrossed with the examination of a mosque she'd found. The inscription implied that those resting within represented an historical event. Having fully satisfied her curiosity, she started to

GRANNY'S PLACE

walk down a path she'd discovered that led straight through the cemetery. As she walked, she passed Joy leaning over a flat gravesite.

"Found something Joy?"

"Yes, Glenda. Take a look at this," Joy replied. "This grave is just a slap of cement but the writing on it caught my attention." The girls got down on their knees and gently brushed away patches of moss, tangled vines and loose leaves.

"Isn't this beautiful? Look at the gothic swirls, roses and leaves bordering the edge of the slab," Joy said.

"This is a real find Joy. The lettering is remarkably clear and well preserved. This will make a great charcoal rubbing, don't you think? Glenda said."

"Yes...it will but has something else sunk into that brain of yours yet?"

"Ummm...let me see. Well...It looks like someone has taken good care of the site and it's awfully small. Wait a minute, Joy! Read the engraving!"

"Jamaal, come here quick!" Joy yelled as he came towards them. Leaping over tombstones in his path like they were merely hurdles on a track course, Jamaal reached the girls.

"What's all the hollering about? You guys find something? I found a..."

"Nevermind about that Jamaal just read what Joy found," Glenda said.

Jamaal began to read.

LIZZIE MAE TAZELL
OCTOBER 31, 1899 – DECEMBER 25, 1904
REST IN PEACE LITTLE ANGEL

"This is the grave of Granddaddy's little sister who died of pneumonia," Joy said. "She was only six years old when she died. Granny said my Mom and Lizzie resembled each other so much that they could have passed for twins."

"It's too bad we don't have a picture of her," Glenda said.

"It must have hit the entire family real hard," Jamaal said.

GRANNY'S PLACE

"Can you imagine...we are staring at part of our heritage," Glenda said.

"Let's give her some respect and bow our heads for a minute," Joy said. Joy did the rubbing in silence and rubbed one for Glenda too.

Not far away, Joy began a charcoal rubbing of another gravesite. It wasn't as old as Lizzie's but proved to be just as interesting. Glenda helped her hold the paper in place. Jamaal spread out in the grass between two 'Here Lies' and bathed in the sun.

"Wow, I just thought of something!" Jamaal shouted.

"You almost made us jump out of our skin, Jamaal," Joy said. "What's wrong with you? What did you notice that's so important?"

"Don't tell me 'Miss Brains' didn't see it either?"

"Jamaal, notice what!"

"...the birth date of Lizzie. Joy...you and Lizzie were born on the same day. I wonder if that could mean anything. She's family and all you know."

"You're nuts, Jamaal. So what if she and Joy have the same birthday. It happens sometimes you know," Glenda said tersely.

"Jamaal could be right, Glenda. It could be some sort of code or something."

"You two are nuts! It's just some kind of coincidence. A date is just that...a date," Glenda said.

Joy didn't dismiss Jamaal's observation. She sensed a connection of sorts but couldn't figure out the real meaning. In light of the mysterious discoveries, the cousins decided it was best to explore together but each was determined to find the oldest tombstone anyway. Jamaal went his separate way but kept the girls in sight...especially Joy.

"EE-K-K!" Glenda screamed.

"Not again," Jamaal said, running in the girls' direction. By the time Jamaal reached them, they were standing side by side as motionless as one of the statues in the cemetery.

"What is it this time? Maybe I made a mistake suggesting we come here."

"Over there...on the tombstone," Glenda whimpered like a baby.

Jamaal cautiously walked towards the grave marker until he stood directly in front of it. His eyes bulged and his heart raced as he read the writing on the tombstone.

THEUDAS JAHDAI JONES
1683 – 1893
SON OF JOSIE AND HARMON JONES

"It can't be…it impossible! T…J…Jones," Jamaal quietly said. "According to this…TJ is two hundred and ten years old."

"Did you read the names 'Josie'? That's what he named his mule," Joy managed to say.

"How about the name Harmon? Harmon-ica!" Jamaal said.

"It can't be the same person! It's got to be some sort of mistake! Maybe whoever carved the letters in this tombstone was trying to be funny," Glenda said trembling.

"Good try, Glenda but who'd take the time to carve a tombstone for a practical joke. That doesn't make any sense," Jamaal said. "Joy are you brave enough to make a rubbing of this? We've got to show it to your grandparents and see what they have to say. "…and there's something else."

"What now?" Joy moaned.

"Look at the condition of the headstone. It doesn't look like it's gone through two hundred and ten years of weather to me. In fact it doesn't look five years old."

"Hurry and do the rubbing Joy so we can get out of this place. I've had enough exploring for one day," Glenda said helping Joy hold her paper.

The tombstone rubbing of Lizzie's resting place…Granddaddy's tales of things going bump in the night…Rufus and James Williams… the youth lynch and left hanging on a tree limb…and now this TJ mystery and grave marker discovery was too much for anybody.

"There…all finished," Joy said relieved, rolling up her art work.

"Good because I'm starved," Jamaal said, patting his stomach. "Let's sit under the bench under the weeping willow and eat our lunch."

"Jamaal, how can you think of food at a time like this?" Glenda asked.

"Why not sit and relax, Glenda. No one is going to complain around here," Jamaal teased. "Aren't you guys going to eat too?"

"No you can have our sandwiches," Joy said.

"I want to leave…now!" Glenda said hysterically.

"Okay scary cats, let's go," Jamaal said, digging in his lunch bag.

Joy and Glenda said nothing as they walked back down Eight Street and the shortcut towards South Fourth Street.

"Do you suppose we've been taking hay rides with a two hundred and ten year old ghost whose mother is a mule and whose father is a harmonica?" Jamaal asked.

The three stopped in their tracks…and howled with laughter.

THE ENIGMA

TJ finished his last handyman job for Dave. Josie was meandering around the shaded side of the barn enjoying whatever pleasantries she could find in the grass.

"Say TJ, Pervis wants you to stop by his place when you're done here. Will that be okay?"

"Yessum, Mr. Dave. I's finished heah now." Mysteriously, TJ already knew of the cemetery discovery.

"Okay TJ, see you another time," Dave waved.

"Come on old gal. L'll Miss needs our help." As he rounded the corner of the Wilson home, he met Jamaal coming up the path.

"How do, Massah Jamaal?" TJ greeted tipping his weathered, grease stained hat. "You and the little missies were scratchin' roun' agin?"

"Yeah…or something like that," Jamaal answered.

"Dat's nice. See ya 'roun din."

Jamaal stood on his front porch steps watching the ancient, mysterious figure until he was out of sight. He thought about Jericho Cemetery and the tombstone. "I wonder could it be true. 1683 to 1893?"

Pervis finished putting away his equipment in the workshop and was locking up when TJ arrived at the yard gate. His heart pounded with nervous anticipation as he watched TJ settle Josie under the magnolia tree. Pervis walked towards TJ with his hand extended for a handshake to meet the mystifying visitor once again. TJ returned the gesture.

"Let's sit down on the front porch and take a load off," Pervis suggested.

As the men chitchatted about this and that, in his mind, Pervis wondered how he'd begin to tell TJ why he asked him to come by the house. Eva was still taking her afternoon nap on the sofa which was most unusual for her to do because it was now late in the afternoon and the signs of evening were approaching.

"Have a seat, my good man," Pervis said pointing to the glider.

"Thank ya kindly," TJ responded exposing the only four teeth he owned.

"I don't quit know where to begin, TJ but…"

"Mr. Pervis, I's hea' 'cause yo' grandbaby is in trouble. How's kin I help?"

"How did you know this was about my granddaughter?"

TJ slowly removed his hat and sat it on the glider. As he began to speak, his physical appearance changed. A rainbow encircled his whole being. All the patches on his clothing disappeared and his mouth was filled with perfectly white teeth. He became a picture of perfection and started speaking.

"Pervis, you don't have to say another word. I'm whatever you need me to be. I smile because even though I dress odd, drive around with a horse and wagon, speak in a way one can barely understand, you and Eva extended nothing but kindness to me. You offered me food and water. You trusted me with your granddaughters. You and Eva are genuine and it's good when love abounds. Mainly…you didn't judge me."

"I've been given permission from Him to share information with you. My assignment from the Lord of Heaven and Earth is to guard Joy all of her life. I'm her guardian angel and have been with her since she was in her Mother's womb. I chose to reveal myself to you now because I knew no doubt would exist in your mind if you knew the truth about me. We're allowed to do that sometimes. You and Eva have made praying a daily reality. Actually, praying is exchanging words with the Word Himself who is the Master of the Universe. Continue to do this. The Alpha and Omega loves to hear Eva read what He expressed in Psalms 91 through King David."

"I know you want to discuss Arvis. Let me say the only One who knows the number of days one will spend on this earth is the Almighty. Don't hold any bitterness about losing her at an early age. Arvis was precious to Him and He wanted her to come home…to her original home. She had fulfilled her mission here…she gave birth to Joy. Don't fret for her because you may be persuaded to entertain doubt about

Him. He is the giver of life…not death. I know you miss the vessel that housed her spirit but you and Eva will see her again."

Pervis began to weep outloud. It was as if his emotions about his daughter had been locked away but were now freed. TJ smiled. After some minutes, Pervis wiped his eyes and cleared his throat. Eva was standing in the doorway crying like a baby. She never thought that one day she would see and talk with a miracle. She flopped down in her rocker.

"Now that Eva is with us…we must discuss what the immediate future will hold for Joy and there is much I have to share with you. You begin first because you have much on your mind."

"Yes TJ, I do. Let me begin with Jasper who plans to drive down from New Jersey in a week and pick up Joy."

TJ nodded his head in quiet awareness as Pervis related details of everything that had been happening concerning Joy.

"…and so you see TJ, we hope that Henry will have all documentation filed with the courts by then.

TJ rose from his seat on the glider. "Know all is in His hands and the results will be in your favor but…are you a fighter, Pervis?"

"Yes TJ."

"Do you believe in Him?"

"Yes TJ."

"Then I'll be back at noon tomorrow. We have the victory already."

With that comment…he disappeared from sight. Pervis and Eva began to praise the Lord. All was well with their souls. Joy and Glenda came downstairs after both had taken a bubble bath and chatted a bit.

"How are my Sweetmeat and Peaches doing?" Pervis said.

"Fine Granddaddy," Joy said.

"How was your outing to Jericho Cemetery?" Eva asked.

"It was most interesting," Glenda said.

"…and I got some excellent rubbings. We put them up on my bedroom wall before we came down. Was that okay, Granny?"

"That's was fine, sweetheart," Eva said.

"We're going back upstairs Granny. We're sort of exhausted from today's outing," Glenda said, but something else was on her mind.

"Yep, and my bed is calling me too," Joy added.

GRANNY'S PLACE

The cousins kissed their grandparents...and that was that. Eva and Pervis couldn't believe it. After a long moment, they continued the main topic of the evening.

"I'm not frightened anymore, Pervis. TJ said he was anything someone needed at the moment. I know now that I understand everything because of faith in what He has said in His Word. I now fully understand what Jesus meant when He said '...if you have faith like a mustard seed'. I don't care if people think I'm crazy for believing He exist today and works in our behalf. It's as if a light turned on in my head." Pervis listened ardently. His wife's thoughts intrigued him.

"I'll explain what I mean by using an example of what I know... my kitchen. When I'm cooking or making something for a special occasion, I sometimes mix a special ingredient to create a whole new dish using a basic recipe. Let's suppose TJ is that special ingredient and our lives are the original recipe. The pan used to fix the dish is our hearts. The other two ingredients are trust and belief. Prayer, the final ingredient sets the temperature for perfect results."

"Eva...you never cease to amaze me. Your explanation was absolutely beautiful."

They stared into each other's eyes and the same question was in their minds. They both wondered what recipe would be used to include the ingredient...Jasper Bailey. The wise old couple sat in the quietness of the night. All that could be heard were the sounds of nature at night and the rhythmic motion of the metal rockers on the porch linoleum. Each meditated on events of the past and the incredible events since their daughter's death...and the happenings to come. They're thoughts were interrupted by the telephone.

"Hello?" Pervis answered. "I'm listening. But you said August sixteenth! It's only two weeks from the end of July! Now you're telling me you'll be here in three days? What do you mean Joy needs to be near you? I don't give a hill-of-beans about a change in your pathetic wedding plans. You don't need our grandchild there so you can make a whole new mess in her life. What? You better watch your mouth you empty-headed heathen. Have you forgotten who you're talking to? I see...you don't care. Well lame-brain, you can act like a big man on the phone but if I had you here...it'd be a different story. Threaten me will you. Well, Mr. Big Shot bring it on and we'll see who gets their shoes dusted first!"

Pervis slammed the phone down, stormed into the kitchen and poured a glass of ice tea. Eva followed and knew there was no need to ask the identity of the late night caller.

"That insolent, disrespectful idiot will be here for Joy at ten o'clock…in three days."

"Oh no Pervis, if Jasper get's his hands on that child before we get those papers filed, I shudder to think what will happen to her. Peace darling! Let peace reign."

"You're right Eva. I've calmed down. That man makes me so mad. There's only one kind of future for our grandbaby and that's a future without Jasper Bailey!" Pervis said. "Her leaving this house is not going to happen."

"Pervis please believe all will be made right. We don't know what's going to happen next but you have got to realize that we've already won. Anyway, do you know what TJ's plan is?"

"I have no idea but he must be told that Jasper will be here before August. "TJ used the same word you used in your 'recipe' tonight, Eva. I've got to trust and not doubt to see the rest of the plan unfold. I wish I had your faith and confidence."

The telephone rang again. "If that foolish man has called again I'm going to tell him a thing or two. Hello? TJ? You already heard about Jason's early arrival? Yes TJ, trust and obey. You'll be here early in the morning? Fine and we'll be waiting for you."

"In a little while, we won't have to put up with anymore of Jasper's nonsense. Let's get some sleep now. We've got to be up and meet with TJ…remember? Eva said."

This time…Pervis read Psalm 91.

JOY'S THIRD DREAM

Having gone to bed without dinner or one of their grandmother's treats, Joy and Glenda felt the pangs of hunger. It was four-thirty in the morning. They tipped past their sleeping grandparents and went down to raid the refrigerator to munch on anything they could find.

"Granny and Granddaddy sure acted strange before went to see," Joy said as she and Glenda chomped cold chicken legs and homemade rolls.

"Strange isn't the word for it," Glenda said, with her mouth stuffed full of chicken.

"You know Glenda? I had the weirdest dream last night."

"What was it about," Glenda asked, swallowing from her glass of cherry Kool-aid.

"It was all about TJ. He didn't look like he looks now but somehow I knew it was him."

"Tell me his new look then."

"He was very handsome and taller than he is now. His hair was shoulder length and jet-black and he didn't have a mustache. His skin was dark-brown and smooth. What made all this so peculiar was that there was a light surrounding his head…like a halo and…"

"And…"

"He had on a white robe with a gold waist band."

"Really? A robe? Maybe he'd just gotten out of the shower."

"Come on Glenda. I'm serious and you're making jokes."

"Sorry. You were saying?"

"There was a peace about him and he didn't use broken English when he talked either. Mom told me about angels before and he was dressed just like she described."

"It sounds like your describing one of those Christmas angels."

"Right, Glenda…an angel."

"You know what I think, Joy?"

"What, Glenda?" Joy asked anxiously.

"I think you got too much sun at Jericho Cemetery," Glenda chuckled.

"Oh Glenda, you're hopeless.

THE LAST PREPARATIONS BEGIN

It was six o'clock in the morning and Jasper would arrive early that evening. As if knowing of his arrival, the rays of the sun were shrouded by the grayness of an overcast sky. Misty rain was falling. Mother Nature was weeping softly. Not a bird sang, not a leaf stirred. The silence was like the stillness before a storm. Old Colonel didn't crow this time. He stood still as if listening for something or someone. The hens were huddled together protecting each other from impending doom. Not one egg was laid either.

"Whoa Josie, whoa," TJ said as he turned his wagon around in the yard. Pervis and his wife came to the kitchen screen door when they heard TJ's voice. Although the weather was damp, Eva's knee didn't ache one bit.

"You're a sight for sore eyes, TJ," Eva said.

"I don't have much time, Pervis. Do you know the old Woodson Plantation house that's deserted now?"

"Yes, I do. It's the one that sits on a hill about a mile from the back entrance of Jericho Cemetery."

"I'll be back at exactly two o'clock instead of noon like we originally planned. Make certain you and your family is ready to leave when I return."

"TJ, before you leave, I want to tell you that Jasper called last night and…"

"Sorry to cut you off, Pervis but I'm aware of that already and that's why plans have changed. Don't let what the man says to upset you so. Listen to your wife. Here's a list of the things you'll need to bring. I have no doubt Eva will know how much food you'll need to take with you. I have to leave for the Wilson home now."

"Dave, Debra and Jamaal are coming too? But why are they coming?"

GRANNY'S PLACE

"I have explained to you before He has assigned me to children. Jamaal and Glenda are in danger too. That's all I'm allowed to reveal. Just get prepared to leave."

In a twinkle of an eye, TJ was gone. "...*in the winkle of an eye* are words I'll always remember," Pervis said.

Eva was in the kitchen heating up the oil to fry chicken. Pervis got two large picnic baskets out of the downstairs hall closet. If filled to the brim, they'd hold enough food for a trip to Mars and back. While the oil was warming, Eva sat a plate of buttered raisin bread and two coffee cups on the table.

"I'm glad the girls are resting. Most of their clothes are already in the diningroom on the ironing board.

"Good Eva. I want to collect all the items on this list that TJ told me to bring. I want to be sure I don't forget one thing."

"Eat a bit and drink your coffee first."

Ta-flop! Ta-flop! Ta-flop!

Eva and Pervis stopped chewing their toast at the same time and looked up at the kitchen ceiling.

"Looks like you're going to have plenty of company in the kitchen, Eva."

"I know Pervis but I've never known them to get up so early...ever."

"Well...I'm going to see about this list. It seems like I'll have to call Dave for a few items though."

"All right, Pervis. I have to get started organizing and filling these baskets but one more thing before you go. How do I explain this sudden outing to the girls?"

"I guess I have to take care of that one, Eva," Pervis said as he walked to his workshop.

Glenda and Joy stomped sleepily downstairs and went into the kitchen yawning with their hair all over their heads.

"I've got buttered raisin bread and hot chocolate for breakfast this morning."

"Just a cup of hot chocolate for me, Granny," Joy said.

"Me too, Granny 'cause I'm not very hungry either," Glenda added.

GRANNY'S PLACE

"You know, Glenda you're Mom is going to be so proud of you when she notices how much weight you've lost. You've trimmed down so nice. You've come down from a size fourteen to a size nine," Eva said.

"My clothes do fit looser too and I feel so much better," Glenda answered. "It won't take much to convince Dad that visiting Suffolk for the summer is a lot cheaper than all those expensive summer camps."

Pervis came from the workshop carrying two large cardboard boxes. He sat them on the glider and walked back to the kitchen. When he saw his granddaughters, he grabbed them lovingly.

"Guess what Sweetmeat and Peaches? You're Granny and I decided we're going on an adventure trip together today. In fact, TJ is going to take us on his wagon and guess what else?"

"The Wilsons are going to come along too!"

"What a terrific surprise. I was wondering why Granny had her picnic baskets out," Joy said excitedly.

"Too much!" Glenda shouted.

"Where will we be going for the picnic," Glenda asked.

"We're going to camp out at the old Woodson Plantation mansion. Jamaal's Dad contacted the owner who now lives in another city up north. They gave us permission to be there today. The wing we're going to use is all prepared for us. It's a wonderful chance to see how another part of the world lives and being indoors will keep us out of the weather too. There's even a fireplace we can use if we want to roast marshmallows."

"Oh Granddaddy, that sounds absolutely wonderful," Glenda shrieked. "You know what Granddaddy?"

"What Peaches?"

"I saw a mausoleum with the same name of 'Woodson' at Jericho Cemetery. Do you suppose it could be relatives of the people who lived in the mansion?"

"It's the very same family, Glenda. When your grandmother and I first moved from New York, my first job was working for the Woodson family. In fact, I earned extra spending money for my family by building that very same mausoleum."

"Gosh! I'm so excited I could faint right here," Glenda said.

"Please do, Glenda. I've always wanted to throw a bucket of water on someone who's fainted," Joy teased.

The kitchen filled with laughter and the girls had swallowed the bait. They raced upstairs to dress for the most important day of their lives.

"Better dress in long pants and bring down your jackets and two quilts on off the trunk in the hall," Eva hollered behind them.

Pervis hastily finished his coffee and continued to collect the supplies listed by TJ. Keeping an eye on the clock, Eva spread out on the kitchen table all she wanted to put in the picnic baskets and soon the kitchen table resembled a smorgasbord of country delights. A large huge platter of fried chicken, a platter of sliced country ham, fried fish fillet, twenty slices of meatloaf, potato salad, collard greens, pickled string beans, a platter of candied sweet potatoes, macaroni and cheese, three jars of watermelon rind pickles, three peach pies, an angel food cake, a coconut cake and three dozen rolls completed the contents of the huge wicker picnic baskets.

The cousins made their beds and tidied their bedrooms. Today, Glenda brushed her hair one hundred times.

"Glenda I can't get rid of the feeling that this outing is more than meets the eye. Somehow, today's events are connected with that dream I had last night. The dream bothered me but it didn't frighten me."

"You know, you might have a special gift like 'prophecy' or something. The Bible says there are nine of gifts…I think. We had to deal with learning them and what they meant in Vacation Bible School last summer."

"…or maybe it's just artistic intuitiveness," Joy said, waving her hand with an aristocratic air.

"Now that's what I call spreading it on thick," Glenda giggled.

"You two ready yet?" Eva yelled upstairs.

"Yes Granny!" the cousins yelled back.

Returning to the kitchen, Pervis sat at the table and had a final cup of coffee while Eva put her last touches on the packed picnic baskets. The telephone rang. Fearing the worst, Pervis and Eva froze.

"Hello? Oh hello, Harvey," Pervis sighed with relief. He turned and winked at Eva to assure her that the call was friendly.

"Pervis I'm calling to warn you about something" Harvey said.

"What's up, Harvey?" A deep frown creased his brow.

"I picked up three rowdy soldiers at the Greyhound bus station. You could smell the liquor on their breath. I dropped them off in South Suffolk about ten minutes ago. While they were in the cab, I overheard them say why they'd come to town. They talked of Jasper and said they'd be glad when the job was done."

"What kind of 'job', Harvey."

"They were bragging about some tricks Jasper had up his sleeve and now they were to meet him at your house a six o'clock tonight. They spoke of 'real fun on South Fourth Street'."

"Thanks for letting me know Harvey. God bless you for telling me this," Pervis said.

Pervis told Eva everything about the call and everything Harvey said. "It looks like we'll have the victory party and the food to help us celebrate, Pervis."

Glenda and Joy were on the front porch when TJ came through the opened gate. Jamaal and his parents were already sitting on the bunk board.

"Hey Jamaal! How are you Mr. and Mrs. Wilson?"

"Hi! Looks like we're in for some fun," Dave said.

"Come help me carry these baskets to the wagon girls," Eva said.

"I'll help you with them, Miss Eva," Jamaal said, jumping down off the wagon seat. "Pervis, you and Dave load the rest of the stuff on the wagon."

Pervis took an extra moment to make sure the house was secure and climbed on the wagon and sat next to TJ. Eva and Debra made themselves comfortable on two low sitting chairs Dave had rigged up for the ladies. The hikers sat on the back edge of the wagon jabbering and swinging their feet but the ladies kept a close eye on them. The three friends were elated about the family outing but they all concluded that there was something a bit out of the ordinary about this sudden family gathering.

Harvey, Mr. Percy and the trustworthy ladies of the W.B.F.C. followed TJ's plan to the letter. They'd deliberately spread the word around town that the Tazells, Wilsons, and young folk would be at the Woodson Plantation so when Jasper arrived in Suffolk, he'd be sure to find where they were going. So far, the plan was working beautifully and the trap was being set.

Mother Nature was doing her part too. A misty rain was falling and thick clouds blocked the blazing sunlight allowing the entourage to the Woodson Plantation to enjoy pleasant weather. Despite all that was happening, Josie didn't let one iota slow her steadily trot.

"You know, Joy. I can't wait to hear TJ try to explain the eulogy we found in Jericho Cemetery," Jamaal said.

"It will be awfully interesting to hear his explanation about many things," Glenda said, feeling like quite the detective.

TJ smiled.

THE WARNING

Some people who knew him tried to figure out what had made Jasper so bitter. Radonia Bailey, his mother, worked long hard hours at Planter's Peanut like many of Suffolk citizens. Jasper's father William Bailey was a military man too but died of cancer when Jasper was fourteen. He was the oldest of five male stair-step siblings. Six years after his father's death, Radonia married Eugene Beale. Eugene was an ordinary, kind-hearted, hard working, church man who was a loving father to his stepchildren. He owned a small construction business. To their union was born three girls who all graduated from college and are teachers by profession. They're married and still live in Suffolk. Radonia children and her stepchildren all knew of Jasper's bad behavior. Now nineteen and near school dropout, Jasper was the rotten apple in the bunch.

Eva and Pervis last saw Radonia and Eugene at Arvis' funeral. They loved Arvis like a daughter too. News got back to them about Jasper's mistreatment of Arvis and to show their disapproval, they sat nowhere near their son during the funeral service. It was Radonia who sent over the large bowl of potato salad by the W.B.F.C.

In his youth, Jasper wasn't as spiteful and vindictive as he is now. At one time he had considered entering the ministry and was an avid Bible student. Folks who knew him then were proud and supportive of him and aided his efforts to study theology. Then like the wind changing, he became bitter and rebellious and his entire demeanor did a three hundred-sixty degree flip. Since then, it was as if he was constantly fighting a war inside himself. So far…he was losing the battle. He rejected anything to do with Bible study, theology or spiritual subjects. He mocked hymns and would blast rock-'n-roll just to annoy the neighbors. Church became like catching a plaque and he made blasphemous comments about church only to irritate his mother.

As it happened, Eugene died one month after Arvis. Details reported in the Suffolk New Herald indicated he'd died from a nasty fall, sustaining massive head injuries while climbing his ladder to do repairs to the roof of his home. Two broken ribs pierced his lungs and he died of internal bleeding. Before his death, folks learned that Eugene had a fierce argument with Jasper concerning his cousin Petula caring for Joy in New Jersey. Some believe that the argument was the reason why Eugene's lost his footing while on his ladder. One night, a neighbor of Eugene's snuck to the backside of the house where the ladder rested. A stair at the top of the ladder had been partially sawn in half. No one could find out what really happened…except Jasper.

Radonia had become despondent over Eugene's demise because he was a loving husband and caring father. Grief robbed her of the will to live. According to an ever present close relative, her last word to Jasper was a warning. She'd told him he'd better stop mocking life and put an end to his evil ways or life would mock back at him. After twenty-five years of marriage to Eugene, she joined him for all eternity. Jasper never took heed of the final warning.

THE FINAL ADVENTURE

It was a long bumpy ride but it was fun. Josie hauled the wagon along a wide cobblestone driveway in the front of the Woodson Plantation. It was the biggest domain Joy, Glenda or Jamaal had ever seen. The house loomed against the sky like a ravenous dinosaur about to devour an unsuspecting prey. Huge white columns on the first floor stood gallantly from one end of the house to another and joined the second floor overhead. The second floor was a long porch. The porch was decorative with a massive hand-carved iron railing and 8'x7' floor-to-ceiling bedroom windows. Devil's Shoestring vines and English Ivy grew between and around each window. The moss covered branches of a weeping willow tree hung like jellyfish tentacles and created an umbrella of shade on the front lawn.

It was now four-thirty in the afternoon. Time was passing quickly and like a medieval warrior, an angry looking was cloud rapidly forming in the distance sky.

"This is great! It's got to be the most fascinating place I've ever seen. I've been all over Suffolk Dad, but I've never come across this," Jamaal said.

"It is spectacular Jamaal but these are places exclusive to certain kinds of society folks only," Dave said.

"If this place is an example Mr. Wilson, that's fine with me but Jamaal is right. What do you think, Glenda?" Joy said.

"Oh…it's okay I guess." The three rolled with laughter.

"Y'all betta start unloadin' now," TJ advised.

Everyone grabbed an armload while TJ opened the mammoth doors to reveal a vast marble black and white checked floor in a colossal foyer. Eva had seen huge houses before but never something like this. She shivered with delight at the sight before her. A huge gold family crest hung above the door within a gigantic glass stained window that illuminated the stairway.

GRANNY'S PLACE

"Dis way, ladies," TJ directed towards the stairs. "Da entry ta yawls wing is up dah."

Eva and Debra held on to the banister as they went up the winding stairs case.

"Look at this," Glenda said. Have you ever…?

"No," Joy finished. Jamaal found no words as he walked up with his parents and Pervis close behind. Already at the top of the stairs, TJ opened another set of huge, delicately carved double doors that were twenty feet tall. Eva stepped in first. Debra was on Eva's heels followed by Dave, Jamaal, Joy, Glenda and Pervis. They stood transfixed.

"I never knew people enjoyed such luxury," Debra said. "How can they know what to build?"

"Would you believe God said He has a mansion more spectacular than this waiting for each of us?" Eva said reverently.

All the way on the opposite side of the room was an enormous fireplace framed in marble and gold leaves. It was so vast that six people could stand side-by-side and play a game of tag without touching the bricks. A floor-to-ceiling window with tufted paaisley cushioned bench seats was positioned on each side of each window. The towering windows opened up the enormous room to a fantastic panorama of lawns and gardens outside on the ground floor.

"Eva, there's enough room in this place to fit both our houses inside," Debra said. "Have you ever seen such a room?"

"Not since Pervis took me to see *Gone With The Wind* in New York theater."

"I's got ta see 'bout Josie now," TJ said.

The families arranged their household goods and the picnic baskets were unloaded. Eva set up the large marble and glass-topped coffee table smorgasbord style then the adults sat in oversized, luxuriously padded wing back chairs placed at each corner of a huge table. Joy, Jamaal and Glenda sat crossed-legged in one of the giant picture windows.

"The view is awesome," Jamaal said. "Can you imagine coming home to this after school?"

"No," Joy and Glenda chimed together.

"It's like looking down through the window while taking off in a plane," Glenda said.

GRANNY'S PLACE

The cobblestone road they'd used to get to the mansion looked like a long twisting snake. The sun was going down so Eva had Pervis and Dave turn on the chandelier light. Then the men lit the fireplace. The flickering flames created shadows that danced across the room like giant puppets. The table became the center of a delicious buffet style dinner for all to share. Jamaal and the girls carried their plates back to the window seat.

"Where did TJ go?" Joy asked.

"He probably went to see about Josie," Pervis said.

"You know, he's the nicest person I've ever met," Debra said. Everyone nodded in agreement.

"Let's show them the rubbing you made in Jericho Cemetery, Joy," Jamaal whispered.

While Dave and Pervis selected a sandwich off the coffee table, Joy stood in front of the fireplace with her rubbing rolled up in her hand. "Can I have everybody's attention please?"

"What do you have there, Joy?" Eva asked.

"It's a rubbing of something Jamaal, Glenda and I want to show you," Joy said, while unrolling the rubbing and holding it up for all to see.

"It's wonderful," Eva said.

"You did a terrific job," Dave added.

"Yes and I have to agree. Your art work is terrific," Pervis said.

"How long did it take to do it?" Debra asked.

The youth were stunned. "Has anyone read what it says on the rubbing?" Joy asked, totally confused. "Doesn't anybody see the connection here?"

The four adults howled with laughter. "We already know about TJ, kids," Pervis said.

"Yep we sure do," Dave said, placing two more logs on the fire.

"Well...I wish somebody would tell us what's going on," Joy said, pouting. The jovial mood in the giant room changed to seriousness when the adults saw how upset the children were. Glenda and Jamaal joined their comrade in front of the fireplace.

"Somebody please say something," Glenda said with a trembling voice. "Why all the secrecy?"

Pervis spoke up first. "It's not that no one wanted to tell you about TJ. I was only able to confirm the truth about the man a few days ago. If we told you what we know now...would you have believed us? Would you have believed TJ was who he said he was?"

"You're frightening me, Granddaddy," Joy whimpered. "What is it you want us to know about TJ?"

"I want you to know this, Joy. Sometimes what we think we a falsehood and by that I mean...," Pervis observed the look of confusion on the youngsters.

Pervis retold the story about the fishing trip experience with Frank and Charlie. He also told them about yesterday's front porch conversation with TJ. When he finished, the children were astonished. Joy and Glenda began to cry. A shaken Jamaal walked over to his parents, stood between them and held their hands.

"So...all this time, you've been in the presence of a..."

"...angel." Debra said, finishing her husband's sentence.

"TJ said he was assigned to 'children' and that he was assigned to safeguard Joy for the rest of her days. What dumbfounds me is the fact that we all have been privileged to have such a wonderful encounter."

Silence fell over the spacious room. Everyone meditated on Pervis last statement. Only the crackling flames in the fireplace could be heard. After a long time, Pervis broke the silence.

"Joy," Pervis said. "Last night your Dad called and informed Eva and I about his plans to take you back to New Jersey."

"Oh no, you and Granny promised I wouldn't have to leave," Joy blubbered and sniffed sitting on a hassock beside Eva.

"Now hold on a minute, darling. Eva and I have not agreed to let you go. We've put a plan in action that will stop Jasper in his tracks. You're grandmother and I have contacted Uncle Henry who immediately filed the necessary papers to prevent Jasper from taking you anywhere."

"You mean to say that I'll be legally adopted by you and Granny?" Joy asked.

"That's exactly right, Joy," Pervis said.

"I'm so glad she won't have to live with that mean thing again," Glenda said, sitting on the other side of her grandmother's chair. "I told you adoption to the right people was a blessing, Joy."

"Yes honey, that's exactly what I mean, Glenda," Pervis replied tenderly.

"Is this the real reason for this mansion picnic? Don't get me wrong, Granddaddy because we all love the place but there are so many loose ends to tie together. Why is everything happening tonight?" Glenda asked.

"…because Jasper changed the date of his coming to Suffolk and taking you back to New Jersey. Then Harvey Ellis called and told me that some of Jasper's buddies were in town and talked about helping him in this matter. Bits and pieces of Jasper's reasoning began to fall into place. The night before all this was to happen is when I found out about TJ and who he really was. He's the one who made all the plans for a special trip here to the mansion."

"Oh I get it now. Joy's Dad had some kind of plan to grab Joy and his friends to help him and…and…" Jamaal said.

"…and get rid of Eva and me," Pervis added. "Murder!"

Jamaal sat in a chair next to his Dad. His mind whirled as he digested each bit of the newfound fact.

"What's the rest of the plan, Granddaddy?" Glenda asked.

"I don't know, Glenda. Like TJ said, everything is by faith."

"What's that suppose to mean? How can a person have faith at a time like this?" Glenda asked, obviously irritated. No one answered except Pervis.

"Excuse me Glenda, but do you remember when I explained that TJ is Joy's guardian angel and he was assigned to all children?"

"Yes, I remember."

"Don't you and Jamaal fit into that category too?" The conversation was ended.

"Because we learned that Jasper's plan was to slip into town early, Pervis and I prayed for a miracle. TJ was that miracle," Eva said. "He wants to touch all our lives somehow."

"Oh Joy," Glenda sighed. "We're going to be sisters after all."

"Somebody pinch me so I know I'm not dreaming," Joy said.

"There's something else too," Pervis said. "Henry also found out through some contacts in New Jersey the real reason Jasper wanted to cut Joy's vacation short."

"This is incredible Pervis," Dave said.

GRANNY'S PLACE

"Henry found out Jasper had gotten traveling orders and was taking Joy to Hanau, Germany but he needed to get married first to meet the government regulations concerning families. The woman he's marrying is only six years Joy's senior in age. She thinks he's marrying her for love."

"She'll be sorry," Debra said.

"It's a crying shame to mess up another's life like that. TJ said tonight we'll all be witness to what happens when a heart has turned to stone. Like all of us, Jasper has had chances to mend his ways but I actually feel sorry for the man," Eva said.

"Granddaddy, Mom wrote in her letter to me that you must forgive when a wrong is done to you. How can I forgive Dad for what he's done to me and to Mom? She's not even here anymore. He took her from me."

"I'm sure in the letter, Arvis told you to forgive your Dad of his wicked ways. She had all the right to harbor hate but she chose not to and she wants you to do the same. Hatred can eat away like acid and your granddaddy and I don't want that for you," Eva said.

"But…how do I begin to forgive?" Joy asked.

"That's something only you can do…and believe me…you'll know." Eva said. "Remember the story I told you and Glenda about Rufus and his brother at the well?"

"I remember the story, Granny," Glenda chimed.

"Do you remember the reason I told the story in the first place, Joy?"

"Yes Granny, I understand you now," Joy said. "Whatever seeds you plant in this life, one day you'll have to reap the harvest you grow."

"Listen well, Jamaal," Dave said. "You'll hear all the words your Mom and I have been trying to teach you for all of your life."

"I'm listening, Dad. Boy! Nobody will believe I've got friends that hang around with heavenly aliens!" The room exploded with laughter once again.

"I'm hungry again. Let's all get something else to eat. Eva and Debra prepared all this delicious food and it would be a shame to let all this go to waste," Pervis said.

"I'll put more logs on the fire. It's getting chilly in here," Dave said.

"I'll do it for you, Dad," Jamaal said. He looked into his father's eyes and each knew the look meant 'thank you'.

Eva was as proud as a peacock at the way her husband handled the whole situation. Pervis imagined what she was thinking and blew her a kiss. Joy, Jamaal and Glenda saw them and playfully mocked by blowing kisses in all directions. After the silliness, the youthful trio each grabbed a meatloaf sandwich and returned to the window seat.

"Pervis," Dave began. "Now that we know why the rest of you are here, why did TJ want my family here too? He could have dealt with Jamaal's character on one of those visits to our home."

"Oh for Pete's sake Dave," Debra interrupted. "Think about it, honey. Each one of these children is special but even more so, they're special because they have one thing in common."

"What...?"

"...all three are eleven month babies!"

"That's right, Debra. I completely forgot all about that. It's said that if it takes eleven months for a baby to get here, that baby would meet it guardian angel," Eva said excitedly.

"Well I'll be hogtied," Pervis grinned. "Arvis was an eleven month baby too."

Dave wondered what Jamaal's involvement in this life would be. He looked at his son seated on the window seat. His caring for animals so adamantly always penetrated his thoughts but there had to be a reason.

"Eva, do you remember the nurses talking to you about some sort of membrane being over Arvis' face at birth?"

"Yes Debra, I sure do. They never really explained why it was there."

"It's a symbol that the child is gifted with 'sight' and would be able to predict the future," Debra said.

"You're right, Debra and an angel disguised as an earthly being would intervene for that child all of its life."

When they finished their conversation, all cast their eyes towards the window seats and starred at the youngsters. Their thoughts were interrupted by the sudden appearance of TJ.

A brilliant light filled the room. He no longer appeared as the torn and tattered handyman they had seen. There wasn't a rip or sewn tear in his clothing. His hat looked brand new and was now donned with a gold band. He smiled revealing a mouthful of teeth as white as pearls. Unmentionable peace filled the massive room. When TJ finally spoke, his voice was booming yet commanding yet gentle to the ear.

"It's time. Do not leave this room. You can look out the windows by the fireplace only. Jasper will have one more chance to change his heart because my Master is longsuffering. You have all purified your hearts with forgiveness and have been forgiven by the Alpha and Omega.

As Theudas Jahdai turned and left the room, the brilliant light left too. Glenda's mouth hung open and at the same time, she recalled the dream Joy told her about TJ this morning and the joke she'd made of it all. She and Joy looked at each other as if reading each other's minds. Together, they tore up the charcoal rubbing about TJ into tiny pieces.

"Look everybody, headlights," Jamaal shouted.

Eva sat on the window seat with the youngsters and Dave, Pervis and Debra sat in the other window. Just as Jamaal said, headlights were approaching the mansion.

"It's Jasper! I don't recognize the other fellows," Pervis said. The car screeched to a halt in front of the huge edifice. The soldiers got out of the car. They walked like threatening lions towards TJ who had positioned himself in front of the entrance of the mansion. Jasper shook his fist in TJ's face.

"What do you mean we can't go in," Jasper asked angrily. The other three soldiers inched their way behind TJ. They tried to break down the door but the door seemed to be made of steel.

"Lord, don't let TJ get hurt," Joy prayed silently. "…and let Dad come to his senses."

"Gosh, you guys. We can hear everything they're saying like were watching TV or something," Jamaal said.

"Of course we can. TJ said we'd be witnesses to everything so how could we be witnesses if we couldn't hear?" Glenda retorted.

"Hush up you two and just listen," Debra said.

One of the bullies pulled a crowbar from under his jacket and was swinging it back and forth.

"What kind of trick so do you think you're playing? Do you know who you're dealing with?" Jasper shouted.

GRANNY'S PLACE

TJ said nothing and smiled.

"We've got to help TJ," Pervis said.

"No Pervis. TJ told us not to leave the room. Remember?" Dave said.

"Look Jasper, I see them up in the windows!" One of the ruffians said.

"I'm warning you Pervis Tazell and I'm warning that Battle Ax wife of yours too and both of you had better send that gal down here right now or you'll have hell to pay," Jasper said, shaking his fist up at the window.

Stomping towards TJ, Jasper tried to push him aside. TJ grabbed him by the back of his collar and belt and held the squirming and cursing soldier over his head like Jasper was made of air. With one powerful motion, he tossed Jasper like a rag doll. Not wanting a taste of the same, the three so-called buddies took off running in three different directions. Joy gasped.

"Great day in the morning," Pervis said. "Did you see that?"

Before anyone could answer, the earth began to tremble but the mansion stood perfectly still. A fierce wind began to blow. It blew so hard that the Mercury Jasper was so proud of was rolled over and over until it resembled a tangled mess of green metal. The wind snapped the trees in half and uprooted many. TJ had disappeared.

Jasper struggled to his feet. The earth continued to shake but Jasper was angry and continued to curse. Suddenly, the ground split open a few feet from the angry man. The split looked to be a block long. A thick cloud of black smoke belched through the widening crevasse. Horrible earsplitting shrieks resounded from within. The earth continued to quiver and Jason lost his balance. He tried to belly crawl away from the crevasse and the diabolical screams. He got kneeled down on the ground but the smoke still burned his eyes and throat. He couldn't see what it was but something with superhuman strength grabbed his ankle. Jason scraped the ground with his fingers trying to get break free until his fingers bled. His face was twisted with horror.

"Please Dad say you're sorry for everything. Change what's in your heart. That's all you have to do," Joy said.

Glenda put her arm around Joy and bowed her head and whispered the sinner's prayer. Dave hugged his wife and Jamaal. Pervis and Eva wept because of the crop Jasper was harvesting.

A hideous colossal apparition resembling a dragon appeared from the crevasse. Its eyes glowed as red as coals. It picked up Jasper but the foot and shook him like a wet rag. Jasper cursed at the apparition and tried in vain to free himself. A talon tipped finger grabbed his collar and held him onto him like yesterday's laundry. With a satanic grin, the hideous incubus bared its fangs and watched with evil delight as Jasper grimaced in pain as the monster dug a talon finger into his back. It was as though the apparition was toying with Jasper. With a flick of its wrist, the scaly demonic phantom flung Jasper against a nearby tree. Jasper moaned and his back felt like it had been snapped like a dried twig. Jasper spewed forth more curses at his assailant. Then, the scaly, monstrous lowered its lizard shaped head until its eyes peered into Jasper's.

"Don't you have something you'd like to say or have I got you completely. It's up to you," it hissed with a blast of putrid breath.

"Now Dad, repent of everything now," Joy said.

"…say something about what? I don't deserve this, damn you. I haven't done anything wrong," Jason shouted.

"Damn me? I don't think so little soldier boy," the dragon hissed.

Someone was standing behind the creatures huge scaly legs. Jasper heard chains rattling. It was Theodore Bowers standing in the midst of many unknown faces.

"I'm begging you, Jasper Bailey. Admit your wrongs while you still have the chance to repent. Don't wait until it's too late like I did."

"You old fool; I don't know what you're talking about. Get away from me."

"Can't you understand why all this is happening to you? It's your heart, man. It's all because of the monstrosities you're harboring in your heart. That's what you see before you now. The monster is your sins. It's a mirror of what's in your heart. Don't be a fool like I was," Theodore pleaded. Without warning, the scaly apparition snatched Theodore back into the smoky crevasse.

The Tazells and the Wilsons knelt in front of the fireplace. All heads were bowed. They were praying for Jasper. They said the sinner's prayer and then raised their hands in praise to the Lord for his saving grace. Joy prayed especially for her father. She had witnessed what others only assume and have never seen.

The gargoyle like creature reared its head back and let out a dreadful shriek…as if it was in pain. "I can't do what I want because those things up there are praying for this man," it snarled. "That prayer is holding me back but I have no doubt we shall meet again."

The monstrosity swung around and with a giant leap, disappeared into the black smoke. The earth ceased to tremble and the fierce wind stopped. When Jasper came to his senses, he saw TJ sitting in a white iron chair on the front porch of the mansion. He took out his harmonica and began to play.

Jasper looked all around and found no evidence of what had just happened. It was if he were in a dream. There wasn't a scratch on his body and his army uniform was untouched. The trees in the front of the house stood erect but all of nature was silent. His buddies had fallen into a drunken sleep on the backseat of his perfectly shiny green Mercury.

Jasper, still cocky and contemptuous, stared at TJ with abhorrence and then looked up at the folks in the windows.

"You can have the brat," he hollered to Eva and Pervis. "She'd only get in my way." With that, Jasper jumped into his car and drove away.

The atmosphere in the large room was solemn but reverent. The two families packed up their belongings in silence. Each was enthralled in their own thoughts and reflections of what they'd eye witnessed.

Debra and Eva took their seats in their chairs on the wagon. Dave and Pervis sat next to TJ and Joy, Jamaal and Glenda let their feet swing off the back of the wagon. A glimmer of gold and orange began to spread across the horizon. A new day was dawning. July flies began to sing their song warning that another sultry day was arriving. TJ dropped the Wilsons home first and then drove the wagon to the Tazell house.

There were no more adventures that summer. Old Colonel crowed two hours late as usual. The hens greedily pecked the ground to try to find the last bit of grain. Sheets and towels fluttered in the wind on the clothesline while Eva was on the telephone taking orders for pies and cakes. Pervis walked to the end of South Fourth Street to catch his van for work.

Joy took her first train ride with Glenda to upstate New York. Jamaal increased in his knowledge of animals and decided he wanted to be a veterinarian.

Jasper never made it to Hanau, Germany. Instead, he'd been admitted to a veteran's hospital with a room in the psychiatric ward.

"Say Melvin, check out that fellow over there."

"Oh yeah, he's on my caseload," Clarence replied.

"Something must have really messed up the boy's mind."

"Do you think it was the war?"

"Nope and according to his case history, something happened that literally short circuited his brain. It's like his brain switched off or something."

"Look Melvin, look what he's doing now? What's that all about? I don't have time for this kind of foolishness. I've got to put a diaper on room number twenty-five."

"Man I don't know all the whys. The doctor's can't even figure this one out. He always drops to the floor and belly crawls a few feet every night about this time. Then he gets up, sits on the edge of his bed and won't move a muscle. See? He's sitting now just like clockwork," Melvin explained.

"What's he muttering?" Clarence asked.

"It sounds like…'I'm sorry'…and then he says nothing. Then he opens that Bible of his."

"He opens his Bible?"

"Yeah, his daughter sent him a Bible. At the exact same time each night he repeats Psalm 91.

"You never know what's going on in these guy's heads."

Mother Nature had changed her clothes for the fall season and a melodic sound of harmonica music drifted over lush forests, meadows and farmlands.

The End

www.ingramcontent.com/pod-product-compliance
Lightning Source LLC
Chambersburg PA
CBHW071956070526
44583CB00015B/1212